D1337053

PROSPECT AND REALITY
Great Britain 1945–1955

T.E.B. HOWARTH

PROSPECT AND REALITY

Great Britain 1945-1955

COLLINS
8 Grafton Street, London W1
1985

William Collins Sons & Co Ltd
London Glasgow Sydney Auckland
Johannesburg Toronto

BRITISH LIBRARY CATALOGUING IN PUBLICATION DATA

Howarth, Tom
Prospect and reality: Great Britain
1945–1955.
1. Great Britain—History—George VI,
1936–1952 2. Great Britain—History—
Elizabeth II
I. Title
941.085   DA588

First published 1985
© T. E. B. Howarth 1985
Photoset in Plantin Light by Ace Filmsetting Ltd, Frome, Somerset
Made and printed in Great Britain by
William Collins Sons and Co Ltd, Glasgow

CONTENTS

INTRODUCTION

LIKE ALL STUDENTS OF BRITAIN in the aftermath of the Second World War, I am the beneficiary of a vast corpus of highly professional historical writing. Particularly in the field of biography we now rival the Victorians in our output of monumental and meticulously researched studies, as typified, for example, in the work of Alan Bullock on Bevin, Kenneth Harris on Attlee, David Carlton on Eden, Michael Foot on Bevan, Bernard Donoghue and G. W. Jones on Morrison, Philip Williams on Gaitskell. The same thorough and exhaustive approach is to be observed in a more general work like Anthony Seldon's *Churchill's Indian Summer*. K. O. Morgan's *Labour in Power, 1945–51* is an indispensable authority. Every year the emergence of newly released official documents adds to the density of source material. Diaries, memoirs and autobiographies abound.

The sheer weight and uncompromising professionalism of published material on the period may, I suspect, prove daunting for the common reader. In which case there may be some justification for a work which at best is an exercise in high vulgarization, to employ an English translation of a French phrase – an attempt, so to speak, to delineate the shape of the wood without benefit of too many trees.

So relatively modest an aim has of course been successfully realized before now, notably in Harry Hopkins's brilliantly evocative *The New Look* (1963) and, for part of the period, in *The Age of Austerity* (also 1963), a series of penetrating essays edited by Michael Sissons and Philip French. While I cannot profess to have improved on the sharpness and range of their social observation, the lapse of twenty years has afforded me an incremental hindsight which allows for some different perspectives – a new look at the New Look, so to speak. In that connection I have had continually to wrestle with the notorious difficulty of writing about a period of which I was an eye-witness for a generation of readers, some of whom – and perhaps the ones I most want to reach – were not yet born in 1955, the point at which this study ends.

I should like to thank Malcolm Muggeridge for help and encouragement based on discussion of a similar exercise of his own called *The Thirties*; Lord Blake for most helpful comments on the typescript; Philip Ziegler of Collins, who allowed me to extend my contract for two years, so enabling me to undertake an unexpected assignment in Greece; Roderick Suddaby of the Imperial War Museum for the use of manuscript material in the Museum's collection; Michael Sissons; Dominic Hobson and Martin Chick, recently first-class History graduates of Magdalene College, Cambridge; and Beverley Storkey, late of Girton College, who alleges that she enjoyed the typing.

NOTTING HILL, LONDON   1984

·I·
The Prospectus

War is the locomotive of History
KARL MARX

THE BOHEMIAN JOURNALIST Hannen Swaffer, inventor of the modern gossip column, lived for many years in a flat overlooking Trafalgar Square in order, as he hoped, to have a front seat when the British Revolution broke out. The Labour victory in the General Election of July 1945, if something less than a revolution, nevertheless aroused in a war-weary Britain a mixture of excitement, elation, and, in some quarters, apprehension. Swaffer, who worked for the Labour *Daily Herald*, soon addressed himself like many others to the problem of how this famous victory had come about and concluded that no single man was more responsible for it than William Temple, Archbishop of Canterbury, who had died, perhaps more widely mourned than any of his predecessors since Becket, in October 1944.

Since the days of Laud and Sancroft, Archbishops of Canterbury have not been prominent in controversial politics, and Temple in his writings, his broadcasts and his frequent letters to the press was always at pains to emphasize that the social gospel, as he envisaged it, transcended day-to-day politics. However, his Penguin Special, *Christianity and the Social Order* (1942), which sold over 150,000 copies, strayed some distance beyond the strict confines of pastoral theology. Karl Marx, he wrote, 'was not far wrong' in declaring that the triumph of the bourgeoisie had left no other remaining bond between man and man than 'naked self-interest and callous cash payment'. Although he condemned slum housing as 'a wanton and callous cruelty', he

9

regarded it as a lesser scourge than unemployment, 'the most hideous of our social evils'. Even those fortunate enough to be in work found themselves challenged by the Archbishop's question: 'Why should some of God's children have full opportunity to develop their capacities in freely-chosen occupations, while others are confined to a stunted form of existence, enslaved to types of labour which represent no personal choice but the sole opportunity offered?' Temple favoured in general terms what is nowadays called worker participation, holding that labour should share 'at least equally with capital in the control of industry'. He advocated not only the nationalization of the Bank of England but that of the joint stock banks as well, and held views of distinct rigidity on the matter of dividends: 'whenever limitation of liability is given, a maximum rate of dividends should be fixed'. Above all, he proclaimed in tones of ringing conviction an idea which had begun by 1942 to seize the minds and consciences of a majority of his flock (believers and unbelievers alike): 'No one doubts that in the post-war world our economic life must be "planned" in a way and to an extent that Mr Gladstone (for example) would have regarded, and condemned, as socialistic.' Henceforth, the nation's wealth would not be allowed to fructify in the pockets of the people as Gladstone recommended. The formidable and frequently caustic Bishop of Durham, Hensley Henson, endeavoured to restrain his superior by reminding him that *dolus latet in generalibus*, a relatively polite manner of telling him that it was time his feet touched the ground. This was, however, in vain, since in Temple generosity of spirit was matched by generally acknowledged superiority of intellect, and his ideas took on for many a prophetic authority and grandeur. An exception was the observant Conservative MP Chips Channon, who wrote in his diary that the Archbishop had a fuddled, muddled brain.

Temple's was, of course, far from being the only voice which during that seemingly interminable war called for a radical transformation of society. Tom Hopkinson, the editor of the illustrated weekly *Picture Post*, watching the announcement of the Labour triumph at the General Election in the Dorchester Hotel, was left in no doubt by his fellow guests that his 'bloody *Picture Post* was responsible for this'. While modestly affirming the greater claims of the *Daily Mirror* as the midwife of radical post-war reconstruction, he had no need to underplay the formidable impact of *Picture Post*'s politics from 1941 onwards. At the beginning of that year Hopkinson had revived Disraeli's concept of two nations by applying that title to the caption of what became a famous and much reproduced photograph of two traditionally garbed and apprehensive little Etonians in the close vicinity of two very ragged but perky-looking street urchins. At the same time *Picture Post* anticipated the Beveridge Report by coming out in favour of full employment, all-in contributory social insurance, and a health service, and went further by advocating a minimum wage, child allowances, slum clearance, and the integration of the public schools. There was a striking article entitled 'Work for all – the first necessity in the New Britain' by a young Hungarian academic from Balliol, Thomas Balogh, with an accompanying illustration of cheerful, smiling workers at the factory gate. Balogh advanced the proposition that work can be made universal, pleasant and secure by proper planning of the national resources. In February 1941 the high-priests of planning, the octogenarians Sidney and Beatrice Webb, were appropriately eulogized in an article entitled 'A tribute to two wonderful lives' by George Bernard Shaw, illustrated with a photograph of Beatrice sitting under a portrait of Lenin. The Webbs' masterpiece, *Soviet Communism*, which somehow succeeded in being at one and the same time popular and unreadable, was described by the great dramatist, who had once criticized Shakespeare for having no message for his age, as follows: 'Finally came the work in which those who believe in Divine Providence may like to see its finger. . . . In their last two volumes they gave us the first really scientific analysis of the Soviet State, and of its development of our political and social experiments and institutions, including trade unionism and co-operation, which we thought they had abolished.' In March 1943 Hopkinson told his readers that the government had filleted the Beveridge Plan and that as far as Parliament was concerned it was dead and defeated, 'but once before, over the Hoare-Laval pact, this country spoke its mind, and the government had to follow'.

It was not perhaps unreasonable in the wartime circumstances of early 1943 to pan in general terms rather than to legislate precisely, to 'peer through the mists of the future', as Churchill put it, when he described himself and his colleagues in the government 'as strong partisans of national compulsory insurance for all classes for all purposes from the cradle to the grave' in his broadcast of 21 March 1943. But Hopkinson took the lead in a concerted movement to cast doubts on the degree of commitment to any future Welfare State of the wartime Coalition by concentrating on the pessimistic, if not wholly unrealistic, utterances of senior Tory backbenchers, like Sir Arnold Gridley and Sir Herbert Williams. The latter had for long represented nobody much except himself and ran true to form in giving it as his opinion during the Beveridge debate that, if the scheme were postponed till six months after the end of the war, it would be rejected by the then House of Commons by a large majority as being beyond the financial resources of the nation. This prompted Hopkinson to write: 'Exactly. If we don't get the foundations of a new Britain laid while the war is on, we shall never get them laid at all.' Hopkinson's evangelical zeal for a new Britain was always inclined to brush aside economic as well as political obstacles, as when he wrote in 1943: 'And what of the export trade? Well, what of it? To me, and to those who think as I do, the idea that after the war we are all going straight back to cutting one another's throats in the effort to export more and import less . . . is delirium. There could only be one answer to that – a general refusal. A world strike!' He urged his readers to reject altogether the idea that the British people needed to reduce their standard of living for the sake of trying to undersell the Japanese.

Hopkinson was a member of J. B. Priestley's left-wing ginger group called the 1941 Committee, as was *Picture Post*'s owner, Edward Hulton. Paul Addison in *The Road to 1945* gives us an imposing roll-call of the Committee's membership, comprising as it did the cream of the left-wing establishment – Victor Gollancz, publisher, mystic, and founder of the Left Book Club; Kingsley Martin, whose editorship of the *New Statesman* not infrequently suggested that for him comment was sacred whereas fact was free; other journalists in Gerald Barry, David Astor and Ritchie Calder; Konni Zilliacus, genial and tireless apologist of the USSR; Tom Wintringham, Spanish Civil War veteran; Sir Richard Acland, leader of the short-lived Common Wealth party, which frequently won by-elections on behalf of the Labour party, still hobbled by the prevailing electoral truce; Thomas Balogh of Balliol and Douglas Jay, formerly of All Souls; the influential social scientist Richard Titmuss; and A. D. Peters, literary agent and indefatigable hob-nobber. But the most dazzling member of the *Linksintellectuelle* and the object of much anxiety on the part of Churchill and Beaverbrook alike was the Chairman of the Labour Party in 1945, Harold Laski.

Laski, like his hero Tom Paine, would have been at home in the atmosphere of the Jacobin Club of 1791. There was in him the same generous espousal of all radical causes together with a rage for declamatory over-simplification. In pre-war years he had been something of an advocate of revolution *tout court*, as when he wrote to his friend the American judge Felix Frankfurter in October 1931: 'I stay with the Left of Labour and, if necessary, I go to the extreme Left.' He described his 1933 book *Democracy In Crisis* as a 'philosophical-historic explanation of why Capitalism and Democracy are incompatible', and what he came to call revolution by consent he more or less defined to a Labour party conference in 1942 thus: 'The age of competitive capitalism is over. A democracy means nothing less than a society of equals planning full production for community consumption.' Laski was an exceptionally influential Professor of Political Science at the LSE from 1926 to his death in 1950. During the war years at Cambridge he was not in good health – one of his many friends recording that on the ledge before the gas-fire in his rooms there was always a benzedrine-inhaler warming – but his energy and zeal in the propagation of his views were relentless. He was a remarkable platform speaker, partly as a result of a phenomenal memory, with which he used to vanquish athletically-minded student hecklers at the LSE by his total mastery of the cricket averages since 1880. He described his indefatigable lecturing activities at military installations in the war as those of 'a walking delegate for the trade union of ideas', and his 1943 book *Reflections on the Revolution of our Time* was widely read by young serving officers. He frequently wrote to President Roosevelt, as for instance on 4 September 1939: 'I do hope you will be able to keep America out. At some early stage we must have vital mediation,' or again at the end of 1942: 'I am confident that the need for fundamental change has now the force of unbreakable dogma in the minds of ordinary men . . . .' (Indeed, he always liked to think of himself as influencing affairs at the summit. Malcolm Muggeridge recorded in his diary: 'He talks rather well, apart from the fact that nearly all that he says is imaginary – his interview with Stalin, the day he spent at the Politburo, his intimacy with Churchill, etc., etc.'.)

If Laski was right, why did ordinary men demand fundamental change? There was, as we shall see, a great proliferation of exciting and positive ideas for social and political change building up during the war years. There was also, however, a negative factor of cardinal importance which was the widespread discrediting of almost all the older Conservative and National Liberal politicians, except Churchill himself. Large parts of the nation, particularly the young, had turned in revulsion from a generation of rulers who were deemed, not always fairly, to carry the burden of responsibility for the breakdown of the international order leading to a long, painful and often peculiarly dreary war. This process was well under way long before the end of the war, the historian Denis Brogan writing in *The English People* in 1943: 'In their silent, unrhetorical, undramatic way, the English people seem to be registering a vote of no confidence in their recent rulers.' In addition, as standard-bearers of capitalism, these self-same rulers were associated in the public mind with the genuine and well-publicized social evils of the inter-war years – large-scale regional unemployment, slum housing, poverty, malnutrition and insecurity in old age. It was increasingly overlooked that 4 million new houses had been built between the wars; that infant mortality had halved between 1910 and 1938; that in 1935 the nation had consumed 23 million barrels of beer and 165 million pounds of tobacco, 22 million bunches of imported bananas and 11 million hundredweight of oranges; had bought $1\frac{1}{2}$ million cars and 500,000 motor-cycles and had occupied 4 million cinema seats nightly. As time went on, memories of the real improvements in the standard of living of the great majority in the inter-war years were largely obliterated in favour of a stereotype hate-figure of a stern-lipped Tory politician, garbed in funereal black and a starched collar, administering the hated Means Test with a callous disregard for suffering humanity. The prevalent demonology included as stock figures the grotesque Colonel Blimp; Montagu Norman and other wicked bankers; 'upholders of the Raj', as satirized by Noël Coward; and wearers of the old school tie, as guyed by the monocled music-hall comedians the Western Brothers.

Priestley in his *Letter to a Returning Serviceman* (1945) summarized the new orthodoxy as follows: 'Whatever their faults, the Bolsheviks had put their hand to the great task and were trying to lift the load of want, ignorance, fear and misery from their dumb millions, while the Americans – as they fully admit now – were living in a fool's paradise of money-for-nothing and Martinis, and we were shuffling and shambling along, listening to our Tory politicians talking their old twaddle.'

Amongst the shufflers, shamblers and twaddlers most readily doomed to immolation on the altar of the new radicalism were two erstwhile heroes of the recent past. Stanley Baldwin had been greatly admired for his concern to heal the social wounds of the General Strike, his continual espousal of 'sound' government on the principle of 'safety first' and his skill at the time of the Abdication crisis. There were indeed many who thought of him in the terms used by Field Marshal Birdwood in 1928 as 'a real, true, straight, brave Englishman without a single thought of unkindness'. And it was the Liberal G. M. Trevelyan who wrote of him: 'he remains the most human and lovable of all the Prime Ministers.' Yet in wartime retreat in Astley Hall he was furiously vilified, with some of the press insisting that the presentation railings round his house be pulled down to help with the war effort. No less spectacular was the fall from grace of Neville Chamberlain, a politician with a more than respectable record behind him of social reform and for a few short months widely adulated as the prophet of 'peace in our time'. There were as yet no excuses for the appeasers, condemned to contumely and apparent oblivion in Churchill's own words: 'they are decided only to be undecided, resolved to be irresolute, adamant for drift, solid for fluidity, all powerful for impotence.'

Together with the politicians of the past, there was a widespread disposition to repudiate the whole capitalist order of society for which they stood. Sir Richard Acland, the leader of the Common Wealth party, looked forward in a broadcast at the end of June 1945 to a Britain where in due course there would be no Stock Exchange, no company promoters, no share certificates, no mortgaged title-deeds. Four months after the Election, A.J.P. Taylor in one of his frequent broadcasts expressed the view that 'nobody in Europe believes in the American way of life – that is, in private enterprise; or rather, those who believe in it are a defeated party which seems to have no more future than the Jacobites in England after 1688.' It seemed rather easily forgotten that the Americans had suffered 2500 casualties on Omaha Beach alone.

Arguments against capitalism and private enterprise were marshalled by the nation's sages in terms both of morality and expediency. J. D. Bernal, with the austere authority expected at this period of the great scientists, wrote in the *Modern Quarterly* that because collective action is the only effective action it is the only virtuous action. The novelist John Cowper Powys told his wireless listeners that the ability to make money requires only the lowest qualities of the human character, an opinion which would have much irritated Dr Johnson, who believed that no man but a blockhead ever wrote except for money and that in any case there are few ways in which a man can be more innocently employed than in getting money. Warnings urged in certain quarters about the risks involved in the birth of the new order were swept away with persuasive briskness. Talk of the supreme importance of exports for national survival, for example, left Aneurin Bevan unimpressed in 1944, since at that time he saw expanding exports as 'the will-o'-the-wisp private enterprise is compelled to pursue by under-paying its own workers and thus limiting its home market'. The leading articles of the historian of Soviet Russia, E. H. Carr, in *The Times* had persuaded many of his readers to agree that the desire for monetary gain had ceased to work as the motive power of the economic system. Conservative suggestions that too much Civil Service control might hamper industrial production were swept aside in the *New Statesman* by Ian Mikardo, the new member for Reading and the author of *Centralised Control of Industry* (1944), with the comforting reflection that 'most of the red tape, in fact, is tied round dividend warrants and will disappear as public controls give way to public ownership.'

There was much unbounded optimism in the spring and summer of 1945 among the supporters of public ownership. At the Labour party conference at Blackpool in May, Aneurin Bevan drew much laughter with his remark that 'only an organizing genius could produce a shortage of coal and fish in Great Britain,' which as a prophecy was true in part as the nation was to have its fill of fish in the meatless years ahead, although coal

16

would be rather a different story. The Labour Speaker's Handbook for 1945 recommended in broad outline: 'A plan for the nation's food, deciding how much is to be imported and how much produced, should be drawn up by a Ministry of Food. Such a plan will be expansionist, i.e. will seek to provide everyone with an adequate diet, with considerable variety and ample consumers' choice.' The reality for some years to come would be rather more a matter of eating the air promise-crammed. In another area of public concern Sir Ernest Simon, contributing to a May 1945 publication called *Post-War Britain*, was unwise, as it turned out, to envisage 'the abolition of the slums within one generation and the provision of a good home for every family on a well-planned estate in pleasant surroundings at a rent or price it can afford to pay'. As to strikes, there was George Woodcock, at that time Secretary of the Research and Economic Council of the TUC, concluding a broadcast with the encouraging pronouncement that the question of strike action by trade unions in nationalized industries should become almost entirely theoretical. Sir Stafford Cripps, the new President of the Board of Trade, a little later, on 13 February 1946, modified this only slightly when he told the House of Commons that he was prepared to endorse the legitimacy of the strike weapon as long as capitalism and private enterprise persisted, a proposition which he was quite satisfied to argue 'on the basis that capitalism will exist for another year or two in this country'. The Town and Country Planning Bill impelled the buoyant Dr Dalton to sum up prospects with a quotation from H. G. Wells: 'For a moment I caught a vision of the coming City of Mankind, more wonderful than all my dreams, full of life, full of youth, full of the spirit of creation.' (Wells had long since abandoned views of this sort, substituting the acute pessimism of his *Mind at the End of its Tether*.)

The widespread enthusiasm for planning was largely derived from two sources – the experiences of wartime and the achievements of the USSR. Churchill had a premonition of what would come to pass when he urged the House on 13 October 1945 to be careful that a pretext was not made of war needs to introduce far-reaching social or political changes by 'a side wind'. It needed no pretext for the nation to effect important and beneficial social changes under pressure of the blitz in medical and child care services, in factory regulation, in care for the disabled, in communal feeding and in many other fields, admirably set out in Angus Calder's *The People's War*. But in addition central government was assuming more and more responsibility. The wartime coalition absorbed three-fifths of all production, one-third of personal expenditure was controlled by rationing and five-and-a-half million citizens were under arms. The civil service was about to enter on its heyday, its ranks expanded by 1943 to 184 per cent of its pre-war strength. (After the war it never fell below 175 per cent of the 1939 figure until 1951.) And for none of this did the nation appear to be beholden to private enterprise. As Cripps pointed out, you don't talk about Smith's Grenadiers or Jones's Fusiliers. If an operation as complex and successful as the Normandy landings was based on centralized planning, then surely that must be the right formula for the great enterprises of peace. Few people paused to ask whether methods eminently suitable for achieving the single aim of destroying the enemy were equally applicable to the multifarious purposes of peace. For the next forty years politicians would periodically urge the nation to recover the elusive Dunkirk spirit, not of course easily recoverable unless you were actually required to evacuate Dunkirk. But as the war ended people were inclined to agree readily with Labour's Evelyn Walkden when he said: 'We can endeavour to carry over the fruits of victory into the days of peace and thus ensure for all concerned those material comforts that make life more tolerable,' without necessarily reflecting that the fruits of victory were the loss of our overseas investments and a mountain of debt. Ellen Wilkinson in a 1944 lecture to the Fabian Society presented what she saw to be a clear contrast between trained and tested intelligent planning on the one hand and national needs being met by 'the ethics of the poker-table' on the other.

Trained and tested intelligent planning was believed by many to be the particular achievement of the USSR. It would be some time yet before it sank fully into the British consciousness that in the new civilization, so extolled by Shaw and the Webbs, there existed a state apparatus of terror without parallel in human history. The heroism of the Red Army as allies in the great cause; the sufferings of the Russian people during the long years of war; the sustained agitation in left-wing circles for a second front; the activities of organizations like the Anglo-Soviet

Public Relations Committee and the Society for Cultural Relations with the USSR – all these led to a climate of opinion about Russia both sympathetic to the aspirations of state socialism and hostile to its capitalist detractors. On 16 August 1945 Churchill told the House that he thought Mr Stalin was a very wise man and that he himself would set no limits to the immense contribution the Soviet government would make to the future. As late as 7 November he developed the theme as follows: 'Here I wish to say that Generalissimo Stalin is still strongly holding the helm and steering his tremendous ship. Personally, I cannot feel anything but the most lively admiration for this truly great man, the father of his country, the ruler of its destinies in times of peace, and the victorious defender of its life in time of war. Even if as, alas, is possible – or not impossible – we should develop strong differences on many aspects of our policy, political, social, even, as we think, moral, with the Soviet government, no state of mind must be allowed to occur which ruptures or withers these great associations between our two peoples which were our glory and our safety in the late frightful convulsion.'

Such views were, not surprisingly, echoed with more confidence by the opinion-formers of the Left. In April 1946 Bernal gave a broadcast talk on the social responsibility of science, in which he announced that science had come of age, a phrase more often associated in later years with radical theology. In organizing society, he said: 'We have before us the example of the Soviet Union, where the first efforts towards a national communal plan were made. That example inspires the world today, even those who would repudiate the inspiration. It underlies our plans for industry and agriculture, it will underlie the future organization of world production and world trade. . . . In the new world everyone has the responsibility, not only of doing well in his own job, but of seeing where and how his job fits in with collective human effort. As Lenin said, "every cook must learn to rule the state".' Other fellow travellers busied themselves with praising different aspects of Soviet moral and political superiority. D. N. Pritt, KC, MP for Hammersmith North, in an angry correspondence with a fellow Wykehamist, the historian R. C. K. Ensor, conducted in *The Listener*, wrote: 'The secret police of the USSR do not seem quite so secret as those of this country, or the USA or Canada.'

As for torture, 'doesn't Mr Ensor know that this allegation has been made dozens of times and never proved?' He went on to add, 'that their labour camps are humanely run has been established by a number of outside witnesses'. On a later occasion he was to tell the House that 'in the Soviet Union the country is ruled by the masses of the people, and consequently so is the Press.' Pritt described Russian foreign policy in a debate on Yalta thus: 'The USSR has a very distinguished record, for what records are worth, of not wanting puppets around her.' For those less inclined to be convinced by the more strident voices such as those of Pritt, there was Konni Zilliacus who was a great believer in Russian kindness to minority populations and suggested that on the strength of that the USSR might with advantage be brought into the Palestine question. Neither was there any shortage of distinguished academics with reassuring things to say about the great Russian experiment. G. D. H. Cole in *The Intelligent Man's Guide to the Post-War World*, which came out in 1947 with 1142 pages and only one joke (about the American hotel which boasted it had more soap than any other hotel), stated emphatically, 'I do, then, accept Soviet democracy as a legitimate form of democracy, and reject altogether the notion that it is merely autocracy in disguise.'

Sections of the press also presented a view of Russia more favourable than the facts warranted. Alexander Werth, born in Russia and brought up in Glasgow, infiltrated himself successively into the *Sunday Times* as diplomatic correspondent, and the *Manchester Guardian* as Moscow correspondent, and was a favoured contributor to Kingsley Martin's *New Statesman*. From these vantage points he was steadily at work putting the most favourable interpretation on Russian domestic and foreign policy. In the early post-war era *The Listener* regularly printed extracts from Moscow broadcasts without comment or elucidation.

As we shall see, disillusionment with the USSR would soon build up even among the intellectuals, and there was no sympathy among most of the Labour leaders, especially those with a trade union background, towards Communism in this country. Only two overtly Communist members of Parliament were elected in 1945. Nevertheless, throughout 1945 and 1946 admiration for the USSR contributed significantly to the general popularity of social planning.

Of all aspects of planning, the highest hopes were entertained for the nationalization of key industries. In January 1949, by which time the Labour government had carried out nearly all its manifesto commitments in the field of nationalization, the Policy and Publicity Sub-committee of the Labour Party reported to the National Executive Committee that 'we must recognize that the spiritual results of nationalization are not as good as we hoped.' To a later generation, predominantly agnostic, to say the least, about the spiritual merits of nationalization, such language may be hard to credit. Yet it should be remembered that for Beatrice Webb, as she expounded her creed in *I Believe*, a symposium of advanced thinking published in 1940 and reprinted in 1947, 'In planned production for community consumption, the secular and the religious are one.' The same publication contained an essay by John Strachey explaining that the only way to produce a distribution of income sufficient even to make it possible for the population to buy the total product of industry and so keep themselves in employment is, in the long run, to redistribute the means of production themselves, which is the source of income, to the mass of the population. But you cannot distribute big modern means of production such as railways and power stations by cutting them up and giving little bits of them to individuals, so you have got to place them in the collective ownership of the whole population. Until that is done it will not be possible for people to live decent lives. 'But that is all you have got to do. And that is socialism.' It was the need for equitable distribution which E. H. Carr had stressed in a celebrated *Times* editorial at the time of Dunkirk, when he wrote that in any talk of economic reconstruction the emphasis would be less on maximum production (though that too would be necessary) than on fair distribution. Nationalization was seen to be the prime agency in the task of cutting the national cake into fairer slices.

State control of the nation's economy together with welfare provision was widely seen to be the answer to social deprivation, the existence of which had increasingly impinged on the social conscience in the Thirties and with the outbreak of war. No one had done more to draw attention to a wide range of social injustice than the chairman of the Labour party conference in 1945, the diminutive but fiery Ellen Wilkinson. She had achieved her first, but by no means last, sensation in the House on the second reading of the Coal Miners' (Hours) Bill in 1926 by exhibiting a contraption called a guss, which was a coil of rope which went round a miner's legs together with a hook which fitted on to the tub which he dragged along. She then read out a letter from a miner: 'Many a time I've scraggled along on my belly with the guss on, tugging my put [barrow of coal] more than twenty yards with only nine inches between floor and roof.' As MP for Jarrow she had accompanied the famous Jarrow marchers in 1936 and Victor Gollancz's Left Book Club had published in 1939 her book on the subject, *The Town that was Murdered*, with the sub-title 'A Picture of Capitalism at Work'. Ellen Wilkinson, although only four foot ten, was a difficult person to stop, a friend recording that one night when they left a restaurant together she found her car had been hemmed in on the kerb, so got in and charged it backwards and forwards till she had made enough space to manoeuvre herself out.

To the grievances of the miners and the miseries of means-tested unemployment was added, as the war broke out, a startling revelation of social deprivation among urban children which had come to light as a consequence of evacuation at the beginning of the war. While not everybody's experiences were as lurid as those described in Evelyn Waugh's *Put Out More Flags*, middle-class families found their susceptibilities disagreeably assailed by a number of infantile attributes on a scale they had never previously encountered, notably obscenity, lice and incontinence. *The Lancet* documented the latter problem in 1939 as follows: 'Somewhat unexpectedly, enuresis has proved to be one of the major menaces to the comfortable disposition of evacuated urban children . . . every morning every window is filled with bedding, hung out to air in the sunshine. The scene is cheerful, but the householders are depressed;' and the Medical Officer of Health of the Stewartry of Kirkcudbright reported a Glasgow mother upbraiding her child: 'You dirty thing, messing the lady's carpet. Go and do it in the corner.'* H. C. Dent, editor of *The Times Educational Supplement*, summed up the effect of evacuation in 1944 as having 'lifted the lid to reveal a seething stew of social degradation hitherto unsuspected – or if suspected, ignored – by increasingly comfortable and comfort-loving middle and upper

* R. M. Titmuss, *Problems of Social Policy*, Longmans, 1950. (*History of the Second World War*, U.K. Civil Series).

working classes'. Angus Calder in *The People's War* states that during the war sixty million changes of address took place amongst the civilian population of about thirty-eight million. If this degree of civilian mobility is taken in conjunction with the years of nomadic existence endured by most members of the armed forces it is small wonder that the post-war prospect most consistently craved for by the majority of the population was simply to 'settle down'. During the VI attacks on London in September 1944 20,000 houses a day were being damaged, and during the war as a whole 458,000 houses had been completely written off and many more damaged. There was much damage too from causes other than enemy action, whether in Waugh's Brideshead at one end of the scale or the local Home Guard headquarters in the Parish Hall at the other.

Quite apart from war damage, there was an obvious need for slum clearance and better housing. In the six years before the war over two million new houses had been built, but only just over half a million were council houses, and slums were not only widespread but abominable. Bessie Braddock, the new MP for the Exchange Division of Liverpool, who at fourteen stone was as vast as Ellen Wilkinson was tiny, but equally formidable, was only slightly overstating her case in her maiden speech when she said: 'In industrial areas our people are living in flea-ridden, bug-ridden, rat-ridden lousy hell-holes.' It was not therefore surprising that an exercise by the *News Chronicle* on 18 June 1945 in the relatively new field of opinion polling showed that easily the most important election topic was housing at 41 per cent (followed by full employment 15 per cent; social security 7 per cent; nationalization 6 per cent; and international security 5 per cent). It was also a top priority in the thinking of the Coalition government's Reconstruction Committee, Oliver Lyttelton recalling that the responsible minister, Lord Woolton, in one of his periodic forays into the blindingly obvious, had observed: 'I have come to the conclusion that the key to the housing problem is to build more houses.' A great deal more would be heard on the subject in the next few years. Meanwhile, Woolton, in a preface to *Post-War Britain*, edited by Sir James Marchant, was happy to commit himself to the encouraging view that there was reason to conclude that housing conditions over the next quarter of a century would be vastly superior to those in the past.

Although nationalization, as such, was not a main preoccupation of the electorate, to judge by the *News Chronicle* poll, it featured largely in the plans for the new Britain of the Labour party, being described by one of its most attractive and energetic campaigners, Christopher Mayhew, as 'the mainspring of our Socialist faith'. The question was – just how much nationalization ought there to be? To start with, the establishment of national or local government agencies for controlling parts of the nation's affairs was something with which people were to some extent familiar in practice. There had been Electricity Commissioners since 1919 and a Central Electricity Board since 1926; the BBC was set up in 1927; and the British Overseas Airways Corporation in 1939. Londoners were familiar with the Port of London Authority, the Metropolitan Water Board and Herbert Morrison's London Passenger Transport Board, created in 1931. Indeed the popularity and success of Morrison's Labour-controlled London County Council in building the new Waterloo Bridge, creating the green belt, clearing slums and reforming public assistance had given a generation of Londoners a respect for public provision not subsequently accorded in the same measure to the Greater London Council, its lineal descendant.

Consequently, a relatively modest programme of nationalization was unlikely to prove particularly controversial. Churchill himself in 1943 had prefigured what was to be called in due course the mixed economy by looking forward to a situation in which, as he put it, 'state enterprise and free enterprise both serve national interests and pull the national wagon side by side.' Whether it succeeded or failed, nationalization of the coalmines in particular was felt to be essential. The philosophy of the matter was carefully explained in the book *New Deal for Coal* (1945) by the recent Director of Economics and Statistics at the Ministry of Fuel and Power, Harold Wilson: 'It seems an inescapable fact that the men will not make their fullest effort under private ownership, but will make greater efforts when they know they are serving no private interest or profit-making agency but producing for the service of the community.' It was true that a note of rather prophetic scepticism about that particular view was struck in another book called *Coal*, written anonymously by 'A Colliery Manager', and appearing at exactly the same time, but for the moment Wilsonian optimism went largely unquestioned.

Mr Noel Newsome, the Director of Recruiting in the Ministry of Fuel and Power, combined faith in the future of coalmining with a wider national vision, perhaps by way of an incentive for his manpower drive. 'I am certain,' he said, 'that Britain's days as a Great Power, and a great force for good in the world are not numbered – that we are at the beginning of a splendid new era in our long history in which Britain's moral and, let it be said, spiritual leadership of the world will once more be forthcoming, backed by a strength fairly based on her industrial prosperity; and the miners will be the backbone of the new Britain.' Dr Dalton, who sat for a mining constituency, picked up the theme when he told the House in January 1946 that the government had decided that among the nation's industries 'in the great forward march of socialist accomplishment, the miners shall lead the way.'

As to the practice of nationalization, as opposed to its philosophy, war had once again been the great agent of change. Although the question of the ownership of the mines remained a matter of political controversy, the management of them had been effectively taken over by the Government in the interests of war-time efficiency since 1942. A National Coal Board had been set up to oversee the 800 separate private companies and their 1500 pits (involving a million acres of land) and to establish some sort of uniformity in terms of production targets and industrial relations. It was clear that many, though by no means all, of the owners simply did not have the resources to modernize their pits by the installation of such devices as coal-cutting machines or washery plants. Some South Wales mines had been worked for over a century. Many owners who had already seen mining tithes and royalties nationalized in 1938 were not averse to abandoning what was not always a particularly rewarding activity in return for compensation (which eventually totalled £164,600,000). Nor was it without political significance that the miners in 1945 comprised over 400,000 of the Labour party's $2\frac{1}{2}$ million affiliated trade unionists. So the case for nationalization lock, stock and barrel seemed to many both overwhelming and urgent. No one in the Labour ranks seems to have advocated a limited experiment in terms of nationalizing the weaker, inefficient mines and leaving the others to continuing private enterprise. That this might not have been an impossible concept is indicated by the following description of a model pit at Comrie in Fifeshire in August 1945: 'I could see no ugly rows of colliers' houses, for the Comrie miners drive in comfortable motor-buses to their homes in towns and villages, and you might mistake them for city clerks, because their working togs are in hot-air lockers. I was astonished at the wide green lawn with its ornamental fountain and goldfish.'*

Electricity as we have seen was already sufficiently organized on a national basis to fall readily into the planners' lap and the overwhelming arguments for the nationalizing of electricity generation were widely felt to be applicable also to the supply side of the industry. It was known that Sir Geoffrey Heyworth, Chairman of Unilever, who was presiding over the committee which was looking into the future of the gas industry was in favour of nationalizing what he regarded as a natural monopoly. The desire to nationalize the Bank of England had its origin to a considerable extent in the detestation entertained by Labour's economic theorists for what they regarded as the sinister influence of Sir Montagu Norman, Governor from 1920 to 44. As an instance of this, Harold Laski told his American friend Felix Frankfurter that in the 1931 financial crisis the French Prime Minister Flandin had told Tom Johnston that the French were withdrawing gold from the Bank at the definite request of Monsieur Norman. Glenvill Hall, Financial Secretary to the Treasury, explained what he and his colleagues felt to the House on 19 December 1945: 'All of us in this House have lived through the period of the Norman Conquest. We know and remember that the unemployment and the misery, the uncertainty and the dislocation of the pre-war years were largely due to the power which the City could and did exercise to frustrate the work of any Government which called itself progressive. . . . The City and the Bank will be the servant of the people, and not, as it has been in the past, its master.' The theory of the hidden hand has much potency. In France it had been a matter of *les cent familles*; in Britain Montagu Norman – and in later years the gnomes of Zürich.

In the field of transport, a generation which owed its survival to the Royal Air Force was unlikely to question the desirability of nationalizing civil aviation, which was not in any case an

* *The Listener*, 16 August 1945.

26

amenity which many of them envisaged using. The railways by the end of the war were in a terrible mess, their 52,000 miles of track and 20,000 steam locomotives in urgent need of renewal on a scale widely felt to be beyond the resources of the private companies which owned them, despite some proud traditions, especially on the Great Western. The *New Statesman* echoed a widespread fear: 'Unless the transport industry is unified under public ownership a demand for increased charges is certain.' At that time it was not envisaged that the nexus between public ownership and ever-increasing charges would prove to be quite as enduring as events were to show.

So far then, the programme was unlikely to provoke excessive controversy. However, for the theorists of collectivism no advance towards securing for the state the commanding heights of industry could be remotely complete unless it included the great iron and steel industry. Here paradoxically in the Labour ranks there was a notable sceptic in Herbert Morrison, the very man who would be at the centre of the nationalization programme in the succeeding years. The industry had not had an unsuccessful record during the war, many of the firms were well managed and productivity, if not particularly impressive by international standards, was adequate, largely because the wage structure had a big element of payment by results. The consequent debate exemplified the dilemma which was to bedevil the history of the Labour party in the second half of the twentieth century whereby 'those behind cried "Forward" and those before cried "Back".' A document produced by the National Executive entitled *Economic Controls, Public Ownership and Full Employment*, which confined itself in terms of nationalization to the largely symbolic acquisition of the Bank of England failed to impress the party conference which met at the Central Hall, Westminster, in December 1944. The still comparatively unknown enthusiast for the centralized control of industry, Ian Mikardo, earned himself enduring fame on the left of the party by engineering a motion, which was carried by a large majority, for the public ownership of the land, large scale building, heavy industry, all forms of banking, transport, and fuel and power. The conference went on to demand 'that the national assets, services and industries shall be democratically controlled and operated in the national interest, with representation of the workers engaged therein and of

27

consumers'. It was time for those before to cry 'Back' and although the Labour campaign manifesto *Let Us Face the Future*, drafted by Herbert Morrison, included the nationalization of iron and steel, there was no mention of the joint stock banks nor of large scale building nor of anything at all precise about the land. Since Herbert Morrison was the leading advocate of the public corporation, nationalization when it came would not be conspicuous for the representation either of the workers or of the consumers, as demanded by the party conference. But for the moment the seeds of dissension between right and left in the party were barely visible in the ground and there was much optimism and general euphoria at the Blackpool conference of May 1945, where Morrison, a great dancing man, led Ellen Wilkinson in the last waltz. It would be time enough later on to recall that the notorious clause four of the party's constitution talks not only of the common ownership of the means of production, distribution and exchange, but also of 'the best obtainable system of popular administration and control of each industry or service. . . .'

State ownership was not the only form of social planning which engendered heady optimism in progressive circles as the war ended. The climate of opinion was in many ways reminiscent of the eighteenth-century Enlightenment. Reason would prevail over privilege and prescription. To echo Burke, the age of economists and calculators, if not of sophisters, seemed to have arrived, and with it a new science of government, instead of what was widely seen as the muddle and corruption of the *ancien régime*. The mood of the moment was perfectly caught by the planning consultant to the Middlesbrough Corporation, Max Lock, ARIBA. As he told listeners to a broadcast, Middlesbrough was a town of 138,000 inhabitants and called for a people's plan for re-development in three stages – a five-year plan, a fifteen-year plan and a thirty-year plan. All that was needed was to consult the people and exercise 'sufficiently wise urban statesmanship'. 'Middlesbrough is the key town in a growing industrial area with plans afoot for a great expansion of steel and chemical manufacture, engineering and shipbuilding.' He employed fifteen- and sixteen-year-old boys in carrying out traffic surveys, measuring the amount of soot and dust falling in the town, and reporting to his 'team of geographers, economists, sociologists, town-planners and architects, rather like one of the Russian Planning Brigades'. Part of the problem, as he saw it, was 'to bring the warmth of the slum areas to the dull and socially rather sterile housing estates'. The idea of the planning brigade much appealed to the eminent biologist C. H. Waddington, who felt society needed 'far more pyschologists, far more sociologists, far more anthropologists and others with long names and useful functions'. Talking on Science and the Humanities in a BBC series called *Challenge of Our Time*, Waddington affirmed: 'We know that, given twenty or even ten years of uninterrupted effort, we could brush aside the old spectres of poverty, disease and famine over most of the world at least.' The future lay, it appeared, with the scientists and their homologues, the psychologists and the sociologists. Another biologist, J. B. S. Haldane, harnessed the atomic bomb to his familiar argument for the supremacy of a science-based morality: 'Science does in the long run make us behave better because it magnifies the effects of evil conduct till they become utterly intolerable.' As he went on to explain, collective wrong-doing is largely economic, or due to economic causes, and the remedy for it 'is not a lot of good deeds by individuals, but planning by the community'. A. J. P. Taylor caught the mood, but with one important reservation: 'Scientists can do anything, if you give them the money.'

It was widely believed by many, though not for long as it transpired, that the money would be available because of the magic properties attributed to Lord Keynes and his attractive theory of demand management of the economy. Keynes's enthusiasm for planning was in fact limited to a belief in the advantages of a central framework of broad principle, within which private enterprise and individual initiative could operate. Nor had he any doubts about the social evils of inflation. Unfortunately, his death in 1946 denied him the opportunity of restraining his more imprudent followers, and there was therefore a measure of truth in Brendan Bracken's view that 'with all his beguiling power of expression and great but disordered force of intellect, Keynes will be best remembered as the man who made inflation respectable.' For Professor Waddington and many of Tom Hopkinson's *Picture Post* readers alike, the new economics and the spirit of the age could be relied on to banish the old spectres.

Standing ready in the wings to play a more extensive role

than ever before in the nation's history was the civil service, greatly expanded, as we have seen, as a consequence of the administrative demands of total war and of what was called the home front, which involved for example a million more old age pensions and the feeding at school of 1,650,000 children. Just as the armed forces had added to the common fabric of the language monosyllables like blitz and jeep and prang and scrounge, so the administrators had evolved a new vocabulary of ceilings and priorities and working parties. In progressive circles opinion varied on the question of the social background and capacities of the civil service. From the far left, shortly after the election, William Warbey worried in the columns of the *New Statesman* that, although the old ruling classes had at long last been overthrown by the victory of the common people, there was still the danger that the victory could be frustrated 'by the retention in positions of power and influence of people who are closely linked, socially and psychologically, with the defeated classes'. R. H. S. Crossman, on the other hand, argued that efficiency rather than ideology should be the criterion. His schoolfellow Douglas Jay had tried to enhance the status of the civil service, and in the process coined a phrase which will earn him immortality, when he had written in *The Socialist Case* in 1937: 'Housewives as a whole cannot be trusted to buy all the right things, where nutrition and health are concerned. This is really no more than an extension of the principle according to which the housewife herself would not trust a child of four to select the week's purchases. For in the case of nutrition and health, just as in the case of education, the gentleman in Whitehall really does know better what is good for people than the people know themselves.' The gentleman in Whitehall was in for a good deal of overtime.

It was not only far Left politicians like William Warbey who envisaged a new attitude to class and privilege in the post-war world. Was there indeed the possibility of looking forward, if not to a classless society, at least to a great extension of the principle of Equality? The paramount importance of equality had been influentially propounded in the inter-war years by the Fabians, especially R. H. Tawney, whom Hugh Gaitskell described as *the* democratic socialist *par excellence*, and Beatrice Webb as the saint of socialism. A contemporary of Temple's at Rugby and Balliol, Tawney practised what he preached about equality by refusing a commission in the Great War and extolling the comradeship in misery of the trenches. The Second World War in its turn necessitated both in the field and on the home front, in areas such as billeting, evacuation and a whole range of voluntary activity, much more rubbing of shoulders between the social classes than had commonly prevailed before the war. In particular the jealously guarded differences between the lower middle- and working-classes had been greatly eroded in barrack room and canteen. The upper and middle classes were not given to queuing before 1939 but from then on, whether in the armed forces or not, you waited your turn in the queue and the nation grew rapidly accustomed to new phrases like 'queue-jumping' or 'anti-social behaviour'. Barbara Wootton, author in 1941 of *End Social Inequality*, testified to the unhierarchical nature of wartime firewatching at Chatham House, 'where we might very well find one of the porters was in charge of our unit and we must regard everybody in this context as equal'. Clement Attlee too had written in *The Labour Party in Perspective* in 1937, 'the abolition of social classes is fundamental to the Socialist conception of society,' a process which in Churchill's view had been much accelerated by the war, as he told the boys of Harrow School in December 1944: 'During this war great changes have taken place in the minds of men, and there is no change which is more marked in our country than the continual and rapid effacement of class differences.'

On the other hand, the awkward Dean Inge of St Paul's thought that the average Englishman did not care twopence for equality, though he highly valued liberty. 'It is no use to deny that man is essentially a competitive animal. He would be bored stiff in a Fabian farmyard, and the importance of boredom in politics is often underestimated. If we were made differently, we should long ago have stabilized our civilization on a communistic basis like the social insects. We should live in beehives, a suffragette millennium run by maiden aunts.'

High also on the post-war agenda was the desirability of greater equality between the sexes. In a particularly characteristic 1940 postscript to the nine o'clock news, Priestley praised British womankind at war: 'Here's this big bully, Goering, who for six years has been given all the resources of Germany to create the most terrible and merciless weapon of oppression

Europe had ever known – the German Air Force; and he arrives in Northern France to command it himself, and to tell it to do its worst; and there are launched all the thunderbolts of the Teutonic fury, and the whole world holds its breath. And what happens? Why, a lot of London girls – pale-faced little creatures living on cups of tea and buns, who go tripping from tiny villas and flats with their minute attaché-cases to tubes and buses and then to offices and shops – defy this Goering and all his Luftwaffe and all their high explosives and incendiaries and machine-guns – and successfully defy them, still trotting off to work, still carrying on, still trim and smiling. Isn't that a triumph? I've just had a message from an American friend, concluding with this cry: "What a great race you are!" But I shall tell him that our men wouldn't be so fine if our women at this fateful hour were not so magnificent. There isn't an airman, submarine commander, or unnamed hero in a bomb squad who hasn't behind him at least one woman, and perhaps half a dozen women, as heroic as himself.' The census of 1931 had shown that a million women (and for that matter 36,000 men) were in domestic service, of which 706,800 were resident. By 1939 there was probably a drop in this number of the order of 25 per cent. Thereafter cooks, housemaids, parlour maids and scullery maids disappeared in their thousands into the women's services – WRNS, ATS, WAAF – into ordnance factories, into hospitals, on to the land as landgirls, to discover a new independence and a vigorous new sense of their own potential in society which they had no intention of relinquishing. From December 1941 the principle of conscripting women for war work was accepted. Calder calculates that by 1943 nine single women out of ten and eight married women out of ten, between the ages of eighteen and forty, were in the forces or in industry. A new comradeship, born of shared adversities rather than anything approaching militant feminism, was the prevalent mood. Once again war had effected a profound social change, which would be irreversible, in demonstrating to large numbers of men that women were capable of performing excellently many more tasks than had been traditionally assumed.

The desire for greater equality and the preservation of what was seen as the wartime spirit of national unity were most eloquently expressed for many in a book called *The Last Enemy* by Richard Hillary, a young Oxonian Royal Air Force pilot who died on a training flight after being horribly burned in the Battle of Britain: 'Was there perhaps a new race of Englishmen arising out of this war, a harmonious synthesis of the governing class and the great rest of England; that synthesis of disparate backgrounds and upbringings to be seen at its most obvious best in RAF squadrons . . .? Would they see to it that there arose from their fusion representatives, not of the old gang, deciding at Lady Cucuffle's that Henry should have the Foreign Office and George the Ministry of Food, nor figureheads for an angry but ineffectual Labour party, but true representatives of the new England that should emerge from this struggle?' Soon after the war ended, the nation had its opportunity to choose what it thought to be its true representatives by voting at a General Election for the first time since November 1935. The occasion recalled for Michael Foot a phrase from Tom Paine: 'the candidates were not men but principles.'

Of the eventual outcome of the Election, Aneurin Bevan wrote in *Tribune*: 'The General Election was not an argument with the issue in doubt until all sides were heard. It was the registration of a change which had occurred in Britain before the war began.' That was perhaps an example of being wise after the event, since there was a general disinclination in a pre-psephological age to accept as significant evidence the mounting success of the Common Wealth party in circumventing the wartime electoral truce and so registering the desire for political change. In three successive years – 1943, 1944, 1945 – Conservative seats were lost at Eddisbury, Skipton and Chelmsford to Common Wealth candidates with swings which would have seemed formidable even in peacetime by-elections. Although Common Wealth harboured among its 10,000 or so activists in its short existence between 1942 and 1945 a wide variety of political extremists such as the Communist Spanish War veteran Tom Wintringham, its inspiration derived largely from Sir Richard Acland. Acland's baronetcy dated from the Civil War, as did most of his ideas, which would have found ready acceptance from Ranters, Diggers and Fifth Monarchy Men. A typical Acland manifesto read as follows: 'Common Wealth does not ask for "Public Control over Big Business"; we don't believe it will work. We don't ask for the mere nationalization of three or four key industries as a matter of practical convenience; it's not enough. We insist that all our great resources – all land, mines, banks, railways, yes, and all substantial industries and factories of every sort and kind, shall be owned and run by all of us in common. We ask this not merely in order to cure unemployment and to produce more goods. We ask it above all as a matter of high moral principle. . . .' He set a personal example by handing over his substantial Devonshire estates to the National Trust in 1943. Common Wealth support played a large part in the sensational defeat of the Marquis of Hartington in February 1944, in what was regarded as the family seat in West Derbyshire, by an independent Socialist. After that particular campaign the Duchess of Westminster observed presciently that 'duchess's kisses are not what they used to be.' But even West Derbyshire paled in comparison with Chelmsford where, as late as April 1945, Wing-Commander Ernest Millington converted a Conservative majority of 16,624 to a Common Wealth majority of 6431, a swing of 28.3 per cent. The Conservative loser had conducted his campaign exclusively on Churchill's reputation and popularity; Millington, a popular bomber pilot, described his as benefiting from 'a great sort of Christian Socialist evangelical pull', whereby, as he put it in a letter to the *New Statesman*, Chelmsford had 'voted for a new way of living'. Not far from Chelmsford a rather unconventional evangelist for Socialism in the person of Tom Driberg had done almost as well at Maldon in the summer of 1942 where the Conservative share of the vote fell by 22 per cent.

That the writing should have been on the wall for all who had eyes to see was confirmed also by tests of public opinion, such as then existed. Gallup Polls, in those days exclusively published in the *News Chronicle*, showed a Labour lead over the Conservatives of 13 per cent at the end of 1943, of 14 per cent in February 1944, of 18 per cent in February 1945. At that time there were still 12 per cent of 'don't knows', but by a month before the election all questioned had made up their minds and the Labour lead was still 13 per cent. The American journalist Drew Middleton even claimed to have discovered a man who told him that he would have voted Labour had he not been a Tory candidate.

Why then, in the face of such palpable evidence, were so many, in high places and low, so markedly unaware of what was about to occur? The *locus classicus* on the subject is the entry in

34

the Channon diaries for 6 September 1944 which reads: 'I had a long talk with Robin Barrington-Ward, editor of *The Times*. He thinks that politically there is no serious swing to the Left; and says the country is "centre of centre"; so much for the foolish prophecy of that very nice ass Harold Macmillan who goes about saying that the Conservatives will be lucky to retain a hundred seats at the election.' At the end of October Channon recorded that the Prime Minister seemed in such high spirits 'that no one doubts but that he will lead the Conservative party triumphantly to victory at the polls'. By 23 March 'political gossip has it that the Conservatives will be re-elected with a reduced majority'. The day after Churchill's most celebrated election broadcast on June 4 in which he linked Socialism with the Gestapo, Chips Channon 'met Attlee in the lavatory and he seemed shrunken and terrified, and scarcely smiled, though Bevin seemed gay and robust enough. I personally feel that the prevalent Conservative optimism is overdone. Everyone today was chattering of "another '31 or at least another '24"''. Everyone is cock-a-hoop.' The old gang, intent on winning the war with the help of their Labour allies, had increasingly lost contact with any other reality. Their understandable but excessive reliance on Churchill's popularity concealed from them two very unpalatable facts – that large sections of the electorate admired Churchill as a war leader but had made up their minds not to vote for him and entertained no enthusiasm whatever for any of his Conservative colleagues. In fact, though Channon was well enough informed of opinion at Westminster, it was probably true that the upper echelons of Parliament as a whole were peculiarly insulated during the Coalition years from the drift of political opinion outside. Neither Attlee nor Dalton thought Labour would have a working majority, curiously underestimating the general popularity of their own doctrines and discounting the mass appeal of diatribes by their followers against the old gang, such as the pamphlet *Guilty Men*, the work of Michael Foot, Peter Howard and Frank Owen. Kingsley Martin was nearer the mark in the *New Statesman* on the morrow of Millington's victory at Chelmsford: 'However grateful they may be to Mr Churchill, another Tory Parliament and the satisfaction of the uncontrolled appetites of monopolists and speculators may seem too high a price to pay as a reward.' But even he was writing of a 'general consensus that the election will be a close thing' as late as 23 June, and on 14 July he referred to the totally incalculable results.

It is uncertain to what extent the final result was conditioned by the electoral campaign and especially the broadcast speeches. Attlee's biographer waxes indignant at Churchill's use of the 'savings scare'. However, the warning 'there is no man or woman in this country who has, by thrift or toil, accumulated a nest-egg, however small, who will not run the risk of seeing it shrivel before his eyes' may be faulted on grounds of rhetoric, but was to prove a more or less accurate prophecy of the outcome of the steady course of inflation on which the nation was about to embark. The Conservative attempt to elevate the busy Professor Laski into a sort of red bogey was beyond the comprehension of the average voter because of its concentration on the constitutional intricacies of the Labour party. The effects of the celebrated 'Gestapo' speech were perhaps more significant. Churchill's actual words were: 'I declare to you, from the bottom of my heart, that no Socialist system can be established without a political police. . . . No Socialist government conducting the entire life and industry of the country could afford to allow free, sharp, or violently-worded expression of public discontent. They would have to fall back on some form of Gestapo, no doubt very humanely directed in the first instance.' That is of course accurate in respect of Eastern European Socialism as we know it, but what Attlee and Morrison had to offer was generally felt to stop a long way short of Communism, or even of Aclandism. Morrison, for instance, on 29 June promised a nationalized iron and steel industry based on efficiency, low costs, high wages and full regard to public interest, which if not prophetically accurate sounded comforting enough at the time. Above all, Labour proclaimed itself emphatically as the party of moral superiority, as instanced by Philip Noel Baker on 16 June: 'A Labour government can work international institutions because international brotherhood means more to us than international cartels.' Churchill in talking of the Gestapo had evidently taken too much to heart Professor Hayek's uncomfortable observation in *The Road to Serfdom*: 'Socialism was embraced by the greater part of the intelligentsia as the apparent heir of the liberal tradition; therefore it is not surprising that to them the idea should appear inconceivable of socialism leading to the opposite of liberty.' The electorate was in no doubt that you could vote both for collectivism *and* liberty. It was time for a new start. When another diarist, Malcolm Muggeridge, accompanied his wife to church on 9 May 1945 the parson intoned: 'Let us pray for a new world.'

The electoral landslide which ensued was to be without parallel for the next thirty-eight years. On 26 July when, with the service vote garnered in, the declaration was due, Beaverbrook's *Daily Express* surpassed its own not inconsiderable record of editorial miscalculation by informing its readers that 'there are reasons for expecting that by tonight Mr Churchill and his supporters will be returned to power.' Whatever Lord Beaverbrook's reasons may have been, they were not valid. In the Prime Minister's own constituency at Woodford Alex Hancock, standing as an independent, polled 10,000 votes with a programme advocating one hour's productive work a day and the development of a philosophic community. Constituencies like Wimbledon and Winchester, Barnet and Bexley fell to all-conquering Labour. Sir Herbert Williams, who seemed as immovable as his political convictions, was defeated in Croydon South. Labour, rather more predictably, gained Accrington, though somewhat surprisingly in the person of Captain W. S. Elliot, described as having spent some years in the cotton trade in India and being the laird of Arkleton; a public school headmaster, E. M. King, gained Penryn and Falmouth; Lieutenant-General Mason Macfarlane beat Brendan Bracken in Paddington North; and Viscount Corvedale, son of Stanley Baldwin, won Paisley from the Liberals. It was a great day for railway signalmen, three of them being successful respectively in Newcastle-on-Tyne, Derby and the Hartlepools (a Labour gain); in addition a railway clerk, who had evolved into a signals corporal, gained North Kensington. Of eleven Durham members in the new House, seven were miners or miners' agents, who joined Dalton, Shinwell and Ellen Wilkinson. Altogether there were thirty-four members sponsored by the mining union. But it was commonly observed that for every two of the new MPs who could be described as horny-handed there were three who were horny-spectacled, like one of the new Coventry members R. H. S. Crossman. There were some forty practising journalists on the Labour benches and forty-five teachers of one sort or another, which seemed to a disgruntled Tory supporter 'rather a lot in a place which has never been notorious for taciturnity'. Conservative ministers were defeated, as *The Times* put it, in swathes, as was the party chairman, Ralph Assheton. But then so too was Sir William Beveridge, who stood in the Liberal interest at Berwick-on-Tweed and was beaten by a Conservative. There were many that day who echoed the view attributed to Harold Laski that if Labour did the right things there would never be another Tory government. The *Daily Herald* celebrated the first anniversary of polling day as follows: 'For Britain as a whole we can claim this: that on 5 July 1945 her citizens lived their sweetest hour in a long decade.'

What had happened was that Labour had secured 393 seats with 48 per cent of the votes cast on a 72.7 per cent turn out. The Conservatives had 213 seats with 39.8 per cent of the vote and the Liberals twelve with 9 per cent. Although there were thus nearly twice as many Labour seats as Conservative, for every four voters who wanted a Labour government there were three who wanted a Conservative one. And while it was true that some five times as many voters wished for a Labour government as compared with a Liberal government the ratio of seats acquired as between the two parties gave the Liberals considerable grounds for dissatisfaction. Some of the regional swings were remarkable, for instance 23 per cent in Birmingham, where Labour won ten out of thirteen seats. The circumstances of the election have made detailed analysis of the result more than usually difficult but it seems on balance likely that, as in 1979 and 1983, there was a considerable shift of allegiance in the lower middle-class and among the younger voters.

So, after 1902 days in office, Churchill resigned. Alistair Cooke, reporting from America, then as now, described the Hearst newspapers as having practically resigned themselves to world communism, 'against which a brave but lonely Uncle Sam would batter out his brains and money'. *Pravda*, describing the election as the greatest event in the post-war political life of Western Europe, held that 'the British people have emerged from the war enriched with great political experience and with an ardent wish to arrange their life in a new way.' Kingsley Martin rejoiced that for the first time the Parliamentary Labour party was unquestionably a socialist party and not merely the political wing of an industrial movement, but went on to warn his readers that, 'we must strive to end within the party both Trade Union domineering and irresponsible "Leftism",' thus giving early voice to subsequent Social Democratic anxieties. Quintin Hogg, in the intervals of active service, had done much to reconcile large sections of the Tory party to the Beveridge proposals, which he described as 'an opportunity to re-establish a social conscience in the Tory party'. With greater realism than some of his elders he had not expected a Conservative victory, but he was greatly surprised by the scale of their defeat. It could, he thought, only be explained 'as the consequence of a long pent-up and deep-seated revulsion against the principles, practice and membership of the Conservative party'. He had already in 1944 described the new Conservative as one who 'recognizes that privilege based on birth or wealth has served its ends and looks forward to a classical democracy in which differences of education and technical skill have taken their place'. The Conservative phoenix would rise from the ashes rather more quickly than Harold Laski suspected.

It was the opinion of Jennie Lee that if Ernest Bevin and Clement Attlee had had their way there would have been no Labour victory; 'we would have been a minor party in a coalition government, trailing behind Churchill's chariot.'* Nevertheless, and however much she disliked it, she and the Labour party would have to put up with an Attlee premiership, a prospect which a slightly bemused nation accepted with equanimity as guaranteeing a high degree of normality. When *Tribune* described Attlee as bringing 'to the fierce struggle of politics the tepid enthusiasms of a lazy summer afternoon at a cricket match', that was not necessarily a condemnation in the eyes of the public, many of whom were looking forward to a number of lazy afternoons at cricket matches. He was eminently representative of a breed of 'safe' politician to whom the British can become addicted for long periods – Salisbury, Baldwin, Wilson. People had been impressed by his radio reply to Churchill's Gestapo speech – calm, polite, pouring scorn on Professor Hayek as a foreign academic economist and generally giving the impression of answering a foolish gaffe by a likeable but rather unbalanced colleague. Quite what he stood for was not always clear. In 1937 he had written in *The Labour Party in Perspective* that 'Socialists cannot

* *My Life with Nye*, Cape, 1980, p. 154.

make Capitalism work,' but ten years later he told the House that 'private interest and public interest should be mingled, and in our planning we are not suggesting that the profit motive should not operate at all.' His leading personal characteristics were accurately summed up by Ellen Wilkinson when she said that he had two fatal handicaps – honesty and modesty. He was essentially a realist and whenever he essayed a rhetorical flourish, as all politicians have to do from time to time, it sounded false. As Bevan put it, his light shone best under a bushel. In fact his silences were generally more impressive than his polemical discourse, which Churchill described as 'ferocious bleating'. Above all, with Attlee at the helm the country was not going to be run by the Labour intelligentsia, whom he described to a lobby correspondent as persons who could be trusted to take a wrong view of anything. (Crossman returned the compliment in his diaries by calling Attlee variously 'a prissy little schoolmaster' and 'a little ball-bearing'.) Furthermore, the nation in wartime had become used to home affairs being, as it seemed, increasingly well handled by Attlee and his principal lieutenants Herbert Morrison and Ernest Bevin. Once the excitement of the hustings had subsided, it would be nice to settle down to peace.

· 2 ·
Peace In Our Time Breaks Out –
Morale, Manners, Morals

'The world did *not* start afresh in 1945. We are what our
ancestors have made us. And you cannot disfranchise the
the dead.'

G. M. YOUNG

THE HIGH POINT of British morale in the Second World War was
celebrated in J. B. Priestley's postscript to the nine o'clock news
of 5 June 1940:

> We've known them and laughed at them, these fussy
> little steamers, all our lives. We have called them 'the
> shilling sicks'. We have watched them load and unload
> their crowds of holiday passengers – the gents full of
> high spirits and bottled beer, the ladies eating pork pies,
> the children sticky with peppermint rock. Sometimes
> they only went as far as the next seaside resort. But the
> boldest of them might manage a Channel crossing, to let
> everyone have a glimpse of Boulogne . . . They seemed to
> belong to the same ridiculous holiday world as pierrots
> and piers, sand castles, ham-and-egg teas, palmists, auto-
> matic machines, and crowded sweating promenades.
>
> But they were called out of that world – and, let it be
> noted – they were called out in good time and good order.
> Yes, these *Brighton Belles* and *Brighton Queens* left that
> innocent foolish world of theirs – to sail into the inferno,
> to defy bombs, shells, magnetic mines, torpedoes,
> machine-gun fire – to rescue our soldiers. And our great-
> grandchildren, when they learn how we began this war
> by snatching glory out of defeat, and then swept on to vic-
> tory, may also learn how the little holiday steamers made
> an excursion to hell and came back glorious.

41

The Dunkirk spirit, recalling folk-memories of Drake and the Spanish Armada, prevailed until the Battle of Britain was won a few months later in September. Thereafter, there would be short-lived moments of excitement and exaltation – Alamein, the Torch landing, the Italian surrender, D-day, the dam busters – but Priestley's 'sweep on to victory' seemed to many as the months and years rolled on more like a patient, dreary struggle for survival. News bulletins were ritual exercises in hope deferred; censored letters reiterated in conventional and unvarying terms little but the desire to be home and finished with the war; the line of coloured pins on the pub maps of the Russian front, hung up near the disintegrating dartboard, advanced and receded at the prompting of cautious and out-of-date communiqués. For many thousands of men and women in the Forces, the term active service was a cruel misnomer. For many in anti-aircraft and coastal batteries, in the Pioneer Corps, in patrol vessels in the safer waters, among lorry drivers on routine and unvarying journeys, and cooks producing identical and largely unpalatable meals, above all for the huge army of clerks and telephone operators, the boredom was intense and excruciating. Life centred exclusively on the prospect of leave; and when leave came, much of it was absorbed in waiting for hours on blacked-out, ice-cold stations like Crewe or Didcot and calculating how late the return journey to Devonport or Thurso could safely be left. It seemed to many preferable in the circumstances to see the world, the ostensible reason for joining the army before the days of conscription. What you saw, however, was rarely what you wanted to see. An army intelligence officer recalled an encounter: 'I shall always remember a man from Blewbury, hard by the Berkshire downs. I came across him sitting beside a dusty track looking across the Irrawaddy to Mandalay. He was sucking his water-bottle pensively. "When I get home," he said, "I'm going to have a bath in mild and bitter every night".'[*] For such people, it was not morale-enhancing to be described as the forgotten army. And if serving your country had meant years in a prisoner-of-war camp, you might feel less than enthusiastic about having to submit to further self-sacrifice and privations in peacetime once the exaltation of liberation had begun to wear off.

If we allow that service in the armed forces is, in popular

[*] David Ascoli, *The Listener*, 1 August 1946.

parlance, character-building, it does not necessarily follow that all aspects of the character so built are equally desirable. Many, indeed, of the young adults of the war generation learned in the armed forces self-reliance, courage, initiative, discipline, comradeship and tolerance – and such qualities were further enriched by the acquisition of skills and aptitudes which they might not have had the opportunity to practise in ordinary peacetime conditions. For such men and women war was a life-enhancing and unforgettable experience. But arguably many more learned to regulate an idle working day by reference to the imminence or otherwise of the next cup of tea. Others developed what was to become a life-time habit (and their principal means of satisfaction) of outwitting all possible rules and regulations enjoined on them for their own and others' benefit. Many in charge of stores and equipment in ships, in army headquarters, in canteens, on camp construction sites, acquired a mastery of petty pilfering and peculation, of 'scrounging' and stealing, about which they would quietly boast to susceptible admirers. The necessarily authoritarian and hierarchical structure of the armed forces induced in others again an enduring distaste for all forms of authority, especially anything resembling that exercised by Warrant Officers and NCOs. The wartime sergeant-major would not find it easy to re-emerge as the peacetime works foreman. Life without any corporals was an eagerly anticipated prospect and one which, once realized, would profoundly transform British work habits.

There were others, too, for whom the wearing of uniform, with or without distinction, had for ever arrested further mental development. They would be found in the post-war years propping up provincial taprooms, their moustaches, handle-bar or toothbrush according to Service, greying and yellowing with nicotine stain, their flow of reminiscence recalling sometimes the Baron Münchhausen, sometimes the Ancient Mariner. Old barrack-room loyalties would enable them to borrow twenty pounds here or a few petrol coupons there, but their hopes of running a nice little pub in Taplow were usually frustrated. However, there was to be no repetition of the spectacle, so common in the inter-war years, of bemedalled and crippled ex-servicemen selling matches and shoelaces on windy street corners. Nor were post-war social relations soured by talk of war profiteers as in 1918, although some highly dubious fortunes were built up by scrap merchants operating among the debris of European tank battles.

Ernest Bevin's demobilization scheme was universally commended as fair and sensible. However, the scale of military commitment in the aftermath of war remained formidable. It included, in particular, the control of twenty-four million demoralized Germans in the British zone, to say nothing of the thirty-nine colonies Britain still possessed in 1950. Thus in 1947 there were still a million members of the armed forces, one-fifth of the number at the end of the war two years earlier. Every year between 150,000 and 170,000 National Service recruits reported to inhospitable barracks and by the end of 1945 there were still eight and a half million men and women in war factories. For many of them this was a twilight, if not a nightmare existence, neither peace nor war and often acutely demoralizing, especially for servicemen in certain dreaded black spots like the Canal Zone.

Priestley, who had spent his twenty-first birthday in the water-logged trenches of the Western front in 1915, addressed a new generation of demobilized veterans thus: 'The citizen-soldier, as distinct from the professional, finds himself at the end of a modern war a sharply divided man . . . one half of whom wants to settle up, the other half wants to settle down. Sharing the same billet in his mind are an earnest revolutionary and a tired and cynical Tory.'* Whether Tory or not, the tired and cynical were to be found in large numbers, and such revolutionary zeal as was evident confined itself for many to the marking of their election ballot paper in 1945.

Despite years of blackout and privation and the loss of 60,000 lives in air-raids, the morale of the civilian population had remained astonishingly high until the winter of 1944–5, during which 6500 tons of flying bombs and rockets descended on them, and the war, which had seemed virtually over in the summer, dragged on into its sixth year. At what seemed a snail's pace, restrictions were lifted, as peace at long last came into sight. That winter you were allowed to have a radio in your car and buy a large scale map. You could release a racing pigeon without police permission. The blackout was partially lifted and then

* *Letter to a Returning Serviceman*, p. 3.

totally abolished and, as the curtains were torn down they released a cascade of dust and dead bats and spiders. The Board of Trade soberly anticipated a limited outburst of national rejoicing with the announcement on 7 May that it would be permissible to buy cotton bunting without coupons provided it was not priced at more than 1s 3d a yard and was red, white or blue.* The people would now at last be able to put out more flags, but on a strict basis of fair shares for all.

When the street lamps reappeared in London, children who had never seen such a sight were dazzled and burst into tears of alarm. Grown-ups were thereby increasingly made aware of their desperate shabbiness. Harold Nicolson found that up to July 1943 all his clothes, of whatever vintage, maintained a high level of neatness, 'and then suddenly in some wild Gadarene rush, they all disintegrated simultaneously and identically within the space of a week', his shirts splitting from top to bottom 'with a sharp sigh of utter weariness', while his pyjamas 'assumed the form of pendant strips, such as might be worn by some zany in a morality play'. He gloomily concluded that by 1947 he would have nothing to wear except his Defence Medal. If you were able to save enough clothing coupons to buy a shirt you would find it had a short tail cut away with horizontal abruptness and cost at least five times more than a much superior pre-war one. Statistics in *The Economist* in September 1944 indicated that Harold Nicolson was not exaggerating: they revealed that the average yearly purchase of shirts was 1·41; of pants 0·69; of pyjamas 0·14; of boots and shoes 1·21. Such modest purchases were to supplement an average surviving wardrobe of 4 shirts, 2·4 pants, 1·4 pyjamas and 3·8 pairs of boots and shoes. Clothes rationing was to last till 1949. For a decade the nation was on its uppers.

The civilian population was not only shabby, but immensely tired, few more so than the King himself, who wrote to his brother the Duke of Gloucester at the beginning of 1946: 'I have been suffering from an awful reaction from the strain of the war, I suppose, and have felt very tired . . . Food, clothes and fuel are the main topics of us all.' There seemed no great likelihood of any relaxation. The rival political leaders were at pains to emphasize the stern path of duty. Churchill told the nation on 13 May 1945

* *See* Norman Longmate, *How We Lived Then*, Arrow, 1973.

that: 'You must be prepared for further efforts of mind and body and further sacrifices to great causes,' and that he would be unworthy of their confidence and generosity if he did not still cry: 'Forward, unflinching, unswerving, indomitable, till the whole task is done and the whole world is safe and clean.' Ten months later Attlee had the same message, couched in more prosaic tones: 'I know that most people are feeling the strain of the last six years. I know how many things there are which irritate and worry you. I know how trying it is not to be able to get the goods which you want from the shops, and to have to wait in queues for them. But there is only one way to fill the shops and get back to plenty and that is to produce more.'

In the weeks and months following VE day and VJ day layer after layer of hopeful illusion was stripped away. Harold Nicolson, once again reporting a Paris Peace Conference, as he had in 1919, summed up the post-war world: 'There is one great difference between 1919 and today which hangs like a fog in the air . . . In 1919 we all of us possessed faith and hope. There is no faith or hope to be found in the Luxembourg today. They do not believe in what they are doing – they do not believe in each other – they do not believe even in themselves.' Admittedly such bitterness and disillusionment as there was only occasionally expressed itself in outbursts induced by unusually severe frustration and irritation – indeed, Alistair Cooke returning to Britain after eight years early in 1946 thought that behind the grime and fatigue the country had never had such dignity. For the most part, conditioned over the years to grin and bear it, the British tacitly decided to shoulder a new set of burdens with a grim fatalism. And such fatalism would be very necessary, especially for the housewife engaged on a shopping expedition in the peace-time summer of 1945 which would characteristically develop like this:*

Request	*Answer*
Children's sandals, size one	(8 shops) None at present
Plain straw hat for school	Board of Trade doesn't allow them
Ladies' shoes, size 6	All gone. No more yet

* From the unpublished letters of W. H. Haslam in the Imperial War Museum.

46

Request	Answer
Bicycle bell	Try at end of week
No. 8 battery	No such thing
Glucose on doctor's note	All sold already
Any parsley?	None
What about the grapefruit allocation?	No sign of it
Any chocolate peppermint creams?	Had some two weeks ago
Can you clean this blazer?	If you join the queue at nine o'clock

If you tried to get away from it all, the only method of being sure of a seat in a train was to carry a baby.

Illusions die last of all with politicians. It was not till 1962 that Dean Acheson told the British that they had lost an empire and had yet to find a role, but illusions of imperial grandeur were limited long before that to old men dreaming dreams. However, for a year or two after the war the feeling persisted that since we had been on the winning side and indeed had stood alone against the enemy in 1940, there must still be some sort of star part for us to play on the world stage. Politicians and social philosophers were for a time fertile with suggestions. In January 1945 Bertrand Russell broadcast on Britain's post-war role on the Home Service of the BBC: 'We can, if we are wise, make up for what we have lost in material power by a gain in moral leadership. In this new role our country can be as great and as beneficent as it has ever been in the past, and what is best in our patriotic emotions can find full scope.' The most favoured idea was that we should somehow assume the moral leadership of the world. By that and various other means we might perhaps act as a sort of third force mediating between the USA and the USSR. Even that seemed to Michael Foot and others too modest a role. As he put it: 'We should not want to act the part of Lepidus in the great triumvirate of nations, for Britain stands at the summit of her power.' Raymond Blackburn, another new Labour member with, as it turned out, less of a future in the party, also staked out a high claim for Britain in October 1945: 'We must now take the moral leadership of the world in a situation that is almost as

47

desperate as 1940.' On the far Left, the wish was frequently father to the thought, as when Konni Zilliacus suggested that if 'we played ball with the Russians they would play ball with us'; or when the veteran polemicist, H. N. Brailsford, recalling his vain efforts in 1924 to bring together Ramsay MacDonald and the Russian trade commissioner Rakowsky, applauded the meeting of Attlee and Stalin, whom he described as 'the masters of two great power-complexes'. 'Is it a dream,' he pondered, 'of a vanished generation that they should meet as the heads of the world's two Socialist governments, linked by a common ideology?'* The Left could call in aid the best-selling journalist Negley Farson, who assured his listeners on the African service of the BBC that in their treatment of the defeated Germans 'the realistic Soviet Russian will begin another huge experiment in the brotherhood of man.' In the higher reaches of the government Herbert Morrison also was frequently inclined to try to bolster national morale with the tonic optimism which enhanced his popularity with the general public, if not always with his fellow politicians. The 1945 election for Herbert Morrison was: 'about whether we are going to be a great power or a small one – leader or hanger-on. . . . Follow the vision of a Britain leading the world as a great popular democracy.' A year later he told an audience that the British, more than any other people, held the key to the question whether the world in future was going to be mad or sane. Euphoria also occasionally seized Sir Hartley Shawcross, as in September 1946 when, conceding that the government held out no easy promises, he prophesied that if we tackled the problems we had to face in the spirit of a free, energetic democracy, we could achieve a golden age of freedom, happiness and prosperity. It was even more rash of Herbert Morrison to tell the party conference at Bournemouth earlier that summer that we had turned our backs on the economics of scarcity, but a politician is not on oath at a party conference.

The leading protagonist of the idea of Britain as a third force restraining and modifying the extremes of East and West by dint of its superior political wisdom was R. H. S. Crossman. In November 1946 he instructed the House of Commons how British social democracy could bridge the gulf between Communism and anti-Communism. 'We know that freedom cannot

* *New Statesman and Nation*, 28 July 1945.

48

survive in a world of either American free enterprise or Russian Communism. We cannot, like either of these two powers, seek to dominate. We can seek to lead if we are bold and independent, and, if we put into practice abroad the principles of our domestic policy, we and we alone can prevent the third world war.' Just what was meant by putting into practice abroad the principles of our domestic policy was far from clear, but the general idea of bestriding the world like a moral colossus had a certain appeal, and even the formidably realistic Ernest Bevin had been briefly attracted by the idea. As Michael Foot put it: 'It is still our duty to show that this country of ours is the foremost champion of tolerance and decency on the face of this planet.'

The common man, much eulogized at this period as the standard-bearer of the future, had a variety of more humdrum preoccupations with which to concern himself than the moral leadership of the world, as indeed did his wife, since merely acquiring food and rendering it approximately edible was to be a formidable task for years to come. It understandably took some time for the public to become aware that the worst rigours of rationing would be experienced not during but after the war.

Working-class diet in the industrial areas before the war had been so defective that it is not now questioned that the health of the nation as a whole had improved considerably between 1939 and 1945. This was particularly true of the children nurtured on milk, orange juice and halibut liver oil, scientifically allocated. Wartime rations of essential foodstuffs, eked out by the ingenious points system, had after five years been more or less philosophically accepted by all sections of society as sustaining life well enough, while not always building up the necessary immunities against epidemics. What was, however, undeniable for those in the middle and upper classes, who had known better times, was the deadly monotony of a diet deficient in butter, cream, fish and the red meat constantly extolled by Churchill, as well as anything which tasted in the least exotic.

One of the most widely read novelists of the time was Angela Thirkell, who achieved after the war a more or less annual production line of would-be Trollopean novels, depicting life in a twentieth-century Barsetshire. Her pages were frequently devoted to the related themes of rationing, shopping, food and clothing. Her characters would sit down at the end of the war to a

49

Sunday lunch comprising 'beef substitute, flannel Yorkshire pudding made with dried eggs, tough potatoes, damp greens, a pie with a leather crust and watery custard powder mess'. At a time when the meat ration was so small that butchers' shops were closed five days a week, she describes a hot day in Barchester with vividly authentic realism: 'Even the bluebottles outside the butcher's were dozing upon a bloodstained placard bearing the inscription "SORRY NO OFFAL TODAY. A REFUSAL OFTEN OFFENDS".' Refusals for that matter were often curt. The camaraderie of war-time was beginning to wear thin. J. L. Hodson quoted a correspondent who wrote: 'Don't you think it about time that all of us stopped accepting the almost unlimited rudeness hurled at our heads quite gratuitously by tobacconists, taxi-drivers, post office clerks, bus conductors, waiters, commissionaires. . . . I'd like to see all of us standing up for our inalienable right to respect from those to whom we accord respect.' Harold Nicolson wrote feelingly on the subject of wine-merchants: 'In the old days when I visited my wine merchant he would dance towards me with pencil and order-pad in hand; when I slink in there today I find him immersed in a huge ledger, indifferent to my concilia-tory cough, and glancing towards me petulantly as at an imperti-nent intrusion.' Particularly stern was the struggle for a monthly bottle of gin or whisky, especially the latter. The relative pro-fusion of the officers' mess, especially as reinforced by captured German and Italian supplies, began to seem a distant dream. Coffee continued to consist primarily of a far from stimulating bottled essence called Camp and even tea was not what it had been, though as Mrs Thirkell testified, it continued to hold its secure place in the affection of the nation: 'England, our beloved country, battered and bullied by THEM, still has one source of real comfort in every affliction. THEY have rationed it; they have caused it to be made of dust and bits of black straw; they allow government offices to glut themselves on it while the working housewife with a husband and children hardly knows how to last till the end of the week; but as long as a spoonful of tea is to be had, England will keep her heart.'

Tea and sugar did not come off the ration until 1952. Al-though milk was finally de-rationed in 1950, butter, fats, bacon and meat were still rationed in 1954. Potatoes were rationed in 1947 and came off in 1948 with jam and bread. The weekly quantities of cheese, bacon and cooking fat were minute. In May 1945 bacon came down from four ounces to three ounces and soon dropped to two; in November 1948 it was reduced from two ounces a week to two ounces a fortnight. The cheese ration tended to be three ounces of what was universally known as mousetrap. The annual allocation of fresh eggs for 1946–7 was eighty-seven per person. Just after Christmas of 1950 the meat ration was lower than it had ever been and it was not encouraging for the populace to learn that henceforth it would have to include a proportion of the greatly disliked ewe and wether mutton. In April 1949 sweets were de-rationed and visitors to Blackpool were observed buying rock in eight pound chunks. This encouraging relaxation was, however, rescinded by the middle of August and it was 4 February 1953 before the children could celebrate as a red letter day the availability of sweets in the shops without coupons, after being restricted to three ounces or so a week as long as they could remember. A civic welcome greeted the arrival of the first post-war banana ship at Bristol in January 1946, but for a long time greengrocers had only exiguous quantities. Home-made 'cream' to go with a banana was a mixture of flour, milk, margarine and a little sugar.

Three years after the war an average man's allowance per week was thirteen ounces of meat, six ounces of butter and margarine, one and a half ounces of cheese, one ounce of cooking fat, eight ounces of sugar, one egg and two pints of milk. In general these privations were accepted with a stoicism which was as remarkable as it was admirable, especially as everyone knew substantial quantities of food were being diverted to Germany and India. Indeed, while we were setting out to dismantle German heavy industry, 60,000 people volunteered to reduce their own rations to make up German food parcels. The irony of this particular situation was not lost on Honor Tracy, describing on the air a visit to Bonn at the end of 1949: 'The shops are full of everything that anybody could possibly want; bulging sausages, mountains of meat, piles of chocolate, much of it English, nylon stockings. . . . I scarcely dared to tip the concierge of the hotel, so long, so fragrant, so *imponierend* was the cigar that protruded from the corner of his mouth. . . . By six o'clock [in the morning] the town is up and about and from seven onwards everyone is streaming to his place of business with the single-minded enthusiasm of a flock of ants.'* If British sausages bulged it was with bread and soya bean; nor did British workers show much ant-like enthusiasm for an early start to work.

Only on two occasions did the British housewife register a significant protest against the powerful forces characterized by Mrs Thirkell as 'them'. Nothing had done more to forge friendly transatlantic links than the relatively copious supplies available of United States dried eggs. Attlee's first Minister of Food was Sir Ben Smith, successively an able seaman, a laundryman, the driver first of a hansom cab and then of a taxi before he earned fame as the leader of the London Cab Drivers' Union, the germ of the Transport and General Workers' Union. During the first post-war winter he proposed to save dollar imports by discontinuing the purchase of dried eggs, but in the face of an anguished outcry he had to back down. More serious than the dried egg 'crisis' was the bread 'crisis' which belonged to the stormy career of Sir Ben's successor, John Strachey, in the summer of 1946. Wartime bread looked grey and repellent but had proved itself wholesome and nutritious, particularly valuable for what was known as filling corners in hungry children. In the summer of 1946 wheat shortages prompted the government, on the advice of the civil servants, to ration bread, a decision explained to the House by Strachey: '. . . one of the most important considerations about rationing . . . is not merely the saving which it gives you, but also the fact that it enables you to operate if you have to do so – you will not do it unless you have to – with a considerably smaller amount in your pipeline. That is, perhaps, the most important of the considerations which have animated us.' Barbara Castle suggested that her fellow MPs should eat less as a good example, lavish meals being 'very injurious to our sense of unity and equality as a nation', while Arthur Lewis, then member for Upton, had been told by the kitchen staff at West End hotels that bread crusts were being thrown away. The Ministry surpassed itself in the ingenuity with which it sought to divide the staff of life equitably among various categories of citizen – babies, two ounces a day; children up to the age of five, four ounces; adolescents, eleven; ordinary adults, nine; expectant mothers, eleven; male manual workers, fifteen. The complexity of the proceedings was enhanced by the

* *The Listener*, 19 January 1950.

fact that for a time you could exchange your bread coupons for points, so that, in a manner of speaking, you could have bread yesterday and jam tomorrow. In the event there was always enough bread to go round, so that even John Strachey lost interest in the scheme, which was, however, to last for another two years, carried along by its own administrative momentum. Churchill ruthlessly poked fun at a government which combined bread rationing with the debasement of the silver coinage with nickel: 'And now the British housewife, as she stands in the queues to buy her bread ration, will fumble in her pocket in vain for a silver sixpence. Under the Socialist government nickel will have to be good enough for her. In future we shall be able to say "every cloud has a nickel lining".' (Since it was necessary to pay back to the United States seventy-five million pounds' worth of silver within five years, the new coins were to be 75 per cent copper and 25 per cent nickel, instead of 50 per cent silver, 40 per cent copper, 5 per cent zinc and 5 per cent nickel. It seemed somehow symbolic.)

Bread rationing was not calculated to enhance either morale or a feeling of confidence in the government and drew from Mrs Thirkell's ready pen one of her fiercest fictional diatribes. Everything in Barsetshire was now 'obscured by Bread. THEY, as everyone had anticipated, had put it on the ration without so much as a by-your-leave, and the British housewife, with death and murder in her heart, set out on yet another series of queues. In addition to pages in the ration book called "Do not fill in anything in this space" and "Points" and "Personal Points" and "Do not write on this counterfoil until instructed" and large capital Ts and Ks and little things called Panels whose use nobody knew, and a thing called a Grid General which meant absolutely nothing at all, the harassed and overworked housewife was now faced with large capital Ls and Ms and small capital Gs, each of which, so she gathered from the bleating of the wireless if she had time to listen, or the Sunday paper which she hadn't time to read, meant so many BUs. And what BUs were nobody knew or cared, except that B seemed an eminently suitable adjective for whatever they were. The net result of this new piece of meddling was longer and better queues, fewer and more unpleasant loaves, and a sudden outburst of very nasty so-called cakes rather like india-rubber bath sponges in colour and consistency.'

In those early post-war queues the vagaries of human nature were sharply exposed. Shopping, an activity which before the war had brought women together except at the sales, had now become disagreeably competitive. It was not even a question of anything so simple as the early bird being favoured with a highly treasured piece of offal. The shops opened at different times, so that, if you staked your morning campaign on being at the head of the grocer's queue at 8.30, you might have to hang about for a couple of hours before the fishmonger opened, and it was a matter of pure guesswork to determine when the second delivery of bread would arrive at the baker's. More and more, the wartime spirit of 'all mucking in together' gave way to a niggling wave of envy that one's neighbour had inexplicably acquired a quarter of an ounce more of margarine than one had oneself. In such circumstances it was not surprising that normally law-abiding citizens were increasingly prone to listen to the siren voices of black marketeers possessed of a dozen eggs or half a pound of steak or a pair of nylons on offer at fancy prices.

For the furtherance of equality and fair shares it had been laid down during the war that a restaurant meal could not cost more than five shillings, and this continued till 1950. However, by 1948, if you were rash enough to order a dinner for eight in a high class restaurant you were liable to find your basic charge of forty shillings supplemented by the following items, all legal in so-called luxury establishments:

House charge – forty-eight shillings
Oysters – thirty-two shillings
Flower decoration – eighty shillings
Private room – twenty shillings
Brandy for crêpes Suzette – forty shillings
Coffee – sixteen shillings

– to say nothing of the wine, such as it was. However, the spate of regulations afflicting the restaurateur or innkeeper rendered life in the catering trade far from enviable. In 1950 a publican received the following written admonition from the authorities: 'You are alleged to have stated that you regarded one *whole* round of sandwich as a light meal – i.e. you are presumably reckoning the number of light meals served per day by the number of sandwiches consumed. This is known as the factorial system, and may only be granted by the Food Executive Officer. Under these regulations, accurate daily record of the number of light meals must be recorded, thus if a person consumes half a sandwich and one glass of beer this must be recorded as one light meal. Similarly, if one person consumes five half-sandwiches, this may only be recorded as one light meal.'

In a laudable attempt to assist the housewife to vary the national diet along appropriate and economical lines the Ministry and the BBC frequently published enterprising recipes, details of which bring back the flavour of the times in more than one sense. There was jam roly-poly with potato pastry, and mock applestrudel; and for the economical and enterprising a wartime concoction which the Ministry described as 'economical scrambled eggs', and rather uninvitingly christened English Monkey. It consisted of one egg (reconstituted), one cup of milk, one cup of stale breadcrumbs, half a cup of grated cheese and one tablespoonful of margarine. Given sufficient ingenuity, you could get by, as the popular song had it, without your rabbit pie.

It did not, however, follow that the public was prepared to acquiesce automatically in everything the Ministry had in store for it. The mass importation of whalemeat in 1947 to fill up the national larder had a mixed reception. Hammond Innes, the popular explorer, helpfully produced recipes for housewives called Ways with Whalemeat. The Women's Press Club debated the problem of whether you eat whale with a fish-knife. Could you make fishcakes out of it or would they be rissoles? The final decision was that it had 'perhaps more of the texture of strong liver'. However, before long whale was accepted as a sort of steak substitute and, properly cooked, earned a modest popularity in some quarters, despite a disagreeable oily tang which hung about it. Noël Coward, contemplating in song the problems of commending the current British cuisine to overseas visitors to the Festival of Britain, concluded:

> We can serve whale steak,
> And when the weather's hotter,
> And in place of entrecôte,
> What's wrong with otter?

If whale was endurable, the strange South African foodstuff

55

TO21121

called snoek (or its Australian equivalent, the barracouta) was a very different kettle of fish. When it came on the market the Ministry of Food thought it had made a killing, although its previous experiments with pilchards and sild had not been a great success. Here was a non-dollar source of limitless nourishment and ten million tins were imported in 1947. It seemed a promising answer to Lord Cherwell, who had just pointed out that according to the Ministry the existing rations and points only yielded 1720 calories a day, whereas 2710 were provided in prisons and 2887 had been the minimum suggested by the League of Nations before the war. So the public were informed that 'if you have not yet tried the new allocation of snoek, you may be wondering what it's like. It is rather like tunny fish in texture, but with snoek it is best not to try serving it as it is, but to break it into flakes and moisten it with some sort of sauce, dressing or mayonnaise.' This led to a great burgeoning of Ministry recipes including the celebrated Snoek Piquante, immortalized by Susan Cooper in *The Age of Austerity*, which tricked out the offending material with vinegar, treacle, onions and pepper. Less ambitious was watercress and snoek spread – four level tablespoonfuls of chopped watercress, four level tablespoonfuls of flaked snoek, onion, pepper and salt – and the so-called Barracouta Envelope. The ultimate beneficiaries were the cat population. Small wonder Cyril Connolly, in one of the last numbers of *Horizon* in September 1947, urged any American readers who might feel well disposed to the magazine to send him a food parcel. The article was entitled 'Our American Begging Bowl'.

Added to these privations was a shortage of consumer goods – Hoovers, electric irons, household linen notably – which made for frustration and friction in households usually encompassing returned warriors, who needed domesticating, and small babies. Such goods as were obtainable in the shops were either markedly unattractive, like the so-called utility furniture, or made of inferior material, so that sewing cotton and needles broke, saucepans burnt through in a few weeks, broom-handles detached themselves, scrubbing brushes moulted, elastic snapped and soles parted from uppers. Married couples found themselves for many months in rented lodgings, sharing with relatives, or nomadic. By 1948, 86 per cent of households had an electric iron, but only 40 per cent had Hoovers, 4 per cent a washing machine and 2 per cent a refrigerator. In the 14 per cent of households without electricity twenty-six hours a week were needed for coping with paraffin lamps, cooking stoves, fires, washing, ironing and cleaning. Of the rural population in England and Wales after the war only 70 per cent had piped water, rather fewer in Scotland, and virtually nobody in Ulster. A remarkable social phenomenon of the time was the speed at which the middle classes, believed to be totally dependent on domestic labour, managed well without. They learnt to answer the front door themselves and often dispensed with the back door; they decided that blackleading fireplaces and whitening doorsteps were no longer essential; the shortage of coupons prevented them overdressing the children; brass-polishing and starching disappeared and the silver was put away; a dinner of snoek or rabbit hardly called for elaborate display. Most important of all, as recorded in a *Listener* editorial of 1947: 'The parks are filled with men pushing perambulators and every evening kitchens contain men doing at least a little of the washing-up.'

Curiously enough, the Labour government addressed itself seriously to the so-called servant problem. After the war two notably public-spirited ladies, Violet Markham and Florence Hancock, were charged with exploring the possibility of setting up a National Institute of Houseworkers. There would be training centres, a specially designed overall and badge, and hostels with restaurants for daily workers. Girls would be 'members of the National Institute of Houseworkers – not Mrs Jones's maid'. Mrs Markham set the tone for the enterprise in ringing terms: 'This is the test today: can women share the work of the home, no longer on any basis of condescension or rank, but on terms of justice and mutual respect and independence? So that "service" will cease to be considered a badge of inferiority but will find its true place as a princely motive for the enrichment of life.' She and Miss Hancock, her trade unionist colleague, proposed predictably a minimum wage, a forty-eight hour week, overtime and a day and a half free each week. Unfortunately, it was soon calculated that, unless you were without children, the service provided would be of little use unless ten hours overtime were involved, which would be prohibitively expensive. So no more was heard of that, except that a maid in a frilly apron was exhibited at Madame Tussaud's.

If the contrast with pre-war conditions affected most sharply the genteel readers of Mrs Thirkell's novels, who hunted them down voraciously on the.shelves of Boots' Library, there was undoubtedly as time went on something of a collapse in morale among a far wider section of the community. A much better writer than Mrs Thirkell testified to this from a differing viewpoint. George Orwell wrote in the spring of 1946: 'For anyone outside the armed forces, life since the armistice has been physically as unpleasant as it was during the war, perhaps more so, because the effects of certain shortages are cumulative. The clothing shortage, for instance, becomes less and less tolerable as our clothes become more and more completely worn out, and during last winter the fuel situation was worse than it had been at any time during the war. Food is as dull as ever, the queues do not get any shorter, the contrast between the wealthy person who eats in restaurants and the housewife who has to make do on her rations is as glaring as it always was, and every kind of privation seems more irritating because there is no war to justify it. Black market activities are said to have increased since the war stopped. Then, again, the housing situation does not improve, and is unlikely to do so for a long time to come, and there is already an appreciable amount of unemployment. On the other hand there is resentment against long hours and bad working conditions, which has shown itself in a series of 'unofficial' strikes. When you listen to the conversations in the fish queue you can hardly doubt that the average working-class person is discontented, feels that the ending of the war ought to have brought him more comfort and amusement, and does not see why our loaves should be made smaller or our beer reduced in order to prevent Europe from starving.' Mass Observation's 1947 survey called 'Peace and the People' also recorded discontent and apathy, their findings summarized by a mother: 'Peace to me means the return of old evils. . . . I have lost my youth, and to what end? I was happier when I lay listening to bombs and daring myself to tremble; when I got romantic letters from abroad; when I cried over Dunkirk; when people showed their best sides and we still believed we were fighting to gain something.' She went on to say that you don't now offer to get Mrs So-and-So some tomatoes – you make sure you get your own first and don't tell her where you get them.

As if Britain's well-meaning new government had not enough to contend with in the psychological condition of the people afflicted by the dollar shortage, the elements began to play a curiously malignant role. People still shuddered at the recollection of the Christmas of 1944, the coldest since 1890, with its unseasonable news of the Ardennes offensive. But worse was to come. March of 1946 was continously wet and the summer cold and miserable. Despite some understandable anxiety on the part of Morrison and others in the government about the winter's fuel supplies, the responsible minister, Emmanuel Shinwell, was invariably reassuring on the matter, pointing out that coal production was rising. But then so also was demand, with factories restocking. James Lees-Milne recorded in his diary that it rained every day without exception in November. By mid-December it was sharply colder and on 30 January the fiercest blizzard for fifty years confirmed the prospect of the worst winter for a century. Shinwell's gamble on there being sufficient fuel supplies for an average winter had failed to come off and between December and February the unemployment figures leapt from 360,000 to two million, as factories closed down.

February 1947 far surpassed in unpleasantness even February 1974 or February 1979. Big Ben froze and the brewers Bass cut licencees' not over-generous quota of beer by half. Offices were lit by hurricane lamps and candles. Concert and theatre-goers took rugs and blankets with them, except to the Arts Theatre which was specially heated for Shaw's *Back to Methuselah* out of consideration for the plight of Adam and Eve. The Board of Trade's only contribution was to end licences for the manufacture and sale of umbrellas. On 5 February six hundred vehicles were trapped end to end in the snowdrifts between Grantham and Stamford, and the next day the Ministry of Fuel and Power announced that 'a most serious situation has arisen in regard to the supply of coal throughout the country'. It was of no particular comfort two days later to hear from Douglas Jay that there was unquestionably a terrible amount of waste by domestic consumers.

On 13 February Lees-Milne recorded: 'Since Monday we have had no heating in our office apart from one electric fire. And now this is turned off from 9 to 12 and again from 2 to 4 each day. Wrapped in my fur coat with three pullovers underneath, my snowboots kept on, I am still too perished to work properly. . . . People are unanimous in blaming the government for a hideous muddle, yet Mr Shinwell still remains Minister of Fuel.' On 24 February London had its first sunshine for twenty-one days; on 26 February the temperature in the capital was just above freezing for the first time for ten days, and 850 Blantyre miners went on strike over the dismissal of one man. Then it all started up again, Lees-Milne recording in the Midlands icicles three feet long on 6 March and on the 11th the not altogether surprising fact that Sibyl Colefax and James Pope-Hennessy were becoming disillusioned with a government they had helped to vote into power. The floods in Worcester on 19 March were alleged to be the worst since 1770; at their height throughout the country as a whole they were to cover an area as big as Kent. Rain and bitterly cold winds ushered in an early Easter. By the autumn of what Dr Dalton described as a pig of a year there were two million fewer sheep and lambs, 200,000 fewer pigs and 30,000 fewer cattle and calves than a year before. The stars in their courses seemed to be working against the government and Hartley Shawcross, the Attorney-General, reflected that this might be 'the end of Socialism in our time'.* However, when the weather finally improved, Philip Noel Baker said it was plain that only nationalization had saved us from disaster.

Part of the trouble from the point of view of the spirit of the people was the extreme shabbiness of their environment. The scars of the blitz took years to heal, especially in London, in Liverpool, in Plymouth, in the West Midlands. Somehow there seemed always to be a crisis looming which postponed any attempt at reclamation, much less modernization or adornment.† J. L. Hodson described a typical railway journey in the summer after the war from London to Newcastle which took eight and a quarter hours with no food available en route. There were no taxis at the station on arrival and when he finally reached his

* David Watt, *The Age of Austerity*, p. 103.

† In this connection, the *Daily Telegraph* of 17 September 1979 carried a news item entitled 'Gun Sites to Go', which read: 'Pill-boxes and gun emplacements built along the Lincolnshire coast in 1940 and 1941 are likely to be demolished at last. Mr Michael Sallors, county planning officer, has recommended a start on demolition.'

hotel his towel was the size of a pocket handkerchief, the sheets on the bed were full of holes and the soap in the basin was worn to the thinness of paper. Another traveller, the sympathetic American journalist Drew Middleton, described the West Midlands: 'as your car moves down street after street of drab brick houses, past dull, smelly pubs and duller shop windows, hideous, lonely churches, you are oppressed.' In the gaping cavities left by the bombs and rockets you were more likely to see yellow ragwort, willow herb, brambles and nettles than Noël Coward's London Pride. Such paint as there was was liable to crack and peel within a month and many householders gave up the unequal struggle. It was peculiarly difficult to keep clean and this applied not only to the four and a half million households of more than one person with no fixed bath and the 690,000 households without piped water recorded in the 1951 census. A notice in a London shop window read: 'Paper collars, 4s 6d a dozen – now being worn by bankers, stockbrokers and MPs.' It was still the era of the coal fire, but in 1947 it was often a matter of coal dust, which you collected in queues at the depot, perhaps in a perambulator. As to the coal merchants, their products were often, as the wags put it, 'never too slate to send'. Cyril Connolly usually affected at this time what Dr Johnson discussing *Macbeth* called inspissated gloom, but his description of London in 1947 was not wholly exaggerated: 'The largest, saddest, dirtiest of great cities with its miles of unpainted, half-inhabited houses, its chop-less chop houses, its beer-less pubs, its once vivid quarters losing all personality, its squares bereft of elegance, its dandies in exile, its antiquities in America, its shops full of junk, bunk and tomorrow . . . under a sky permanently dull and lowering like a metal dish-cover.'* Not surprisingly he wound up *Horizon* at the end of 1949 with a valedictory message: 'It is closing time in the gardens of the West and from now on an artist will be judged only by the resonance of his solitude or the quality of his despair.'

The Britons who endured all this with by and large remarkable fortitude, and for a time in 1948 even looked like turning the corner into a brighter world, have been described for us in a number of social surveys with a wealth of human detail, no

* A shining exception to the prevalent squalor was Brighton. Malcolm Muggeridge was not alone in observing that it seemed somehow to have been less touched than any other town by war and austerity.

longer fashionable in the more sternly academic sociology of today. Of these the most useful for the purpose of trying to acquire some measure of the manners and morals of the time are B. Seebohm Rowntree and G. R. Lavers's *English Life and Leisure* (1951); Geoffrey Gorer's *Exploring English Character* (1955); the works of a particularly observant Pole, F. Zweig, *Labour, Life and Poverty* (1948) and *Women's Life and Labour* (1952); and Angus Maude and Roy Lewis's *The Middle Classes* (1949).

Rowntree and Lavers found it hard to conceal their Quaker-inspired zeal for social reform behind a cloak of analytical objectivity. Indeed, Rowntree wrote to *The Times* early in 1947 suggesting that the shortfall of 500,000 workers in manufacturing industry could be substantially offset by drafting in the 300,000 to 400,000 employed in the betting industry, which, if carried out, would have been a truly remarkable example of social engineering. His two hundred case histories, like those of Zweig, tell us nothing new in demonstrating that whereas some people, whatever the circumstances, manage to extract a great deal out of life, others do not. Indeed, Zweig concluded that there was no more characteristically British observation in these years than 'life is what you make it'. So with Miss E, 'daughter of a working class home. She is 21. The family live in very crowded conditions, the parents, three daughters and two sons, all grown up, in a two-bedroomed home. The father and one son work in a factory. There is no bathroom in the house, which has no garden, and only a narrow concrete yard to separate it from the back of the next house. Miss E performs a miracle in such surroundings, stepping out as clean and smart as any debutante in Mayfair. . . . The area where Miss E lives is a rough one. Incest is not uncommon, rape not rare and fornication is as usual as a square meal (often more usual). Naturally, Miss E "knows all about men", but since she met her fiancé she has "given up all that". She is trying to improve herself. She has got a pamphlet on beauty hints from a woman's magazine and is studying a comprehensive five shilling book on etiquette.' Upward social mobility in Miss E contrasts with social stagnation in the case of Miss U, also 21, and a remarkable illustration of the fact that the genus designated 'flapper' in the nineteen-twenties had survived the rigours of the Second World War. Described as the younger daughter of an upper-middle-class couple living just outside a large town, Miss U neither worked nor intended to and devoted her life to tennis parties, moonlight picnics, treasure hunts, races, theatres, cinemas, flirtations and dances. She was appropriately in love with 'a marvellous young man' (who also lived on his parents' income without working) with a fast car which he drove at night with one hand, while the other arm embraced Miss U. 'Although Mummy does voluntary work,' Miss U says that she, 'doesn't see why I should bother about the working class, they're hopeless.' Miss U, in addition, was a regular churchgoer.

Miss U's tennis parties seemed to be under threat from Mr P, a twenty-three-year-old labourer employed on helping to make a hard court at a private house. He and his three mates were opposed to this particular employment, since they were all Socialists and considered that no one should be rich enough to have his own tennis court. They therefore went slow. On warm days they just sat down, except when the foreman visited them and did perhaps two or three hours' work. On cold days they worked just enough to keep themselves warm. Of contrasting work habits was Mrs K, a farmer's wife aged about fifty. 'The farm is a small one and the buildings are dirty and untidy, for the farmer tries to work it with only the help of his family. They are, however, fairly prosperous. Mrs K works immensely hard. She does all her housework and shopping, milks the cows, keeps the hens and pigs, feeds the calves, and does all the paper work of the farm, for her husband is illiterate. It is quite normal for her to work a hundred-hour week and more at harvest time. She has one day off a year, the chapel outing to the seaside by motor-coach. She has never ridden in a train and never spent a night away from home.'

Not untypical of the bewildering cross-currents of opinion in the post-war era was the case of Mr A, aged twenty and a product of one of the leading public schools. Working as a labourer in a shipyard to gain industrial experience, he had flirted with the idea of joining the Communist party and, although he had renounced that particular solution, believed strongly in nationalization and social security. But 'he is about to give up his employment in disgust at the slackness of the workers who will not give a fair day's work, and take up farming as a career.' Also illuminating are the reasons given for voting Tory by various working- and lower-middle-class individuals, the heirs of Disraeli's angels imprisoned in marble. Miss R, a barmaid, had, like Mr A, inclined to idealistic Communism, but now considered 'men are so beastly I don't care what happens to them', and had in consequence become a Tory. Mr S, a surprisingly well-read and informed Irish roadsweeper in his late fifties, justified his particular allegiance to the Conservative party on the grounds that all politicians were thieves and rogues and it was better to be robbed by a gentleman who would say 'thank you' than by one of your own class. Mr F, a sixty-eight-year-old labourer, still working, is described as disliking modern innovations, and a born Conservative. With a pleasant twinkle in his eye and a good, though slow, sense of humour, he read the Bible, 'but nothing else; no radio; no idea of what's going on'. These somewhat instinctive attitudes contrasted sharply with the reasoned political commitment of a forty-two-year-old foreman in a factory. 'Highly intelligent, well read and with a good sense of humour. He is absolutely convinced that Communism is the right path for human development and equally certain that it will eventually embrace the whole world. He would give his life without hesitation for its furtherance.' He was unmarried and very abstemious 'because he believes working men should keep their brains alive, not dull them with alcohol'. A full-time Trade Union official in 'full sympathy' with the Communist Party, though not a member, shared this aversion to the demon drink, alcohol being in his view merely one of the methods employed by the bosses to keep the workers weak and unorganized.

Drink, smoking and gambling as well as other leisure habits naturally loomed large in the researches of Zweig and Gorer, as well as in those of Rowntree and Lavers. Zweig, after much careful interviewing, came to the conclusion that the new social security provisions and the general rise in wages meant that there was little social or structural poverty, though deprivation undoubtedly existed among those with various defects of health, mind or spirit. This seemed to be borne out by a 1945 study of Wolverhampton's old people which showed that only three per cent were undernourished. Old age was already becoming a much more serious social problem than it had been, with the great increase in the expectancy of life, measured by the fact that, whereas seven out of every hundred persons were sixty-five and over in 1931, this figure twenty years later had nearly doubled. But what Rowntree called secondary poverty, i.e. poverty due to unwise expenditure, continued to take its toll of drinkers, smokers and gamblers on their way to skid alley.

There was an acute shortage of beer in 1945, exemplified by the Yorkshire dales village, popular with West Riding townspeople, where the five pubs, all tied to the same brewery, only received ten barrels between them to last a fortnight including Whitsun weekend. Thereafter quantity, if not quality, picked up. Twenty-five million barrels were consumed nationally in 1938, twenty-nine million in 1948, but it is worth recording that 30 per cent of the population over sixteen were teetotal, as were 40 per cent of all women, it still being widely considered 'unsuitable' for women to be seen in pubs, especially unaccompanied, though there was always a number of more or less cheerful habituées like the charlady who startled Drew Middleton by her reference to a 'nourishing drop of gin'. Considering that the 'regulars' carefully observed by Zweig drank at least four to six pints a night and very often ten pints or more, convictions for drunkenness (0·7 per cent of the population in 1948) remained remarkably low. Gorer considered that two men out of five made at least occasional visits to a pub, which may account for his finding that 14 per cent of men preferred the company of their own sex, given a free choice. Except perhaps in Scotland, Merseyside and the murkier parts of London, the pub was a relatively harmless, if monotonous, part of the British social scene. All the authorities concur in the belief that the road to ruin often followed a path first traced by the astonishing popularity of medicated wine. Rowntree and Lavers were in favour of nationalizing brewing and distilling and prohibiting 'joking references to the subject' on the radio.

No less than 81 per cent of the male population smoked (often exceptionally pungent pipes) and 41·6 per cent of women. The national expenditure on tobacco rose steeply from £177 million in 1938 to £690 million in 1947. From time to time Chancellors of the Exchequer became worried about the dollar implications of tobacco imports. Dr Dalton's autumn budget of 1947 put up the price of cigarettes from 2s 4d for twenty to 3s 4d (they cost 1s before the war), and in his cheery way he announced: 'Smoke

your cigarettes to the butts, it may even be good for your health.'
It was a badge of virility for a small boy to walk the streets with
a cigarette butt lodged securely behind his ear.

Those who indulged in gambling, as well as smoking and
drinking, formed an enormous part of the population. The
tedium of the barrack-room or the gun-site had undoubtedly
enhanced a tendency already engrained in the British working
man – and for that matter in large sections of the upper and
middle class. It was the age of the street bookmaker. Credit was
legal, but cash not. It was not unknown for a factory foreman to
detail one of the workers to take an hour off in the morning to lay
the bets. What you bet on was your own choice. The figures in
millions of pounds are revealing:

	1947	1948	1949
Horses	400	350	450
Dogs	300	210	200
Pools	70	69	67
Other	25	21	18
	795	650	735

The high figure for 1947 over 1948 almost certainly reflects
a great many war gratuities, which were thus not put aside, as
intended, against a rainy day. Zweig in his *Men in the Pits* has a
story of miners so determined to gamble in pubs that in the
absence of any other medium they bet on the raindrops running
down the window pane. In the first quarter of 1949 eleven and
a quarter millions per week did the pools. Particularly tempting
was the greyhound meeting, comprising eight races lasting under
five minutes each, with the remaining 145 minutes left for
studying the form. Greater London by 1948 had seventeen
tracks with thirty-three meetings a week and there were fifty-one
authorized provincial tracks. A weekend crowd at West Ham,
Wembley or the White City would number 50 to 70,000. The
combined profits of Wandsworth, Park Royal and Charlton
rose from £72,033 in 1945 to £432,525 a year later. There indeed
could be seen a growth industry, but not one, as Christopher
Hollis observed, which argued great enthusiasm for a society
where nobody should enjoy an income which he had not earned.

With wages running ahead of prices in the early post-war

years and inflation as yet an insidious but not obviously lethal disease, there was often money to spare on less potentially dangerous recreations than drinking and gambling. There was the dance hall, the football match and above all the cinema. Although in August 1945 the *Newcastle Evening Chronicle* advertised a Grand Victory Atomic Dance in the Heaton Assembly Rooms, the nation's dancers soon adopted for the most part a sedate and settled routine. Four to five hundred dance halls, open on all weekdays (and sometimes on Sundays for club members), catered for some three million clients per week, there being normally a 3 to 5.45 session followed by one from 7.30 to 11. Perhaps one night a week there would be an Old Time dance to pre-1914 music. One chain of dance halls proudly boasted, 'we supply clean entertainment to people who want it'. It was mostly a matter of the foxtrot and the waltz, though you could sometimes encounter an activity called jiving, thus practised at the Paramount Dance Hall in the Tottenham Court Road – 'she holds her partner more or less at arm's length and they both twirl and kick their legs in the air, sideways and without much mutual timing. Her skirt rises from above her knees and she displays a neat pair of knickers and an athletic behind.' However, the more traditional *palais* was liable to proclaim 'no jiving'.

The popularity of the cinema was a prodigy of the age, explicable, given the frequently abysmal quality of much of the entertainment provided, only by the romantic relief it afforded to a society bereft of colour and excitement. There were nearly 5000 cinemas. Eastbourne voted for Sunday cinemas in 1947 and even Swansea by a small majority in 1950. It was the heyday of J. Arthur Rank with his Odeons and Gaumonts and his celebrated dictum: 'I am in films because of the Holy Spirit.' The American stranglehold on the industry was such that not even the ingenuity of the President of the Board of Trade, Harold Wilson, described by Harold Nicolson in those days as a boyish statistician, could loosen it. There was indeed a terrible time in the unhappy winter of 1947 when Dr Dalton tried to tax American films, whereupon the Americans retaliated by simply not sending any more, so that cinema managers were rapidly forced to substitute pantomimes. Despite the near disintegration of the British film industry, Michael Balcon's

Ealing Studios had an *annus mirabilis* in 1949 with *Whisky Galore, Kind Hearts and Coronets*, and *Passport to Pimlico*. More normally, the man in the street and his girlfriend in their utility mackintoshes stood solidly in chilly queues for their weekly dose of Michael Wilding and Anna Neagle. By 1954 the cinemas were closing down in the face of television's rapidly growing competition.

In football, the peak season was 1948–9 when the attendance figure at league matches was forty-one million. The maximum weekly wage of a professional footballer in 1947 was £11 and the record transfer fee at that time was £14,000. In that year Great Britain beat the Rest of the World 6-1. But it was not only the top stars who drew in the faithful and well-behaved crowds. In 1950 49,000 people watched a Third Division game between Notts County and Nottingham Forest; the next year 98,000 saw the amateur final at Wembley between two clubs of markedly different social origins – Pegasus, drawn from past and present Oxford and Cambridge students, and Bishop Auckland.

If Britain, as many hoped or feared according to predilection, was on the point of becoming a classless society, there was still some way to go. Let us join two of Mrs Thirkell's ladies lunching at a women's club. ' "Is there any tripe?" said Lady Pomfret. "Sit down, Lucy dear." "Well, there *is* tripe, my lady," said the Jill-in-office, implying that tripe was low. "Two tripes then, please," said Lady Pomfret, "and then the apple pie. The chef really understands tripe," she continued to Mrs Belton. "We can never get it from our butcher, so I always have it when I come here. I don't like throwing my weight about, but thank God a title still helps." '

Lady Pomfret's satisfaction with her title was not shared by G. D. H. Cole who, in a 1949 Fabian Society pamphlet, described the House of Lords as 'a pestilence ground of snobbery and class distinction which stinks in the nostrils of every decent democrat'. But G. D. H. Cole was a difficult man to please, describing Churchill's politics as aristocracy tempered by the possibility of economic and social climbing, and claiming that, although he could not accept the Communist interpretation of democracy, he greatly preferred it to Churchill's. It continued to be a source of surprise to those with Cole's cast of mind how

many of their countrymen approved of the possibility of economic and social climbing. While it was not true that everybody
loved a lord, some of Zweig's case histories indicate the extent
to which working-class animus tends to be directed against
the middle classes rather than the upper classes. A sweeper
in a public park, working from 6.30 a.m. to 6 p.m. (and on
Saturdays till noon) 'certainly prefers a rich man to a middle-
class one. He thinks that the upper and working classes could
get along much better if there were no middle class. The latter
are false and snobbish, and concerned only with themselves;'
and a worker in a West End club thought 'the upper class is all
right, but the middle class is snobbish, selfish, self-assertive
and money-minded.'

In any case the very rich were a fact of life. In 1954 1 per cent
of the population owned 43 per cent of the national wealth; the
top 5 per cent owned 71 per cent; and the top 10 per cent 79 per
cent. When the Duke of Westminster died in 1953, estate duty
was estimated at £20 million. In August 1945 the Marquess of
Salisbury was still sharing Hatfield with returned prisoners of
war who were being rehabilitated, but rapidly the great, if not
by any means all the lesser, stately homes were once again occupied by their owners – Drumlanrig, Grimsthorpe, Belvoir,
Dunrobin, Arundel, Petworth, Melbury, although part of
Alnwick Castle was let to a teacher training college and it was
1949 before Blenheim was tidied up and fit for habitation.
Despite frequently expressed disapproval by Labour MPs, fox-
hunting rapidly reasserted itself with 183 registered packs. Many
of the great estates remained intact, the Duke of Beaufort, the
Earl of Durham and the Earl of Lonsdale keeping their nine-
teenth-century estates intact with 51,000, 30,000 and 68,000
acres respectively. There were still 573,000 farm-workers in
1948, although thereafter numbers began to drop rapidly with
20,000 a year leaving the land. For encumbered estates there
was always the possibility of the National Trust, albeit with
reservations such as were felt by Sir Robert Abdy, who, according to James Lees-Milne, thought the public should not be
admitted to Montacute House because they smelt. All in all, the
aristocracy were displaying both resource and resilience,
Malcolm Muggeridge overhearing two gentlemen complaining
at Pratt's that Moss Bros had only offered them £4 10s for their

Lord-Lieutenants' uniforms, as they had a surfeit of them, and Lees-Milne discovering Lady Montgomery-Massingberd at the age of seventy-five polishing the stairs on her hands and knees. It was, one way and another, difficult to know what to make of things, as was evidently the experience of a correspondent who wrote to *The Times* in 1949 to report that he had noticed a man in the train reading the *Daily Worker* while whistling the Eton Boating Song.

By 1948 the sociologist M. Abrams reckoned that the standard of living of the average working-class family had risen by 10 per cent since 1938 and that of the 'submerged tenth' by considerably more, whereas that of the average salary earner had come down by not less than 20 per cent. It remained, however, true that the salary earners were still vastly better off than the wage earners. It was essentially a matter of differentials and as the truth of their new situation began to sink in, more and more members of the middle classes came to regret their temporary flirtation with egalitarianism. Though the war may have been a people's war in the sense popularized by Angus Calder, both experience and common sense pointed to the fact that it would not have been won without a massive contribution of essentially middle-class skills and attributes. Awkwardly situated between a vanished world of cheap domestic labour and the later advent of cheap washing machines and as yet unaware how rapidly their lot would improve through untaxed capital appreciation, the middle classes felt disillusioned, resentful and often bitter as they shouldered responsibilities sometimes as onerous in peace as in war. Only eight out of sixty middle-class budgets studied by Maude and Lewis in 1946–7 revealed the ownership of a car. As a grammar school master, one of the eight, put it: 'We could give up the car; but we cling to it as a last link with comfort and luxury, having surrendered so many things, including annual holidays, library subscriptions and golf.' And what was it all designed to achieve? A leading article in *The Observer* in November 1947 echoed the thoughts of many: 'A new class of masters, wielding an impersonal, pervasive authority, seems to be rising at the Government's bidding to replace the old. And this chilly world of forms and regulations, of don'ts and delays and petty interference, is felt to be far removed from the generous visions of 1945.'

Not all members of the government were as impervious to

the cries of anguish of the middle classes as Aneurin Bevan, who had rejoiced that it would now be possible to make the right people squeal for a change. Hartley Shawcross, himself no proletarian, thought he saw the way forward for them in 1949: 'In a year's time the position in regard to education and medical services will be that the middle classes will be able to avail themselves to the full of the social services provided by the state and will want to do so because these services will be better than those obtainable privately.' As we shall see, after some initial hesitation the middle classes showed themselves very ready to espouse the National Health Service. Education, however, was a different matter and the obduracy with which the middle classes in England, if to a much lesser extent in Scotland and Wales, adhered to private schooling continued to surprise the reformers. Mass Observation was told by a parent: 'I don't see why they should go to the elementary school. When you think of the sort of children who go there, the parents have no ambition. I mean, they can't help being poor, but they don't want to live in any better way. When you try to bring children up well, with good manners and dress them nicely, and then to have them mix with those sort of children, well it's not fair. I mean, we're working people, but we do want to give our children the best that we can. There's a very good private school near here. It's really an excellent school, and we're going to manage the fees somehow.' Michael Foot wanted to put her and thousands of other middle-class parents out of their agony by protecting them from themselves. In the *Daily Herald* in April 1947 he deplored the fact that the abolition of public schools did not feature in *Let Us Face the Future*. 'It would be wrong for us to tackle that anachronism without a mandate. But clearly that reform should be high up on the list.' In terms of priorities, this was a reform much higher on Foot's list than it was on Attlee's.

In their attitude to children the different strata of English society had undoubtedly much in common in these years. The social investigators found everywhere a robust realism more consonant with Victorian standards than with the liberal orthodoxy of today. Gorer's sample, showing 68 per cent who thought that children needed more discipline, led him to believe that the typical English view of childish nature was that the young child was inadequately human and that, unless the parents were careful and responsible, it would revert to, or stay in, a wild or animal condition. However, less than a quarter of his sample of fathers believed in 'severe' physical punishment for boys. A young middle-class mother seemed to have the matter well in hand when she told him: 'My boy is easy. One day locked in his bedroom with bread and water would be enough.' Tom Johnston, a Labour Secretary of State for Scotland in two administrations, addressed himself to the problem of what a primary school should or should not be in his native Glasgow, in the *Sunday Times* in 1948. He described a bad school, where one out of four and a half children became juvenile delinquents, as having 'no prefect system, no organization of class clubs, no welfare system, no old school tie or badge of honour, no tuition in social service or public duty, no anything but the bare school curriculum'. This he contrasted with the Abbotsford primary school on the edge of the Gorbals which had all these things as a result of a new headmaster who had transformed the school, which had once been notorious for juvenile delinquency. As he put it, in language of which Mrs Thirkell would have approved, 'the tone has changed.' Even more striking was the able seaman who told Zweig that in his view the right system of education was to pick out the children of high ability and character from 'the husk' since 'only the best should progress.'

If the 'best' were progressing in well-disciplined homes and schools, the 'husk' were an increasing cause of concern. There was a rapid increase in the number of juvenile delinquents, all too conspicuous by 1949 with their long hair, organized in artificial waves, or the heavily greased 'Boston flashback'. They wore striped flannels and belted jackets; large, loosely knotted, plain-coloured ties and often a wide-brimmed trilby. As such, they presented a sharp contrast in the streets with the national servicemen. Shortage of labour meant that their wages enabled them to indulge in conspicuous expenditure, which in this age group was a totally new phenomenon in working-class culture and aroused much head-shaking among their seniors in all sections of society.

Whatever its record of success or failure, the traditional British attitude to child-rearing in home and school was already under attack from increasingly fashionable theorists whose inspiration derived from European and American experiments.

In 1947 James Hemming, assisted by Josephine Balls, produced a book with the startling title *The Child is Right*. Its readers were told that psychology and child observation had demonstrated that a child *wants* to be good and pleasing and acceptable; that in every case of bitter conflict between a young person and society that Hemming and Balls had observed it had turned out that it was the child that had been true to life and society that had been playing the traitor; and that if young people were to be given an opportunity for developing self-reliance through creative interests, the practice of loading them with evening homework must stop. It would not do to try to hurry the pace of development since it gave the child a sense of strain. Rather 'in school much can be done to develop judgment by classroom discussions on subjects that really interest young people, conducted from time to time, not by a teacher chairman but with a pupil in the chair and the teacher on the floor.' The writing was on the wall, if not on the blackboard. Even the sober columns of *The Spectator* in July 1945 carried an article extolling the new teachers' techniques, which announced that 'the antagonism and autocracy in the classroom produced by the traditional teaching must give place to democratic relationships.' A visiting French professor was understandably startled to be told by one of His Majesty's Inspectors of Schools: 'Let the children be happy and the multiplication table will look after itself.' He modestly demurred in a broadcast talk, explaining that he was sceptical about happiness as an educative means and wondered whether there might not be something to be said for making life a bit hard for children so as to train them for the real hardship of life and to show them the value of effort. His scepticism was echoed by Compton Mackenzie, one of the most popular broadcasters of the day, who argued that 'the present tendency to coddle childrens' brains, laudable though the motive may be, is a menace to their future.'

An optimistic contributor to a collection of essays called *Education: Today and Tomorrow* (1945) concluded that 'we may be on the eve of a renaissance more wonderful by far, and more potent, than that of the fifteenth century, a rebirth among the common people of life more abundant – disciplined, creative, wise and joyous.' While there was undoubtedly much to admire

73

in British moral attitudes at the time, there were grounds for a rather more modest assessment than that. If any single figure commanded the admiration and respect of the nation it was not any twentieth-century Renaissance man but the ordinary police-man on his beat. All the sociologists were in agreement that the police were considered by all sections of the community as kind, reliable, and incorruptible – a veritable bulwark against what was to many a puzzling phenomenon, the sharp increase in crime. Morrison, interviewed early in 1946, was shocked by the London crime figures for the previous year – shopbreaking and robberies and assaults doubled and burglaries up 150 per cent. As he put it sadly, 'no one would have thought of stealing second-hand shirts in 1938.' The next year, pilfering on the railways – bulbs, ashtrays, window blinds, spoons, cups, mirrors and toilet rolls *inter alia* – amounted to £2,600,000. Rowntree and Lavers discovered a manageress of a good-class seaside hotel who lost 10,000 coat hangers in fifteen years and a waitress in a good-class restaurant possessed of a well-stocked larder in her small and shabby flat who told them: 'Nobody misses it, you know. It's only a bit for me and my friends. I wouldn't do it serious like, for selling or nothing of that sort.' There was a two-thirds increase of offences in 1947 as compared with 1938, many of them juvenile. Crimes of violence had increased by 58 per cent.

The legislators were worried. In November 1945 a far-ranging speech from Herschel Austin, Labour MP for Stretford, contained some interesting reflections on the growth of juvenile crime. He had a long list of contributory factors – lack of parental control on account of war conditions; abnormally high rates of pay for young people, rendered inevitable by the labour shortage; young girls throwing themselves at the troops. On a visit to Brixham during the war he had been shocked to see, 'and on a Sunday afternoon', a pin-table saloon of all things. In that pic-turesque village there was what was euphemistically described as a 'sports palace' or a 'sportsdrome', or an 'amusement arcade'. He entertained doubts about the moral influence of public danc-ing: 'It may well be that our young people today are improving their style in regard to "jitterbugging" and the other features of acrobatic dancing, but I can hardly feel that it makes them likely to be good citizens in future.' But his worst strictures were reserved for what he called the major evil, the influence of Hollywood on young people. Speaking 'as a comparatively young man' he detected in 'our young people a Piccadilly Circus spirit allied with the "honky-tonk" of the saloons of America'. General Sir George Jeffreys from the Opposition benches advocated the whipping and fining of the parents of deviant children, but the great preponderance of opinion expressed in the debate echoed the Hemming-Balls thesis that the child was the more or less innocent victim of society. In introducing the Scottish version of the Criminal Justice Act of 1948, Arthur Woodburn, the Secretary of State, said that the object of the Bill in general was to make the punishment fit the criminal rather than the crime, and described Borstals as moral hospitals to enable young criminals to get their health back. Rehabilitation, not retribution, was the order of the day and at the beginning of 1949 the Metropolitan Police were 4291 short of their establishment and borough forces outside London 7420 short.

One element of the post-war underworld which flourished with relative impunity in the face of benevolent legislators and overworked policemen was the black market. On one day in February 1947 *The Times* reported two convictions – that of a Glasgow car-hirer who was given six months imprisonment for receiving 82,744 petrol coupons, defending counsel claiming that he was only a pawn in a big game, as something like a million stolen coupons were floating about; and that of a Fulham man charged with stealing 394,000 clothing coupons and 1800 ration books at Guildford. Similarly, one day in July an Oldham farmer was given twelve months for being in possession of 2166 lbs of illegally slaughtered beef; and the same day Joseph and Julian Lyons, father and son, were charged with selling pears and onions above the maximum price. It was alleged that father or son would tell their customers that they could have either pears or onions at the proper price if they paid an additional sum in pound notes, generally £120 for 760 cases of pears.

This sort of exercise was the standard activity of the so-called 'spiv', beloved of the cartoonists with his flashing rings and cufflinks, his striped shirt, curly-brimmed hat and pointed 'co-respondent' shoes. A similar disregard for both the letter and the spirit of the law soon became prevalent at much more exalted levels of society. J. L. Hodson reported what he called an 'authentic conversation, England, 1946 vintage: 'Will you take £600 in cash instead of £800 in a cheque? You'll do far better that way. Just pop it in the bank – no inland revenue. Everybody's doing it, old boy.' The black economy had been born. 'Everybody' included a young, wealthy farmer who found the price of farm implements was such that he had to sell on the Black Market to make ends meet. 'After all, everybody is doing it. In order to dodge income tax a farmer pays, let us say, £2500 for a bull worth much less. He can probably get part of his money back on the side from the seller of the bull, and, anyhow, he can charge the £2500 against income tax.' He had just been offered £1 a lb for butter and sixteen shillings a dozen for eggs. Not surprisingly, confronted with the shopkeeper's curt, 'Are you one of our regulars? No? Then I'm sorry, you can't have any,' the average law-abiding citizen entertained a suspicion that in a society dedicated to fair shares there seemed to be one law for the quick-witted and another for the slow. As early as November 1945 the *New Statesman* described: 'Dusk on a wet Sunday and the smoothies and the spivs come west from Maida Vale. Some in those Packards that do 200 miles a gallon on their basic. Some with their women, a little fleshy, with that heavy brass jewellery that Cleopatra's indigent sister would have worn.'

Without ignoring what was then usually known as the seamy side of life, whether in Maida Vale or Seven Dials, the sociologists were assiduous in trying to establish the norms of sexual morality among the populace as a whole. Their investigations were hampered by a degree of reticence not encountered apparently by their successors in the post-Kinsey era. Gorer came to the conclusion that there had been little or no change in sexual morals since the beginning of the century. He was convinced that half the married population, men as well as women, had had no pre-marital intercourse except with their future spouses. 52 per cent of men and 63 per cent of women in his sample told him that they were against pre-marital sex on principle. He cited as typical of many answers a twenty-nine-year-old working-class wife from Birmingham, who imagined that no decent man after such an experience would regain his self-respect; and a young middle-class Liverpool bachelor who thought that, since every man expects to marry 'an untouched woman', he himself should not have any sexual experience. While such attitudes were undoubtedly prevalent, it was also true that 1947 was a record year for marital instability, with 48,500 persons seeking to terminate marriages, often hastily undertaken in wartime conditions. In 1946 there were 31,871 decrees nisi as compared with 4547 in 1935. Rowntree and Lavers were somewhat surprised at the revelations vouchsafed to them by a divorcée in her middle forties, who explained that she had had four abortions performed by a midwife at £15 each. She explained that she never let the gentleman pay, reckoning that 'if a girl is careless it's her own look-out.' The Labour MP, T. C. Skeffington-Lodge, a Christian Scientist, in a debate on marriage and divorce, told the House that 'however much the finger of scorn may be pointed at Victorian morals, it was certainly not true in those days that 40 per cent of all girls under twenty in England and Wales were pregnant on their wedding day.' There was a tendency in the House to blame these evils on the Press, especially the *News of the World,* but as Tom Driberg, speaking perhaps more as a journalist than as a moralist, put it – 'the Press does not, of course, operate in a vacuum. In a society whose values are largely base or shoddy, the Press will be base and shoddy also.'

Public, as opposed to private, morality was sedulously safeguarded by various forms of censorship, official and unofficial. The Conservative member for Ashford, Edward Percy Smith, himself a playwright, introduced a private member's Bill in 1949 to abolish the censorship of plays, quoting a letter from the Lord Chamberlain about a typographical error in one of his own plays – 'The Lord Chamberlain is prepared to grant a licence for this play on the understanding that the exclamation of the old Victorian lady in Act I is intended to be "Fiddle, my dear" and not, as in the typescript, "Piddle, my dear".' Michael Foot seconded the Bill, but nothing came of it. On the whole, the wireless was well thought of by the guardians of public morality and it was indeed decidedly innocuous, despite which it did not altogether escape the predictable censure of Rowntree and Lavers – 'although on the whole, scripts are kept "clean" there are a good many cases of *double entente* [sic] and of slightly vulgar jokes that are not worthy of the BBC.'

They were encouraged to find that, with the exception of certain American crime magazines, the volume of 'really objectionable literature about could fairly be described as negligible'.

The Editor of the *Sunday Times*, however, felt it wise on 1 May 1948 to warn his readers against a new book called *The Naked and the Dead* by an American author Norman Mailer which he hoped would be withdrawn from circulation immediately – 'Mr Mailer is a writer of exceptional gifts and much of the book has real value, but large parts of it are so grossly obscene that it is quite unfit for general circulation. No decent man could leave it lying about the house, or know without shame that his woman-folk were reading it.' A year later the fastidious George Orwell wrote, à propos *The Conspirator* by Humphrey Slater, that he really thought the modern habit of describing love-making in detail was something that future generations would look back on as we do on things like the death of Little Nell. The days of the Lady Chatterley trial and the Jenkins' Home Secretaryship still lay some way ahead.

There is a deep-seated tendency in Britain to confuse morality and religion, and what were seen in Parliament, and elsewhere, as declining moral values in society were frequently attributed to a collapse of religious belief and practice. Skeffing-ton-Lodge considered that what he called the landslide in behaviour had resulted above all from 'the decay in religious faith and practice in our country'. From the far right Sir Waldron Smithers, described by Crossman as frequently 'squiffy', called for a national religious campaign to combat crime. In a charac-teristic intervention in the 1946 debate on the Address he called the nation sharply to order: 'We in Britain have no written Constitution. Our Constitution is based on the Ten Command-ments, as fulfilled and explained in the Four Gospels. . . . There is a wave of anti-Christ and anarchy all over the world; riots, terrorism in Palestine, murder in India, unofficial strikes causing inconvenience to thousands in this country and in America – and to face this very serious crisis, the biggest in the world's history, Britain has a third eleven of men who do not know the rules of the game, batting in the biggest test match of all time.' Nobody much took Sir Waldron seriously, George Thomas remarking that listening to him he could hardly believe he was in the twentieth century, but there was undoubtedly widespread con-cern that an observable decline in attendance at Church and Chapel might be leading to a general deterioration in behaviour.

If we are to credit Gorer, at least intermittent church-going

and the regular practice of private prayer were still widespread –
though it was a middle-class rather than a working-class pattern,
more prevalent in small towns and villages than in the metropolis
and the suburbs. Rowntree and Lavers analysed the situation of
the churches in the archiepiscopal city of York. In 1946 there
were twenty-nine Anglican places of worship, thirty-one Nonconformist and five Roman Catholic. The average attendance
figures on Sunday in 1935 and 1948 were found to be:

	1935	1948
Anglican	5400	3400
Nonconformist	3900	3500
Roman Catholic	Just under 3000	Just over 3000

The Roman Catholics were still attracting numbers of young
worshippers and the Nonconformists rapidly losing theirs.
Rowntree and Lavers noticed a strong vein of anti-clericalism,
typified by a Methodist parson who ran a successful slum boys'
club as long as he was not seen in clerical dress. When he was
spotted returning from a funeral in a dog collar the cry went up,
'Boys, we've been had. He's a bloody parson,' whereupon they
all left the club. Nor was the simple believer much edified by
the publicity attracted by Dr Hewlett Johnson, the Red Dean of
Canterbury, and Bishop Barnes of Birmingham, whose *The
Rise of Christianity* appeared to espouse a frankly Unitarian
theology. Serialized in Hugh Cudlipp's *Sunday Pictorial*, it
seemed to lend episcopal authority to propositions such as 'a
majority of independent scholars are of opinion that at the Last
Supper Jesus did not say "Do this in remembrance of me";
secondly a minority of such scholars, which seems to me to be
steadily growing, would add that the sentences "This is my
body", "This is my blood" are equally unhistorical.' The agreed
syllabuses and religious instruction enjoined on schools by the
1944 Education Act aroused more optimism among Church
leaders and principals of training colleges than among the
teachers themselves, often too uncertain of their own views to
feel confident about conveying them convincingly to the young.
Nominal Church membership, as measured by baptism, remained high after the war, perhaps two-thirds of the population,
but less than 10 per cent were Easter communicants and many
fewer than that could be called regular church attenders. The

task demanded of the overstretched, underpaid parish incumbents was perhaps now more daunting than it had ever been since the Civil War. Urban wrack and ruin with the social mobility involved was matched as a problem for them in the countryside by the rapid erosion of the old village identity, once petrol rationing began to be lifted. Even the traditional and mutually supportive alliance between the clergy and the voluntary services needed rethinking, as Professor Laski scornfully lashed out at the intervention on behalf of those in trouble, sorrow, need, sickness, and any other adversity 'of gracious ladies, or benevolent busybodies, or stockbrokers to whom a hospital is a hobby'. Visiting the fatherless and widows in the name of true religion, the rector often now found himself anticipated by the Welfare Officer.

Many observers – and not only sociologists – considered that the most striking change in post-war Britain was the new attitude to work and savings. In the autumn of 1944, as the war was drawing to a close, a thoughtful British businessman wrote to a young relative serving overseas: 'So much depends (and of this we at home have no means of knowing) on the attitude of the demobilized sailors, soldiers and airmen. Are they as tired as the civilians at home or are they full of vigour and coming back to civil life full of energy and enterprise? On this so much depends. If they seek security and a planned existence the planners will bind them tightly, and when they awake to their servitude it will take many Samsons to free our bonds.'* In what was bound to be the crucial area of business enterprise the Americans were beginning to suspect something was amiss. The historian Denis Brogan as early as March 1945 reported American scepticism about our pleas for economic spheres of influence, for the avoidance of competition, for the stabilizing of prices, as at best a rationalization of an accepted inferiority or at worst simple laziness. 'We don't work hard enough or effectively enough; we are reluctant to make necessary adjustments, to endure the mental and practical strain of turning from contemplation of our own past economic virtues to the objective study of our greatly weakened economic position today. There is very little hope, as I see it, that American business or the American government will listen with much effective sympathy to mere pleas *ad*

* From W. H. Haslam's unpublished letters in the Imperial War Museum.

misericordiam. The political gratitude due for our stand in 1940 cannot be turned into economic almsgiving.' In the short run Brogan's prophecy was all too dramatically fulfilled, although by 1947 American economic almsgiving was again to come to our rescue in the nick of time.

1946 was perhaps not the ideal year for two million workers to decrease their work load by two hours forty minutes a week, while wage rates went up by 7–8 per cent. Nor did it seem that overtime was at all popular despite the higher rates, Zweig finding that 80 per cent were against it, as it led to higher taxation and interfered with recreation. After much interviewing of bricklayers who admitted that they could lay twice as many bricks as they currently did and painters who worked as much at the weekend for themselves as they did the whole week for their firm and foremen who felt themselves powerless in face of their workforce, Zweig concluded unhappily: 'Thus we see that the policy of planning and full employment requires a complement in a new ethic of work based on the sense of an overriding national purpose and interest.'

By 1948 the government would actually propose to increase unemployment by 50 per cent, since it then stood at 1·8 per cent, instead of Beveridge's figure of 3 per cent, which he regarded as full employment, to say nothing of Ernest Bevin's view expressed in 1943 that a reasonable figure was 8 per cent. Complaints about poor working habits began to proliferate – in bricklaying, in coal, in cotton, in engineering. And to this was added a certain lack of enterprise and desire for betterment which unfavourably impressed Drew Middleton: 'Among the many men I have talked to in the New Towns, I have never met one who was interested in saving enough money to buy his own small business, to strike out for himself. The ideal seemed to be a community of equals protected from economic dangers by full employment and high wages, politically lethargic, unstirred by Socialist or Tory. Everyone earned about the same amount of money, spent it on the same things, and appeared to think and talk alike.' This was rather a long way from the vision of Lewis Silkin, Minister of Town and Country Planning, who looked forward in 1946 to Stevenage, Crawley, Harlow, Hemel Hempstead and East Kilbride producing a new type of citizen, a healthy, self-respecting person with a sense of beauty and culture, of social responsibility and of civic pride.

Zweig found no desire to save among his workers, and sadly concluded that most of them accepted an essentially precarious mode of life, dependent for their security on their trade union. With this went an attitude, more commendable humanly than economically, of class solidarity, which entailed an unwillingness to advance if anybody were thereby likely to be retarded. There was evidence too in areas like South Wales and the Tyne shipyards, now prosperous where they had formerly been derelict, of the old habits persisting, the men having 'nothing to do until the pubs open'. Elsewhere, the Workers' Educational Association was now no match for the cinema and the Light Programme of the BBC. Critical observers drew attention to an increasingly passive and submissive attitude. Before television, there were already signs that the British were becoming, as the phrase had it, 'a nation of spectators'.

In an earlier age a keen student of the British had described them as a nation of shopkeepers. In so far as this was true in 1945 they were very much a nation of small shopkeepers. Of some 745,000 shops, 680,000 were 'independents', that is employing about two assistants each. There were 240,000 co-ops, with a 12 per cent share of retail trade and from which the Labour Party recruited a number of sober-sided MPs; 40,000 'multiples', mostly selling footwear and men's and boy's clothing, of which the archetype was Burton's, the famous fifty-shilling tailors; and just 500 department stores. In London alone there were a hundred markets selling fruit and vegetables and in Britain as a whole perhaps 90,000 small grocers' shops. In 1943 there was one shop for every forty-five inhabitants in Leeds and one for every sixty in Glasgow. The small shop was generally appreciated for its proximity, its flexible credit arrangements and the link it frequently provided between the shopkeeper and the artisan available for small household jobs e.g. the plumber or the electrician running his own store. The 'corner shop' played a vital role in cementing the cohesion of the neighbourhood and as a forum for gossip and grumbling. Boots had over 800 chemists' shops, usually equipped with a lending library, and their future seemed assured since the nation was securely in the grip of the advertisers of patent medicines, a sort of mass suspension of disbelief greeting announcements such as 'Phyllosan tablets, so small, so easy to take – yet when they are taken *regularly*, what a difference they make! Acting directly upon the blood, a regular course of Phyllosan tablets raises the energy potential of the whole organism.' Particularly sought after were antidotes to that most British of afflictions, the common cold – 'Two Serocalcin tablets daily for thirty days provide three to four months' immunity from colds.' A rather more alarming advertisement read – 'All you need are two sniffs up each nostril from your pocket-size Kansodrine inhaler. The effect is immediate. Kansodrine contains the new drug *amphetamine*.'

There were signs, however, of imminent change, as Wolfson's Great Universal Stores and Collier's United Drapery gathered impetus and Jack Cohen of Tesco successfully substituted turnstiles for counters in 1947. A little behind were Sainsbury's, who opened their first self-service store in 1950. The High Street giants, Marks and Spencer, who already had 239 shops before the war, and Woolworths, were still described as 'bazaars' and subject, despite or because of their obvious popular appeal, to much patronizing comment by the middle classes, who preferred the more proprietorial attitude to shopping implied by phrases such as 'my' tailor or 'my' grocer or even 'my little woman'.

The outlook for school leavers in the early post-war years was mixed. On the one hand was the certainty of a job at a wage or salary which their fathers at the same age would not have been able to distinguish from a crock of gold. On the other, higher education was very much rationed. In 1949 there were 83,000 students at universities. A modest suggestion to add another 5000 elicited a comment in *The Times* with a familiar ring about it: 'The widespread belief of university teachers is that standards of entry and education are being forced down by the incoming flood.' Furthermore, as we have seen, for many young men a term of National Service for one, one and a half, or two years (according to the incidence of various international emergencies) filled the immediate horizon. Priestley by 1949 was unimpressed by the merits of National Service: 'to waste so many significant years, to pile up such frustration, all to acquire a lot of resentful, half-trained service men – if this is wisdom, then give me the folly of marching down the High in evening dress chanting that Lloyd George knew your father.'

Individual destinies in National Service varied. You could

spend the time quietly learning Russian in the Intelligence Corps or you could acquire the skills of the platoon commander in training schemes invariably carried out in wet bracken, or you might spend a disproportionate amount of time polishing galvanized buckets. If you joined the Brigade of Guards, your boot polishing impedimenta were two spoons, several candles, an old toothbrush, two yellow dusters, a velvet pad, white Meltonian cream and a bottle of methylated spirits. That the experience was character-forming was not in any doubt, though there was some disagreement, especially among parents, about the character so formed. Before long, however, National Service in various theatres of war would increasingly conform to the 'real thing'.

To summarize, we can call in Priestley again at his favourite task of describing the mood and character of the people – this time in 1949: 'We are a dreary, self-righteous people with a passion for gin, tobacco, gambling and ballet. We are a nation of sabbath-keepers who do not go to Church. We toil to keep ourselves alive, with three tea-breaks, a five-day week and Wednesday afternoon off for the match.' *The Times* reported in 1947 that Priestley himself had bought 2000 acres in the Isle of Wight complete with full mechanized equipment, pedigree Red Poll herds and a registered flock of sheep, so perhaps relative affluence had soured the optimism with which he had once sustained the morale of the nation. However, his censoriousness was echoed by that of T. S. Eliot in *Notes Towards the Definition of Culture* (1948), who saw signs of decline in every department of human activity. It is never of course easy to acquire the status of prophet unless you are crying woe. The march of events was not quite so uncongenial to E. M. Forster, who welcomed the end of 'the capitalist jungle' and accepted the need for planning and ration books and controls. But even he struck a note of warning: 'On the other hand, the doctrine of laissez-faire is the only one that seems to work in the world of the spirit.' To meet the challenge of the time, he felt, it would be necessary to combine the new economy and the old morality.

All in all, it can perhaps be seen that Britain, if it were to meet the varied challenges of the post-war era and at the same time create a new social order, would need a good deal of luck and a marked readiness to forgo immediate gratification in the spirit of unselfish co-operation characteristic of the war years. It was a tall order.

·3·
New Men and New Measures

'We call you to another great adventure which will demand the same high qualities as those shown in the war; the adventure of civilization . . .'   CLEMENT ATTLEE, 1945

'We believe the state, rightly or wrongly, has a duty to perform in the spirit of prayer. We are acting under the Almighty in governing the country.'   GEORGE ISAACS, 1947

THE OLD GANG was out. For a time indeed it was consigned to a rather contemptuous oblivion, typified by Michael Foot's description in the *Daily Herald* of R. A. Butler as having been without protest a man of Manchuria, a man of Abyssinia, a man of non-intervention, a man of Munich, a Baldwinite and a Chamberlainite *par excellence* – and now a Churchillite, charged with working out a Churchillian policy, while the great man wrote his memoirs. 'We are the masters at the moment – and not only for the moment, but for a very long time to come,' said the new Attorney-General, Sir Hartley Shawcross. As the identities of the nation's new masters were revealed, it at once became clear that, whatever else had or had not happened, a great blow had been struck for the principle of the career open to the talents. 43 per cent of the Labour members of Parliament had had no formal schooling after the age of fourteen. While in some quarters it was felt that a number of the remainder had, if anything, been over-educated, the resultant mixture presented the Prime Minister with some problems in the selection of his team, if it were to strike the right balance, in the cricketing parlance he loved, between Gentlemen and Players. In joint harness would be Sir Stafford Cripps, who had been brought up in a forty-roomed house on a 1200 acre estate; Dr Dalton of Eton and King's, the son of a Dean of Windsor; and Ernest Bevin, arguably the greatest Foreign Secretary of the twentieth century, the illegitimate son of a village midwife in Somerset, who had earned his early livelihood as a horse-van driver for a mineral water firm. Many ministerial appointments went to miners – J. J. Lawson at the War Office; George Hall at the Admiralty; Aneurin Bevan, at forty-seven the youngest member of the Cabinet, at the Ministry of Health; Tom Williams at Agriculture; J. Westwood at the Scottish Office. Lawson, one of ten children of a miner, started work in a Durham coalmine at the age of ten and would become Lord-Lieutenant of the county. When ennobled, he continued to live in a minute terraced house in the middle of a coalfield and would show visitors his coal pick polished to the brightness of silver. The popular and effective Tom Williams was the tenth of fourteen children and started at eleven in the Yorkshire pits where his father was blinded and a brother crippled. Hall left school at twelve and Bevan at thirteen. Sir Ben Smith at the Ministry of Food, as we have seen, had been a cab driver; George Isaacs, now in the crucial post of Minister of Labour, had started in the printing trade at the age of twelve before becoming General Secretary of Natsopa. The Home Secretary, Chuter Ede, had been for many years an elementary school teacher and A. V. Alexander, the first Minister of Defence, had left school at thirteen to become an office boy. William Whiteley, the Chief Whip, worked in the mines between the age of twelve and fifteen and might have been a professional footballer with Sunderland United had not his father, a stern teetotaller, burnt his football boots when he discovered that the team was using a pub as a changing room. J. B. Hynd, who combined the grandiloquent titles of Chancellor of the Duchy of Lancaster and Minister for Germany and Austria, had been a clerk with the London, Midland and Scottish railway in Perthshire and a clerk with the National Union of Railwaymen for many years; and Morgan Phillips, the secretary of the party, was the son of an Aberdare miner and left school for the pits at twelve.

This exaltation of the humble and meek into the higher reaches of government was most conspicuously displayed in the contrasted personalities of George Tomlinson and Herbert

Morrison. Tomlinson was initially made Minister of Works and consequently, as he put it, in charge of building materials when there weren't any. He succeeded Ellen Wilkinson in 1947, after her death from a drug overdose, as Minister of Education. He had left Rishton Wesleyan school in Lancashire, where the boys wore clogs and cleaned their slates with their sleeves, to become a weaver in a cotton mill at the age of thirteen. He was paid five shillings a week for a fifty-six and a half hour week. Thereafter, like Ernest Bevin, he had been a mineral water salesman for many years, before becoming a trade union official. No Minister of Education has ever made himself more popular with his officials and the teaching profession at large. His zest for life was so infectiously evident that he probably believed himself when he said that any man who could not be happy as Minister of Education has not within him the power to be happy at all. When asked at a Park Lane luncheon whether he was tired of endlessly eating official chicken he replied: 'Not likely. I started eating chicken much later in life than most of the people here. I have a lot of leeway to make up.' Political dogma played singularly little part in his conception of his duties. A life-long Trade Unionist, he adamantly opposed the Durham County Council's attempt to impose a closed shop on its teachers, and he told the preparatory school headmasters: 'Personally, I do not see the sense of getting rid of something that is doing a useful job of work, or making everything conform to a common pattern. I am all for variety, especially in the field of education.'

While Tomlinson was something of an innocent abroad in the political arena, Herbert Morrison was by contrast an intensely wily politician. Behind a public persona which seemed to typify the cheerful Cockney sparrow, there doubtless lurked some at any rate of the characteristics which led Michael Foot to describe him as 'a soft-hearted suburban Stalin, for ever suspecting others of the conspiracies on which he had engaged himself'.* Yet this immensely experienced and formidably hard-working politician, with his record of success at local government and ministerial level, had traversed a long and hard road before attaining the eminence he enjoyed in 1945. The son of an alcoholic police constable and a domestic servant, he had graduated as a journalist after working as a shop assistant and a switchboard

* *Aneurin Bevan*, Davis-Poynter, 1973, Vol II, p. 288.

operator. In the First World War he had been a strident pacifist, condemning a proposal in 1915 that soldiers should be allowed to form trade unions since he objected to anything which would lead to the army being looked upon as a respectable profession. As a result he spent the last part of the war picking currants in Letchworth Garden City. It was through his pacifist connections that he became secretary of the London Labour party and so began his career between the wars as the most celebrated local government politician since Joseph Chamberlain. The authentic Morrisonian style is captured in his comment on Labour's triumph in the London elections of 1937: 'I believe we can rule London for ever, so when you meet the man who says "it can't be done" pat him on the back, give him a cheery smile and say "Gertcher";' or as when he proudly announced that, the production of prams having gone up 60 per cent, he hoped that enough bonny wee things were being produced to fill them. Commended by Beatrice Webb as 'the very quintessence of Fabianism in politics and outlook', he was a master of the politics of everyday life in matters such as transport, housing, health, education and parks. He defined his supreme purpose in public life as 'the achievement of tidiness'. Responsible for putting nationalization at the heart of the Labour programme, it would fall to him to supervise its implementation on the basis of the public corporation, of which the archetype was his beloved London Passenger Transport Board. Like George Tomlinson, he was no doctrinaire and the degree of his commitment to anything like 'socialism in our time' was highly suspect to the Labour Left, who for the most part greatly disliked him. There was a suspicion at the time, as well as subsequently, that the public corporation as advocated by Morrison might merely substitute for the remote control of the bosses an equally remote control by bureaucrats, but nobody else had worked out a coherent alternative more evidently compatible with Socialist ideals.

Morrison was, like Attlee, untypical of the long-serving members of the party in deriving inspiration neither from dogmatic Christianity nor from Marxism. Of the ministers we have considered, Ernest Bevin in his youth had seriously contemplated being a Nonconformist minister or even a missionary; Tomlinson had trained unsuccessfully for the ministry and was an assiduous lay preacher, as were Jack Lawson and Whiteley;

the political career of Glenvill Hall, the Financial Secretary to the Treasury, was profoundly influenced by his Quaker origins. A different devotional outlook inspired James Chuter Ede, who exchanged a constructive and friendly relationship with Butler in the drafting of the 1944 Education Act for a long tenure of the Home Office. He was President of the International Association for Liberal Christianity and Religious Freedom, and on arrival at the Home Office removed a time-worn copy of *Crockford's* from his desk and replaced it with a volume of his favourite poems. Equally undogmatic but to outward seeming much more fervent was Stafford Cripps, whose mother, Beatrice Webb's sister, had propounded on her deathbed the following religious precepts for the upbringing of her family: 'I should like them to be trained to be undogmatic and unsectarian Christians, charitable to all churches and sects studying the precepts and actions of Christ as their example, taking their religious inspiration directly from the spirit of the New Testament.' The combined service of God and Mammon with which he found himself confronted as President of the Board of Trade, resulted in his addressing the House of Commons in August 1947 in language which united the dispatch box and the pulpit: 'It has been truly said that by our faith we can move mountains. It is by our faith in ourselves, in our country, in the free democratic tradition for which the people of this country have for centuries fought and battled, and for which they must fight again as willingly on the economic front as upon the oceans, on the land and in the air; it is by our faith in the deep spiritual values that we acknowledge in our Christian faith, that we shall be ennobled and inspired to move the present mountain of our difficulties, and so emerge into that new and fertile plain of prosperity which we shall travel in happiness only as the result of our own efforts and our own vision.' Of the two elements traditionally regarded as having most signally contributed to the growth of British socialism, Christianity and Marxism, the former was evidently still holding its own.

The advent of a seemingly powerful Labour government naturally increased the importance of the trade unions, whose status in the eyes of Westminster and Whitehall had been anyway greatly enhanced during the war, largely as a result of the central role played by the Ministry of Labour under Ernest

Bevin. Indeed, it was the power of the unions which Shawcross had in mind when making his much misquoted 'we are the masters now' speech during the passage of the Trade Disputes Bill of 1946. This greatly increased union funds by substituting 'contracting out' for 'contracting in' in the payment of the political levy, and allowed civil service unions to join the TUC. When the Act was finally passed in 1947 Labour MPs sang *The Red Flag* in the lobbies, and understandably so, since the percentage of trade unionists subscribing to their party funds rose from 48·5 per cent in 1945 to 90·6 per cent with the passage of the Bill. The Conservatives' opposition to the Bill was unusually vigorous, rivalled only by their active hostility to steel nationalization. Quintin Hogg reminded the House that the Trade Union Congress was the most powerful corporation that had existed in Britain since the Roman Catholic Church was disestablished at the time of the Reformation. Sir Cuthbert Headlam, whom George Lyttelton suspected of hissing like a serpent at the sight of a socialist, affected to believe that the bill was only introduced to satisfy the *amour propre* of the TUC, but 'in doing so, I am certain they are laying up trouble for future governments in this country, whether Conservative or Socialist, because no man can tell what may be the future political complexion of the trade unions; they may not always be led by the fairly sensible, pink-coloured gentlemen who are now in control.' He may well have had in mind Aneurin Bevan's remark in 1944 that 'the person in this country who is in the most strongly entrenched position, next to the King, is the trade union official.'

The most prominent of the 'pinkish gentlemen', referred to by Sir Cuthbert, were Arthur Deakin of the Transport and General Workers; Will Lawther of the National Union of Mineworkers, formed in 1944 out of forty-one federated unions; Tom Williamson of the General and Municipal Workers; and Lincoln Evans of the Iron and Steel Trades Confederation. Since they were all well to the Right of any significant trade union leaders since, they have earned a special place in the demonology of the Left, Jennie Lee describing them as 'jangling their money-bags and quite blatantly reminding the Cabinet, the NEC and the PLP that he who pays the piper calls the tune'. Williamson was relatively docile but Deakin and Lawther were by any standards powerful personalities. Deakin, the son of a village cobbler, was a Primitive Methodist and a teetotaller, but addicted like Churchill to outsize cigars. When Bevin joined Churchill's Cabinet in 1940 Deakin, also a dockers' leader, inherited the TGWU. By the end of the war he had espoused the doctrine of the mixed economy and talked less and less of 'socializing' industry. Characteristic of his outlook was a speech he made the year before his sudden death at a May Day rally in 1955: 'If the Trade Unions are to maintain that influence and that position in the economy of the country which they claim for themselves, the pattern of their policy must be related to the needs of the community at large in addition to serving the interests of the people they represent.' Nor was this idle rhetoric. He told his union executive in May 1947: 'So far as wages are concerned it is clear that increased wages mean increased prices, subsequently leading to inflation. In my view, we must seek to increase production, reduce prices and increase the purchasing power of money.' This was not language which appealed to all members of Arthur Deakin's executive, nine out of thirty-four of whom were Communists. In 1948 the London dock strike was organized by an unofficial strike committee of forty-eight members, thirty-six of whom were recognized by Deakin as Communists or fellow-travellers. That year Deakin told a Scottish delegate conference: 'The Communist Party stands indicted as the declared enemy of the British working class.' In 1949 he led a walk-out of the non-Communist delegates at the World Federation of Trade Unionists; and in that same year the TGWU voted by 426 to 208 to prevent Communists holding office in the union. Mocked by *Tribune* as Brother Arfur, and towards the end of his life continually at loggerheads with Bevan, Deakin was nevertheless perfectly capable of standing up for his union according to his own lights, as when in 1947 he pronounced that 'under no circumstances is the regulation of wages a matter for the government. The people that I represent are not prepared to play second fiddle.'

Deakin's zeal in fighting Communists was equalled by that of Will Lawther, a large, jolly man who had started in the pits at the age of twelve, had been an MP and was the first miner to be knighted (in 1949). Lawther was in daily touch with Communism since his union's General Secretary, Arthur Horner, was a party member and had an office in the same building, which he decorated with a bust of Lenin. Early in life Horner had been something of a boy wonder in the Baptist pulpit at Merthyr Tydfil, but had long since settled for Communism after a vigorous career as a professional agitator, including a spell in the IRA. He earned considerable opprobrium by denouncing Marshall Aid as a capitalist plot.* Lawther's presidential address to the Union in 1947 included a pointed warning to the delegates: 'It is a crime against our people that unofficial strikes should take place and we advise you, in your own interests, to watch very carefully those who so readily call you out on strike.' Although a well read man, Lawther tended to be contemptuous of the intellectual Left whom he described as 'Sunday corduroy Socialists'. He once went to far, in a speech in Cincinnati, as to describe Bevan, a fellow miner, as a man with his feet in Moscow and his eyes on number ten Downing Street.

Also in a position of power on the far Right of the trade union movement was Lincoln Evans, a much cleverer man than Deakin, who had left school at twelve and worked as a barber's latherboy. He was to be the object of much vituperation from the Left for agreeing to join the Iron and Steel Board in 1951 at a time when the Tories were poised to denationalize the industry. Even more influential in government circles was the Durham miners' leader, Sam Watson, who was a close friend and confidant of both Attlee and Gaitskell. The former told his biographer that he planned to bring Watson into Parliament to succeed Bevin as Foreign Secretary but: 'Sam never wanted to travel south of Durham. Would have been a drawback in a Foreign Secretary.' Among Sam Watson's proudest possessions was a document listing twenty-seven improvements in the conditions of miners and their families – one for each of his years of service at Durham area union headquarters. These included the highest ever wages, a five-day week, pension schemes, modernization of colliery houses and free pit-head baths.

Less than justice has been done to the contribution of working-class leaders like Deakin and Lawther to the smooth working of Attlee's government in a period when affiliated union membership rose from two and a half million to five million in 1950. They were above all realists – about inflation, about the

* Though K. O. Morgan is no doubt right in asserting that he 'derived his prestige as an industrial statesman, not as a party politician'.

limitations of nationalization as a panacea for all industrial shortcomings, and about Communist infiltration and the part it played in fomenting unofficial strikes. The Communists were no imaginary bogey born of middle-class paranoia – they controlled the Electrical Trade Union, the Foundry Workers and the Fire Brigades, and also the Welsh and Scottish miners. The Leggett Committee Report of 1951 on Unofficial Stoppages in the London Dock found that: 'It appears to be incredibly easy to bring dock workers out on strike. We were given repeated instances of men stopping work almost automatically, with little or no idea why they were stopping. In the words of one witness, himself a dock worker: "All that was needed was for a man to go round the docks shouting 'all out' and waving the men off the ships and out they would come." ' By the end of the war the dockers had achieved not only decasualization but average weekly earnings sometimes 20 per cent above the national average. Yet from July 1941 to July 1955 there were sixty-four unofficial strikes, that of September 1945 lasting nearly six weeks. Attlee found himself faced with the uncongenial necessity of using troops in the docks as strike breakers in 1945, 1948, 1949 and 1950. Whatever *Tribune* might feel, there was some merit in Deakin's unusual capacity to call a spade a spade. It had been, after all, a close call at the Blackpool Conference of the Labour Party in May 1945 when the Communists' application for membership had only been defeated by 1,219,000 votes to 1,134,000.

With parliamentary and trade union leadership working closely together, it was not surprising that the country was spared the extremist measures and class warfare which many feared in July 1945. Nevertheless, the government from the outset was evidently in earnest about fulfilling its electoral promises and the tempo of legislative activity was prodigious. Between 1945 and 1950 it passed in all 347 Acts of Parliament – 8640 pages of legislation. In the first session alone there were eighty-three statutes amounting to 1390 pages. Iron and steel required twelve drafts, transport twenty-one and the elephantine Town and Country Planning Act twenty-three. The prevalent mood in government circles was well captured by Christopher Mayhew writing in October 1945: 'The ideas we have hawked round garrets in Bloomsbury, and shouted from street corners and on village greens, are being respectably embodied in Bills and passed on to the Statute Book. It is a great thrill, and if we fail, no one shall say we haven't tried.' Thanks to the pioneering work of the Politics Department of the University of Strathclyde we are beginning to learn more about the machinery that moved this phenomenal workload. Peter Hennessy and Andrew Arends have unearthed from the archives a grand total of no less than 466 committees answering to the Labour government during its period in office, of which 148 were standing and 306 *ad hoc*. Curiously, there was no committee for Foreign Affairs – the unassailable fief of Attlee and Bevin, nor, until the crisis of September 1947 threw up the Economic Policy Committee, any standing committee dealing with overall economic strategy.

The omens for launching a vastly expensive revolution in the structure of society were not particularly propitious. War notoriously distorts the pattern of overseas trade, especially by forcing neutral countries to produce manufactured goods which they cannot obtain from belligerent countries. As a nation which needed to export to survive we had now suffered twice from protracted world wars. International protectionism between those wars had already reduced greatly the volume of our exports, and this was one of the major causes of hard core unemployment, rather than any necessarily fatal defect in British capitalism. When we had been unable before the war to sustain, by exporting, the greatly increased standard of life outside the depressed areas the difference could be made up by the interest on our overseas investments. However, by the end of the Second World War over £1,000,000 of overseas investments had been sold to pay for war supplies, nearly half representing investments in the USA and Canada. That particular mask had been stripped away. The reality behind it was alarming. By 1944 exports had fallen in value to less than a third of the 1938 figure. Furthermore, the terms of trade had turned against us, so that in 1948 about 20 per cent more goods had to be exported than in 1938 to pay for the same quantity of imports. In the event the record of the country under the Labour government in regard to exports was remarkable, even allowing for the temporary incapacitation of some of our most formidable rivals such as Germany and Japan. By 1947 the pre-war volume of exports was equalled and by 1950 the figure was two-thirds higher still. By

1950 there was a £300 million surplus on the balance of payments, before progress was abruptly halted by the demands of the Korean War. But the effort entailed a high price in three different but related respects. First, the degree of austerity involved left people feeling that after six years of peace they were not notably better off than after six years of war. Secondly, the remorseless demands of the export drive combined with a high level of public spending at home left insufficient resources for the essential task of modernizing obsolete plant and equipment. And thirdly – to the mortification of the more doctrinaire socialists – Britain's dependence on the United States became more and more absolute. It was of no great avail for Patrick Gordon Walker to tell the electors of Smethwick that: 'We have to tighten our belts, if necessary, in order to retain our economic independence and not tie sterling to the dollar,' if he then had to vote for Bretton Woods (with its second article of membership enjoining the duty 'to promote private foreign investment') and for a large US loan.

Against this background, for the government to commit the country to implementing in full the party manifesto was a high risk strategy, which would have ended in total disaster in the short term without transatlantic aid and in the long term without the discovery of North Sea oil. But the nation had voted for a socialist programme and this was no moment for faint hearts. After all, it was widely believed that central planning and the national ownership of the means of production would generate far more wealth than the old discredited capitalist system. Magnetogorsk, so to speak, would be a staging post for Eldorado.

However, the stoutest socialist hearts quailed when President Truman abruptly ended Lend-Lease, according to the strict terms of the agreement, just three weeks after Labour assumed office. Dalton had thought that this particular source of US aid would be gently tapered off over many months. Keynes duly negotiated a loan, but not, as was naively hoped, without strings. As he put it in an exasperated telegram: 'We are negotiating in Washington repeat Washington. Fig leaves that pass muster in Threadneedle Street wither in a harsher climate.' Sterling would have to be made convertible within a year, and the need to ratify the Bretton Woods agreement put paid to any devices such as imperial preferences which might enable Britain to cushion herself against the harsh realities of international markets. These conditions were described in the House by one of the new Labour MPs James Callaghan, as economic aggression – and by the *New Statesman* as a devastating appeasement of American capitalism. However the government, not without much misgiving, swallowed its pride and accepted the banker's overdraft at 2 per cent, there being no other way in which they could 'face the future' as they had promised. The welfare state would thus be inaugurated on tick, a tenth of Britain's consumable income between 1946 and 1948 being attributable to borrowing. The world was not what it had been. As Fred Peart sadly observed in a debate: 'There was a time, when, if you wanted to build an empire, you sent the missionary and the whisky bottle. Now one sends Bing Crosby and a tin of spam.' Keynes explained to the Lords that the only alternative was to build up an economic bloc, excluding Canada and the United States, to consist of countries to which we already owed more than we could pay 'on the basis that they shall lend us money which they have not got and buy from us goods which we are unable to supply'.

The new Britain was first and foremost to be underpinned by a policy of cheap food for the people. The government bought foodstuffs in bulk, selling them often below the buying price and making up the difference from public funds. When Leo Pliatzky joined the Ministry of Food in 1947 he was sent on a week's induction course, at which practically every lecturer referred proudly to the fact that the Ministry was spending a million pounds a day on food subsidies. And a very large Ministry it was, comprising 50,000 civil servants, who between them processed a thousand letters of complaint a day. In 1945–6 the cost of food subsidies of one sort and another was £265 million, which rose in the next five years to £465 million. For the most part cheap food could certainly not be justified as a policy of robbing Peter to pay Paul. It paid both Peter and Paul indiscriminately.

Cheap food was a hidden subsidy which people soon came to take for granted; it aroused no apprehension in an agricultural community protected by guaranteed prices and was therefore in no sense controversial. Nor was another basic provision of the Welfare State, the National Insurance Act, introduced in 1946

96

by the ex-miner James Griffiths. Essentially this was the implementation of Beveridge, to which the wartime coalition was committed. The Conservative Osbert Peake saw in it 'very little of what I understand as socialism. . . . It is founded upon the well-tried practice of social insurance with which our people have become so familiar.' Arthur Greenwood for Labour pointed out that 'a social security scheme is no alternative to a constructive economy and social policy,' and Morrison realistically remarked in a speech early in 1946 that: 'We on this side have been too long saying that all the wealth comes from human labour to forget it and believe that Beveridge schemes come from somewhere else. They do not. They have to be earned by toil, by industry. Let us not forget it. . . . If we get more consumption, more taxes, more burdens upon the public purse, more wages, without the production taking care of them, then we shall get not over-production but inflation and a financial smash, a financial crisis from which the working classes will suffer as much as anyone else.' Employing the language of an older generation nurtured on the labour theory of value, and frightened of the social consequences of over-production, Morrison was here displaying the earthbound common sense which so infuriated the visionaries in his party.

An even more sombre warning was soon to come from Beveridge himself. Introducing the 1953 edition of *Full Employment in a Free Society*, he wrote: 'The aim of the Beveridge Report of 1942, as had been stated in it more than once, was the practical abolition of public charity – National Assistance under Means Test: it was to be replaced by security against want given as a right under social insurance, leaving freedom to every citizen to plan his level and that of his dependants above want. Ten years after, in 1952, more than two million needed National Assistance; social security had been destroyed by endlessly rising prices.' He hammered the point home further: 'I have long held the view that maintaining stability in prices is an essential duty of the State, ranking in importance with maintenance of peace abroad and order at home, or abolition of social evils like want, needless disease, squalor and ignorance. . . . There are, of course, in our wage structure today injustices that call for remedy. But do any of these exceed or equal the injustice being done through destroying by inflation the value of pensions and savings provided for old age?' As *The Times* was to write on the fortieth anniversary of the publication in 1942 of his report, Beveridge had a keen sense of the finiteness of national resources.

The Conservative party conference of March 1945 passed a resolution welcoming 'the Government's decision to make a comprehensive National Health Service available to all', thus apparently endorsing Churchill's colourful wartime promise of a service which would secure that everybody in the country, irrespective of means, age, sex or occupation, should have equal opportunities to benefit 'from the best and most up-to-date medical and allied services'. Furthermore, there was undoubtedly a strong undercurrent of support from the rank and file of the medical profession from the outset of the preliminary planning. It is the more surprising, therefore, that the establishment of what would be the most spectacular creation of the welfare state should have provoked such a degree of undignified furore until the Act, passed in November 1946, finally came into operation on 5 July 1948. The forces which prevented the smooth passage of the Bill – the popular press, the BMA and the Conservative party – all made conspicuous fools of themselves by fighting the wrong battle in the wrong way.

At the centre of the conflict was the responsible Minister, Aneurin Bevan, whose portfolio loaded him with the awesome responsibility of implementing the government's policy in both health and housing. He had already been the object of sustained interest in Press circles because of his relentless criticism during the war of Churchill, who had described him as a squalid nuisance. He was incomparably the most colourful figure in a cabinet whose respectability was a great deal more conspicuous than its glamour. Unlike many of his older colleagues from the Welsh mining valleys, he was not cast in a teetotal, lay-preaching mould. His biographer, Michael Foot, described Bevan's socialism as rooted in Marxism, 'whatever modifications he had made in the doctrine, a belief in the class struggle stayed unshaken.' He was a supremely good popular orator in the old-fashioned mode, significantly having no mastery of the radio and always at his happiest talking to a loyal gathering of enthusiastic supporters, who inspired both his finest rhetoric and his wildest indiscretions.

Bevan laid up a rod for his own back as he set out on his task by not consulting the BMA in the early stages of his planning.

The contentious issues about which the debate revolved were the future of the voluntary hospitals, which Bevan's predecessor in the Coalition government, Sir Henry Willink, considered should be allowed to opt out of the service; the extensive powers to be assumed by the Ministry of Health, including especially the right to appoint the members of the regional boards; the method of remunerating doctors and the buying and selling of practices; the proposed Medical Practices Committee designed to ensure that general practice was equitably distributed through the country; and the position of specialists. All these issues were settled in due course. The doctors were to secure generous compensation for losing the right to sell practices, and private medicine was not outlawed, so no question arose of a full-time salaried profession. The specialists were allowed to have fee-paying patients in hospitals. On the third reading of the Bill Bevan declared that 'the only voluntary part of the hospital service destroyed by the Bill is the necessity to sell flags and collect money. Hon. Members opposite, as they represent the party of property, always imagine that the only voluntary act which has any sanctity behind it is the writing out of a cheque.' Herbert Morrison grumbled about the diminution of local government power resulting from the disappearance of municipal hospitals, but was overruled in Cabinet. However, the BMA leaders continued to convince themselves that Bevan entertained the secret aim of destroying the freedom of their profession and converting medical practitioners into salaried civil servants. The Press inflamed the conflict with headlines like 'No Future for us in Britain – Doctors turn to the Empire'.

Bevan lent some substance to the BMA suspicions by talking loosely about a full-time salaried service on the Second Reading: 'I do not believe the medical profession is ripe for it. . . . There is all the difference in the world between plucking fruit when it is ripe and plucking it when it is green.' But all the time he had the support of the general public and he soon acquired the backing of the Royal Colleges. The strong support in the profession which Dr Guy Dain and Dr Charles Hill had built up by their continuous agitation eventually disintegrated, and when the NHS duly started 90 per cent of the general practitioners came in immediately and within two months 93 per cent of the population had signed on. Bevan claimed that Britain now had the moral leadership of the world and that before long people would be 'coming here as to a modern Mecca'.

It was undoubtedly a great triumph, both for the minister and for the government, not least on the floor of the House. The popularity of the concept of a National Health service was such that it was almost inevitable that the Conservatives would appear to oppose the provisions of the Bill just for the sake of opposing them. Possibly their lowest moment in the whole parliament was on 30 April 1946, when Richard Law as opposition spokesman was deputed to face Bevan at his most triumphant moment. Law claimed that the Royal College of Obstetricians had stated that the Bill would lead to a great increase in maternal mortality. Challenged to quote their exact words, he lamely admitted that he had not got the document with him, whereupon the Labour MP for Rochdale, Dr H. B. Morgan, produced it and demonstrated that by no stretch of the imagination could it bear the construction Law had put upon it.

Yet it would not be long before events demonstrated that the National Health Service, for all its merits, was not going to prove the unqualified success promised by Bevan when he enjoined the House to take pride 'in the fact that, despite our financial and economic anxieties, we are still able to do the most civilized thing in the world – put the welfare of the sick in front of every other consideration.' In the real world it is of course not so easy. Bevan was no great admirer of insurance as the key to social policy and persuaded Dalton, from whom he received steady support over the NHS, that only one-twentieth of the cost need come from the insurance fund, explaining to the Chancellor that 'the general figure was bound to be guesswork'. Spectacles, false teeth and hearing aids were all to be included at the outset, despite doubts on Morrison's part. By the beginning of 1949 it became clear that the guesswork about the general figure was already £52 million on the wrong side, which enabled Churchill to taunt Morrison for having perpetrated gross miscalculations.

It was always Bevan's optimistic thesis that once the backlog of medical neglect had been righted, as it soon would be, then the expense would even out and taper off. There would then be no problem about everybody having 'equal opportunities to benefit from the best and most up-to-date treatment'. The reality was to be rather different. The more people you cure the more likely they are to survive into decrepit and expensive old age; the more up-to-date the treatment the more expensive it is likely to be; and the freer the medicine-bottle the more insatiable the demand for it. It soon became all too clear that if you put the welfare of the sick in front of every other consideration you must cut back on housing and pensions and education, which all play a useful part in keeping healthy people healthy. Then if, as a result, you have to limit your medical budget, you must choose between replacing old hospitals with expensive, new ones or neglecting other parts of the service for which there is immediate clamour and more votes. Aneurin Bevan's miscalculations would before long trigger off ideological disputes in the Labour party of an ultimately destructive intensity.

The wartime Coalition had charted the course of post-war policy more fully in the field of education than in that of medicine. It fell to Ellen Wilkinson to begin the post-war implementation of the 1944 Education Act against a shortage of teachers, of buildings and of financial resources. The closed world of educational administration was full of strange new concepts enshrined in the Act – agreed syllabuses, parity of esteem, county colleges and notably something called ROSLA. The latter was an acronym for the raising of the school leaving age to fifteen, which Ellen Wilkinson, despite formidable difficulties and much official faint-heartedness, carried through by April 1947. Some of the more disillusioned secondary modern heads could be heard complaining that they couldn't think of anything to do with most of their pupils detained against their will for another year at school, except to put them to scrubbing the floor, but in general all went well. Her equally bold proposal that the county colleges, the imaginative proposal in the 1944 Act for the further education of one and a half million teenagers, should be established by 1950 was, however, not to be fulfilled.

A Labour party plan for the organization of secondary education had been drawn up by a TGWU official called Harold Clay and accepted by the Conference in 1942. It embodied what was called 'the common school principle'. Ellen Wilkinson went so far in 1945 as to issue instructions that newly built secondary schools were to be 'multi-lateral where possible'. In the prevailing conditions it was rarely possible, although the LCC's Chief Education Officer, Graham Savage, was busy planning comprehensive education for London on the basis of impressions garnered on a three weeks' visit to America in 1925. Ellen Wilkinson, though an idealist, was an intensely practical one, telling Harold Nicolson on one occasion that whereas he dealt with ideas, 'and one can never see how an idea works out, I deal in water closets and one can always see whether it works or not.' This characteristic informed two speeches in the House in July 1946. In one she said: 'I do not wish to dogmatize about the form in which secondary education should be organized at the outset of the great experiment of educating all children according to their ability and aptitude;' and in the other: 'Secondary education does not and should not mean grammar school education for all . . . but I must say that it is not a progressive, but a retrograde step to say that the only alternative is identical secondary education for all.' All this earned the benevolent approval of R. A. Butler, whose attitude to the Labour implementation of what was often known as the Butler Act somewhat resembled that of a proud father periodically visiting the nursery to see how the baby was doing. 'It is through variety in schools,' he said in November 1945, 'that you bring out the best in the pupil. All this nonsense that England is divided into different sects and classes, and that you cream one section and put it into another is out of date. If it is not, then why are there so many people with the old school tie on that side of the House? . . . You must be careful not to import political or other unpleasant changes into education.' While this may not have been an example of Butler at his most logical, it did indicate something of the nearly bi-partisan approach to education which then prevailed. Even the more vituperative comprehensivers like the Welsh headmaster W. G. Cove, MP for Aberavon, were in a state of considerable confusion as to what they were talking about, as exemplified by an article in which he wrote: 'Let it be clearly stated that those of us who accept the principle of multilateralism will not tolerate any lowering of the status and dignity of secondary grammar schools.' As a part-consequence of the relative absence of sectarian dogma, the education service as a whole made remarkable strides in difficult circumstances, with a crash emergency training scheme for what was to prove an excellent generation of ex-service teachers. There were many outstanding administrators both at national and local level. Mrs

Thirkell's eagle eye, it is true, led her to describe an infant school teacher, at that time mercifully uncharacteristic, who told one of her heroines: 'I do the best I can to make the toddlers politically minded. There's such a nice little song "We'll all go down the Big Red Road". The headmistress has another very nice song, "My little Red Home in the East".' However, for some years to come the lunatic fringe in education did not acquire excessive credence, though A. S. Neill was busy telling the *New Statesman* that 'if the emotions are free the intellect will look after itself.' He also produced a book called *The Problem Child*, in which he announced his strong conviction that 'the boy is never in the wrong.' Both Ellen Wilkinson and George Tomlinson knew better than that. But as the first post-war decade wore on, the peace of the educational establishment was beginning to be violently disturbed by the passions engendered by the eleven plus examination. 'Parity of esteem' was not being enjoyed by schools any more than it ever is by individuals. Even if you persuaded yourself that the local secondary modern was as 'good' as the local grammar (which it sometimes was), there still survived into the Fifties 'all-age' schools; and the technical schools which were to have formed the third leg of the tripartite system were mostly conspicuous by their absence. Britain was still a long way short of 'affording' a proper educational system.

Nearer the heart of the electorate in general than schools and social benefits was housing, at a time when the population was crowded into 700,000 fewer houses than in 1939, to say nothing of the three million damaged by war. This initial shortage was accentuated by the fact that, between 1945 and 1948, there were 11 per cent more marriages and 33 per cent more births than in the three years immediately preceding the war. Bevan's officials told him that 750,000 new houses would be required by 1948. Unfortunately this fell far short of what was required.

Aneurin Bevan's approach to his task can be illustrated from two of his speeches in 1949: 'I believe that one of the reasons why modern nations have not been able to solve their housing problems is that they have looked upon houses as commodities to be bought and sold and not as a social service to be provided. . . . A house is far too complex a product of modern society to be left to unplanned initiative. Therefore it is essential that the state should take a hand in the provision of this modern necessity and do so by making housing a service. This can only be accomplished by reposing it in the custody of a public authority;' and again: 'It is not the task of the builder to select the tenants for the houses. It is the task of the builder to build houses and it is the task of the public authorities to choose between the respective claims of the different applicants, so that the houses go largely to those in need of them.' He was also particularly drawn to the concept of 'the social mix', whereby in the towns and villages of the future there would be no segregation by class and income, or as he put it: 'We should try to introduce in our modern villages and towns what was always the lively feature of English and Welsh villages, where the doctor, the grocer, the butcher and the farm labourer all lived in the same street.' It would all be rather more difficult, presumably, if there were more than one street in the town or village. However, Bevan may have had a decidedly optimistic attitude to the housing problem. According to Dalton, he claimed only to spend one afternoon a week on it, since 'housing looked after itself'.

The 1700 local authorities, operating if not on a *tabula rasa* at least in a sizeable vacuum, set out on the giant task, borrowing money at cheap Dalton rates and repaying it with a combination of generous government subsidy, local rates and uneconomic rents. Not all of them relished a task, particularly complicated by the complexities of establishing priorities as between equally deserving and near-frantic applicants and of operating complex licencing systems. Before the war the ratio of house-building was one council house to three private houses. Bevan from the outset planned to revise this completely, so that there would be five council houses to one private house. The trouble was that, whereas private enterprise could build a house in nine months, the local authorities took thirteen or fourteen months, which was all too clearly demonstrated by 1947 from the situation in areas as different from each other as Durham and Hertford.

The whole process was not accelerated by the fact that no fewer than seven ministries became involved, not only Health and Scotland (policy and design); Works (organization, prefabricated buildings*, bricks, glass, cement); Supply (baths,

* Each pre-fab, as they were popularly known, needed over 2500 parts made in 165 different factories. It was a minor miracle that 150,000 were completed by 1947.

nails, screws); Board of Trade (timber, paint); Town and Country Planning, and Transport. Although they did their best to meet regularly and compose their differences, the inevitable outcome was, as Lady Megan Lloyd George described it in October 1964: 'There are seven ministries dealing with this matter, all with separate responsibilities to discharge, all with separate interests to serve, all pulled and pulling in different directions – a tug of war in which time is wasted and energy dissipated.' The word bottleneck assumed a place of great prominence in public discussion of housing. The supply of cement could outdistance that of bricks or timber; the Ministry of Works might have failed to order pipes or bath-taps in sufficient quantities; kitchen-units might arrive on the site well ahead of sand for plastering. There seemed to be a shortage of everything except paper. J. L. Hodson noted, in April 1946, a sight which was all too common: 'Near here some men began foundations for a house, and had a lot of materials on the spot and concrete laid – but now all is at a standstill, and they have departed.' Bevan admitted that private builders got on quicker by dealing with relatively small numbers of houses expeditiously completed, whereas local authorities put out far too many contracts in relation to available supplies. Morrison endeavoured to cheer up a Leeds audience by telling them that the fact that they saw so many bottlenecks was evidence that the economy was expanding.

Furthermore, there seemed to be something rather wrong with the building force. Immediately after the war there was of course a shortfall in numbers and certain aspects of the demobilization scheme – e.g. the release of bricklayers before brickmakers – caused difficulties. But by 1946 the labour force was up to strength. However, by 1948 the Girdwood Committee of Enquiry set up by Bevan reported that a house costing £518 to build before the war now cost £1242, the workers needing 45 per cent more hours and 69 per cent more pay to build just over half the number of houses – statistics which were revealing, even allowing for inflation having doubled over the previous ten years. Zweig was told by a painter: 'At weekends when I work on my own, I do as much, if not more, than I do the whole week for my firm.' A bricklayer told him that he laid 400–500 bricks when on day work as opposed to a thousand on piece-work. A retired builder wrote to *The Listener* pointing out that, between

1900 and 1909, 300,000 to 500,000 houses were being built annually and bricklayers (on piece-work) laid a thousand bricks a day and were much happier as a result. However that might be, there was a curious tendency in London for the building force to diminish just when it was expected to increase, it being darkly suspected that they were busy doing a number of illicit jobs in their own time and on their own terms.

By the end of 1945 fewer than a thousand houses and ten thousand pre-fabs had been completed, and Churchill lost no opportunity of criticizing the responsible minister, as in November of that year: 'Mr Aneurin Bevan, who distinguished himself so much during the war with his bitter taunts at every moment of difficulty and exceptional danger, is in charge of housing. But he cannot find time to rebuild our shattered houses, he is too busy chasing landlords and nightmare profiteers round the ruins.' Thereafter the tempo speeded up. Indeed, Michael Foot in his biography of Bevan makes out a strong case for his hero, who he claims would have anticipated Harold Macmillan's much celebrated triumph by building 300,000 new houses a year in the lifetime of the Labour government but for economies imposed on him by his own Cabinet. Thus by 1948 the annual rate had risen to 227,616, but was then cut back each year subsequently to a figure of 204,117 in 1951. Unfortunately, Bevan was unable to resist making unjustifiably optimistic statements all over the country, explaining how well he was doing. Thus at Durham in July 1946: 'When the next Election occurs there will be no housing problem in Great Britain for the British working class;' at Deptford in October 1946: 'I give you this promise: that by the next General Election there will be no housing shortage as far as the mass of the British people are concerned;' at Coventry in April 1947: 'By the time the next General Election is held we will have broken the back of the housing problem;' and at Cambridge in April 1948: 'By the next General Election the back of the housing problem will have been broken.' That the public thought otherwise was demonstrated by a Gallup poll in January 1949 showing 61 per cent of the nation to be dissatisfied with the government's housing record. The Minister's credibility was not enhanced when he boasted in 1948 that more houses had been built in the preceding three years than in the ten years after 1918, whereupon Ernest Marples, a former builder and now

MP for Wallasey, asserted that the true figure was 900,000 fewer and bet Bevan £500 to be donated to charity by the winner.

A further difficulty in the matter of housing derived from the traditional animus entertained in the Labour party against the private landlord. At the outbreak of the war rents were frozen for all dwellings with a rateable value below £75 (£100 in London), which covered 8·5 million houses and flats. In successive Acts in 1946 and 1949 all Labour did was to extend controls to further forms of accommodation including some furnished premises and new lets and set up rent tribunals to deal with them. By 1947 11·5 million dwellings had controlled rents. By 1950 nine out of ten councils had gingerly raised their rents, although five years later the weekly rent for one of Norwich's eight thousand council houses was seven shillings a week at a time when a skilled worker with some overtime could earn fifteen pounds a week. As far as the inner cities were concerned the choice increasingly rested between luxury flats for the very rich or heavily subsidized housing for the very poor. The majority, who were neither, fled as soon as they could. The addition of subsidized housing to subsidized food played its part in producing spending patterns which can be illustrated statistically as follows:

	1938	1947
	(In £ millions)	
Rent, rates, water	491	564
Drink	235	688
Tobacco	177	690
Entertainments	64	175

It began to look as if the direct subsidy on housing and bread was becoming an indirect subsidy on circuses. In the short run many people could hardly believe their luck. Zweig, for instance, found a contented London road-sweeper in an LCC flat with four rooms and a bath for 15s 9d a week. But the long-term consequences have been much as described by Enoch Powell: 'Imagine what would have been the fate of our motor industry if the majority of its output since 1920 had been purchased for provision at subsidized prices to persons on 1500 waiting lists, while all existing cars were compulsorily priced far below replacement cost. You then have some faint and distant conception of the havoc which the nation has inflicted on its house-building industry.'

Aneurin Bevan had told the House in October 1945 that the Labour party had made certain promises at the election and that they were going to establish a new fashion in government because they were going to keep them. As the pros and cons of the nationalization programme were debated in Parliament a characteristic Labour voice was that of John Diamond, MP for Manchester, Blackley, who declared that as a Socialist and a businessman he was profoundly convinced that nationalization led to efficiency. Iron and steel apart, where as we shall see ideological passion raged, the nationalization programme was relatively uncontroversial and low key in that the enterprises concerned were not by any means shining examples of private enterprise. Most of them had been subject over the years to committees investigating their organization and shortcomings – coal (Reid); the Bank of England (Macmillan); gas (Heyworth); electricity (McGowan). Of these only Heyworth, as we have seen, actually recommended outright nationalization, but none of them shied away from a degree of government involvement. The idea that, efficiency apart, nationalization might in some way regenerate the soul of the nation was not entirely lost sight of but tended to survive in the wake of the arguments advanced for enhanced efficiency under central planning. Thus Harold Davies, MP for Leek, considered that: 'The only justification for nationalization is that it makes for efficiency. That is the test on which we shall stand or fall in the long run – that it is more efficient than private enterprise. The workers under nationalization, while considering wages, will also consider social happiness and enthusiasm, and co-operation between management and men as vital factors in production.' By 1951 10 per cent of the workforce would be in a position to evaluate social happiness and enthusiasm at their place of work in nationalized undertakings.

Whereas taking the coal-mines into public ownership had an obvious emotional appeal to the Labour faithful (and not least to the cohort of ex-miners in the Cabinet), the nationalization of the Bank of England had a special symbolic attraction for the intellectual and Fabian wing of the party. It was seen by them as enabling Labour to manage credit in the interests of trade and employment with overtones of the macro-economics of Lord Keynes. In the event, under Clause Four of the Act, Lord Cobbold, the Governor, found himself with even greater powers. As Oliver Stanley put it rather unkindly for the Conservative opposition: 'We oppose it not because it is a danger but because it is a sham, not because it is going to do harm, but because it is going to do nothing at all.' However, Dr Dalton, responsible for steering this ostensibly daring measure on to the statute book, was pleased enough with it. Since no succeeding government managed to produce a long-term investment programme, it turned out to be something of an *ignis fatuus*.

On 1 January 1947 the nation found itself possessed of 1500 coal-mines, 1000 private companies, a million acres of land, 100,000 miners' houses and 177,000 railway wagons – not all of which were by any means in prime condition. There were celebrations at the pitheads throughout Britain as the blue flag of the National Coal Board was hoisted. Bells rang, hooters blared, plaques were unveiled. The miners cheered and marched behind their bands. As the flag went up at one pit the miners bared their heads; at another they sang *Land of Hope and Glory*. At Penallta colliery in the Rhondda valley, according to the *Daily Herald*, the lodge chairman, still in khaki battledress, shouted into a microphone: 'Private enterprise has had it!' and the valley rang with cheers. Arthur Horner told the nation on the air that under nationalization the miners could be relied upon to produce coal 'right up to the limits of their manpower strength'.

Private enterprise in the coal industry was replaced on the Morrisonian precept by the National Coal Board, a corporation presided over by Lord Hyndley, the son of a vicar who had endured a short period down a Durham pit before turning successfully to the business and administrative side of the industry. He received £8500 a year and was assisted by another coal-owner, a chartered accountant, a scientist, a mining engineer, a barrister, a civil servant and two trade unionists, Lord Citrine and Ebenezer Edwards, who had twice presided over the Trades Union Congress. They were quickly off the mark, shortening working hours and raising wages at a cost of £23 million in the first year. Hyndley was a jolly man and everybody loved Ebby Edwards, who had impeccable credentials in being one of eleven children, down the mine before he was twelve and the recipient of a miners' scholarship at Ruskin College. While it was unkind of the influential *Sunday Times* journalist, G. L. Schwarz, to describe such people as leading a commissar's life without the attendant danger of a swift taking off, it remained uncomfortably true that as far as the workforce was concerned the change in management was less than dramatic. They answered to the same colliery manager, but his office would now be manned by twenty clerks, whereas before they had all scraped along with a secretary, a store keeper and a couple of girls. Under the new conditions the manager was less often seen to be going down the mine as a result of the activities of various new brooms sweeping through the industry. A northern manager complained that he was visited all day on Monday by two financial experts; on Tuesday by the Welfare Officer trying to learn about pit welfare; on Wednesday by an expert on roof control; on Thursday by two senior Hobart House engineers; all of which left him only Friday to go down the pit.* As time went on the NCB had its critics. A well-known mining engineer, Sir Charles Reid, resigned from it ostentatiously in 1948, describing the board as a cumbersome and uninspiring organization. He informed the public that 'without the most radical alteration in the coal board downwards, both in regard to control and personnel, the nationalization of the mines will prove a disastrous failure . . . it cannot deal with the indiscipline so rampant in the mines . . . it cannot keep an effective check on production costs . . . it cannot give confident and effective leadership to management or men.' It was perhaps understandable that Arthur Horner, the secretary of the NUM, thought that the coal industry was well rid of Sir Charles Reid.

It had been hoped that the mines would be self-supporting within five years, but neither this nor many of the other optimistic forecasts for a regenerated and revitalized industry were to be fulfilled. In opposition Shinwell had always emphatically repudiated the suggestion that a reduction in coal output was due to absenteeism. In office he had to admit sadly that it was 'the crux of the problem'. The Ministry of Fuel statisticians revealed a figure of absenteeism as follows: 6·4 per cent in 1938; 16·3 in 1945; 16·0 in 1946; 12·4 in 1947. The miners had secured not

* A. Maude and R. Lewis, *Professional People*, 1952, p. 132.

only nationalization, but also higher wages, a five-day week, special food rations and a large increase in capital equipment paid for in dollars. Yet despite endless exhortation and encouragement, especially from Dr Dalton, who continued to reiterate that the miners were the vanguard of socialism, they seemed disinclined to increase their productivity. Shinwell's plan, for what it was worth, originally envisaged an increase of sixty million tons a year – ten to meet the demands of the home market, fifty for export. The fifty for export were quickly abandoned. By dint of using imported oil on the railways and in a thousand factories the ten million extra tons for home consumption could be reduced to five. He failed to achieve even that, despite leaving no stone unturned, as the critics of the quality of his product unkindly observed. Attempts to blame the coal-owners were effectively rebutted by Lord Swinton, who pointed out that the government had controlled the mines since 1941, and that output in 1946 was twenty-six million tons less than in 1941. Perhaps the trouble was attributable in a roundabout way to the coal-owners, since Labour, while endlessly passing resolutions about nationalizing the mines, had not worked out a proper plan and had had to adopt in the end much of the scheme for the nationalization of the industry proposed by none other than Sir Charles Reid on behalf of the coal-owners. Shinwell claimed that he was impeded by Dalton's refusal in committee to countenance open-cast mining for environmental reasons. 'I advised the government over and over again about this,' he said, 'but nevertheless – I make a confession – I had to make optimistic speeches outside because if I failed to do that it would have been used as an argument against nationalization.' In the end we imported coal from the US to enable some of our own coal to go to Europe at a net loss of seventy million pounds. Herbert Morrison hit the nail inadvertently on the head when he told the House in January 1946 in his calculatedly conciliatory manner: 'It would be a shocking illusion to think that merely because you pass this bill and put the coal-mining industry into the hands of a public corporation you need not worry any more. That is a small part of the business, only the beginning.' However, by 1952 the industry was once more in profit and beginning again to export.

Morrison gave the House of Commons eight reasons why

civil aviation needed nationalizing. It would thereby become more economical and safer; it would have the benefit of public subsidies and publicly funded research; it would enjoy better organization and planning and a better status for its staff; and it would be co-ordinated with the RAF and its whole policy subject to Parliamentary review. This looked on the face of it plausible enough. Yet in the debate on the Civil Aviation Bill, Harold Macmillan thought that he detected a central weakness: 'Here above all, what we need is spunk, not red tape, bravura, not bureaucracy. We want the heady and, if you like, intoxicating wine of youth for competition, not the toast and water and regular habits of old age.' There was, indeed, a distinct element of toast and water in the composition of the boards of the nationalized industries. If you aspired to membership it was a great help to be an alderman, certainly not an office associated with the heady wine of youth. The British Electricity Authority together with its fourteen area boards numbered twenty-two aldermen among a total membership of 128.

It was widely hoped that the public ownership of the railways, still operating steam engines prior to the arrival of the diesels in 1948, would lead to a greatly improved service under Sir Eustace Missenden's Railway Executive. The NUR journal, *Railway Review*, of January 1948, recorded the celebrations consequent on the birth of British Railways. It wrote of a meeting of railway workers and their wives that the keynote of the speeches was service to the community, tolerance and cooperation among all branches of railwaymen, which would be sure to bring efficiency and honour to British Railways. The Minister of Transport, Alfred Barnes, as he took over responsibility for 52,000 miles of track, 20,000 steam locomotives and seventy hotels, told the nation in a broadcast that the keynote of a public system must be efficiency, courtesy and service. 'Each employee should remember,' he said, 'that he is a representative of British Transport, and that by his words and deeds the whole service will be judged.' He was later to boast: 'Give us five years of power and in this field of transport services the people of this country will see more progress than in 500 years of Tory government.'

The public were encouraged to remember always that the railways now belonged to them. Somehow it never felt like that.

Admittedly, there were formidable difficulties to be overcome. There were far more passengers than before the war and far fewer trains, many of them old and battered by wartime service, and railway equipment was being exported. But a pervasive sense of aimlessness and lack of concern for the public began to make itself felt. By 1948 an article appeared in the *Railway Review* which seemed to confirm the opinions of many members of the public: 'Never was there a time when discontent was so rampant as it is today on British Railways. It is with the utmost difficulty that staff can be retained in the service, and, when it can be kept, delinquency rears its ugly head in so many ways as to be a nightmare to very many of the supervisory staff; it has become a problem never experienced in days gone by. . . . The first and most important thing that is wrong is the gradual development of a soulless, dehumanizing and individuality-killing atmosphere. . . . Men – good, honest and trustworthy men – are leaving the railways every week in large numbers, all because of this soul-destroying system of remote control; a control that means nothing to them but a voice giving orders from out of the mouth of a telephone receiver.' This was a long way from the view expressed by James Callaghan in November 1947, when he forecast that under nationalization the railway industry was going to become much more a public service than it had been in the past. 'It will have a spirit pervading it which will enable everybody, at whatever level, to contribute the best he can.' Somehow the engine had gone off the rails.

It was largely in human relationships that the success or otherwise of nationalization would be judged in the early years, since it was too soon to evaluate its economic effectiveness. Richard Pryke in his *Public Enterprise in Practice* has calculated that in the decade 1948–58 the public enterprise sector's output per man hour increased by about 16 per cent, which represents only 1·5 per cent a year at a time when manufacturing industry was going up by 1·9 per cent. Only the airways and the electricity industry come well out of these calculations. But all that lay ahead, as did the improved performance of the public sector between 1958 and 1968. For the moment, there was an uneasy suspicion that, as Christopher Mayhew was to put it, 'contrary to our pre-war expectations, bad labour relations seemed to go with low rather than high profits and to depend very greatly on the quality of management and very little on the ownership of industry'.*Nationalization was beginning to discredit socialism.

Labour, however, had its visible successes, paradoxically for example among the 20 per cent who lived on the land and traditionally voted for their opponents. The inheritors of the William Morris tradition in the party entertained a certain nostalgia for the vanished vision of merrie England. Thus, George Lansbury had written in 1934: 'I just long to see a start made on the job of reclaiming, recreating rural England. I can see the village greens with the maypoles once again erected and the boys and girls, young men and maidens, all joining in the mirth and folly of May Day.' In sober reality boys and girls were leaving the village green at the age of sixteen in large numbers in a new agricultural world in which a tractor could plough forty acres a day where the pre-war horse could plough one. But those agricultural labourers who remained behind were earning 200 per cent more than before the war, with a sharply increased output, and the 1947 Agriculture Act guaranteed the farmers fair profits and stable markets in return for a good deal of form-filling. The government wisely avoided the doctrinaire approach to agriculture advocated by some of its supporters like F. W. Bateson, who argued in a Fabian pamphlet for an agricultural service with state-salaried and certificated farm managers with retiring ages and pensions. The overriding need, to which Churchill constantly recurred, to minimize our imports of essential foodstuffs, meant that in this field, as in others, the wartime consensus was broadly maintained. In an era of rationing the farmer's lot was an enviable one. He had all the butter, cream and eggs he wanted; he could kill two pigs a year and eat as many sheep as he wanted; and an annual visit to the Dublin horse show could be combined with restocking his wardrobe without any coupon trouble.

Nowhere in the kingdom was Labour's advent greeted with such fervour as in Wales, and it was there, among its most passionate supporters, that the government achieved its most apparently spectacular successes. The Distribution of Industry Acts of 1945 and 1950 were the principal vehicle through which a mass of new industrial enterprises were directed into Wales, which even in 1938, when most of the rest of the country was

* *Party Games*, Hutchinson 1969, p. 79.

booming, had had an unemployment rate of 20 per cent. By 1955 only 13,400 were unemployed and for every seven persons leaving Wales before the war to seek employment there was now only one. Wartime ordnance factories were turned into trading estates; the mines, the steelworks, the tinplate mills and the docks were once again busy; and the whole of South Wales being a development area, 179 new factories had been opened by 1949. Harold Wilson at the Board of Trade claimed that there were 75,000 more workers in 1948 in industry alone than in 1938. They were employed in chemicals, paint, gelatine, enzymes, leather, clothing, toys, furniture, hoovers, washing machines and bicycles. The Abbey steelworks at Port Talbot was under way in 1947 and opened in 1951 at a cost of £73 million. In view of its subsequent fate it is ironic to learn that it was locally known as Treasure Island. Output in Wales rose 23 per cent between 1948 and 1954 as compared to 18 per cent in the rest of Britain. But it was not all a success story. The South West Division of the Coal Board reported losses of ten million pounds in 1947 and a further five million in 1948.* Absenteeism at the end of the decade was higher than anywhere else. Four and a half million pounds were invested in a new mining project together with a model miners' village at Nantgarw but the output was so disappointing that it had to be closed. But all in all, there was substance in James Griffiths's boast in 1949 that a revolution had been effected in Welsh social conditions.

Similar initial success in the regional diversification of industry occurred in the Tyne and Tees area, and the West Midlands began soon to enjoy a remarkable boom, notably in light engineering. Scotland, however, remained in many respects an intractable problem. Poverty in the industrial areas was by any standards barbaric. Mrs Cullen, MP for the Gorbals, claimed in 1948 that 4500 families in her constituency lived in one-room apartments and 10,000 families had only two. In 1945 there were 2641 confirmed cases of tuberculosis in Glasgow and in 1948 slightly more. In Scotland as a whole one in every 135 of the inhabitants was a tuberculosis sufferer and there was still a high infant mortality rate. Much more of the housing programme in Scotland was in the hands of local authorities than

* In this connection it should, however, be appreciated that coal prices were deliberately kept low by the government.

elsewhere and so progress was slower, only 150,000 houses being built in the first five post-war years. Glasgow as a port was obviously in decline and the future of shipbuilding precariously dependent on foreign orders. A Cunard White Star liner launched in December 1946 was a fleeting symbol of past glories. The National Coal Board set a target for Scotland of thirty million tons a year, but this was never remotely achieved, twenty-five million being the most ever dug in any one year. War factories in Clydeside and Dundee were converted to peaceful uses and some new industries developed, although overheads were high and markets often distant. Hydro-electric development arrested the decay of the Highlands, but in Scotland as elsewhere it was the farming community which came out best.

While Britain's new rulers were thus engaged in trying to fulfil their election manifesto to create a Socialist commonwealth, they were also confronted with prodigiously difficult problems in the world at large. How effective a part could Britain play in restoring order to a world ravaged and disorganized by war? And what was to be done about the British Empire?

Although Attlee shirked none of the fearful responsibilities which devolved on him both as Prime Minister and, until the end of 1946, as Minister of Defence, the heat of the day in foreign affairs was borne by the formidable Ernest Bevin. On assuming office, Bevin tended to baffle Foreign Office officials at Potsdam by insistently enquiring: 'What is going to be done about S?', by way of reference to Hitler's deputy, without benefit of an aspirate. However, they soon came to hold him in high regard and he for his part defended them stoutly at the Bournemouth Labour party conference in 1946, explaining that he was not one of those who decried Eton and Harrow, of which he had been very glad in the war. He also appealed more than any of his colleagues to the opposition, R. A. Butler describing him as a diamond lying on a vast heap of coke. Professor Laski saw him rather differently, writing to Judge Frankfurter in 1947: 'Bevin is quite pathological in my own view – vain, disastrously ungenerous, quite definitely anti-Semitic in a brutal way.' He was also liable to be mocked in left wing Labour circles for treating the USSR as if it were a dissident branch of his own Union. But unlike the Labour left, who prided themselves on keeping an open mind about Russia, Bevin was forced by real events in a real world to form opinions and act on them.

He was never short of advice on the air or in the public prints. A. J. P. Taylor, in a broadcast as late as December 1946, said: 'In fact the advantages of co-operation between Russia and England are so obvious and the dangers of association with America so blatant that I am amazed that even the fog of a century of suspicion, thickened up by the smoke of ill-informed Marxism, is enough to keep England and Russia apart.' Was it really necessary, Kingsley Martin cried, to identify ourselves with American protests against political arrangements in the satellite countries? After all, he had been talking to American businessmen who had assured him that the West would soon run into an economic blizzard while Russia would 'grow steadily more prosperous'. In any case 'Marshal Stalin has given proof of a sincere desire to have in Poland, as well as in Czechoslovakia and Roumania, "good neighbour" states enjoying real economic and cultural independence.' When in September 1945 Bevin took exception to a suggestion of Molotov's that Tripolitania should be placed under Russian trusteeship, and suggested to the House that one could not help being suspicious if a Great Power wants to come 'right across the throat of the Commonwealth', the *New Statesman* described his policy as a counsel of despair and the politics of international suicide. It all seemed relatively straightforward to A. J. P. Taylor. Negotiate a good Anglo-Soviet trade agreement and then you have 'the most effective answer against the danger of communism. In my opinion, British machine tools are the best weapon for ending the tyranny of the secret police.'

On the other side the air was full of Russian recrimination and slander. The rump of General Anders's Polish army was being brought back to England, they claimed, not to be demobilized but to be incorporated for special duties in the British Army; 'Bevin has become the spokesman of forces working for wars and crimes – against mankind' (26 October, 1946); the British were only in Greece to support Fascist criminals. There were quarrels over reparations; over France as an occupying power in Germany; over the employment in the British zone of dismissed German soldiers to clear up the rubble; most importantly, over the sharing of atomic secrets.

Bevin and the American Secretary of State, Byrnes, were handicapped by the lack of an adequate forum from which to negotiate. High hopes had been held out during the war for the United Nations. In a speech on 22 November 1945 the usually hard-headed and realistic Attlee said: 'The UNO is here present in the world; it was born almost at the same time as the atomic bomb, it is not something vaguely heard of, something quite outside the range of our national life. It is the hope of the world. It is filled with immense possibilities. I want every man and woman in this country and in the world to feel a vivid personal concern in the success of the UNO.' By contrast, the United Nations Organization seemed to Sir Alexander Cadogan, a case-hardened diplomat, a moderate parody of the League with all its failings and no advantages. Instead, the powers had recourse to Foreign Ministers' meetings, which developed into loud-speaker diplomacy, which Harold Nicolson, with memories of Versailles, aptly described as substituting for open covenants openly arrived at, open insults openly hurled. After watching the Russians at work in the Paris Peace Conference in the autumn of 1946, he accurately analysed their technique as asking for 120 per cent of what they really wanted and then after weeks of obduracy making a magnificent gesture by surrendering the extra 20 per cent.

The Iron Curtain had indeed come down, as Churchill proclaimed to the world in his Fulton speech of March 1946. In any case, the chances of Britain maintaining anything other than a precarious hold on its seat at the international top-table were inevitably limited, because of the mounting cost of its widespread commitments. Although Stalin had agreed that Greece should be a British sphere of influence in 1944, he supported the Communist guerillas, who had originally inspired Churchill's remark that democracy is no harlot to be picked up in the street by a man with a tommy-gun. Apart from Greece, the British zone in Germany, and Egypt, there was Palestine, where there were 65,000 British troops, of which three-quarters were living under canvas, as well as various colonial garrisons. This accentuated a serious manpower shortage, which worried Morrison, and in 1946 defence was absorbing a fifth of the Gross National Product, which drove Dalton to threaten resignation unless economies were made somewhere.

Nor could Bevin count on unity in the party ranks. Crossman, although realistic about the Soviets, could not bear to contemplate a Labour party forging closer links with capitalist America. He had visited Washington early in 1946 and found himself tempted to purloin the soap in the Waldorf-Astoria or fit one of their capacious bath-towels into his suitcase. He was much disappointed to find that for the average American, British Labour meant Harold Laski, whom they saw 'as the Lenin of the British Reds'.* His chance came when a group of Labour backbenchers tabled an amendment to the Address in November 1946 demanding 'a genuinely Socialist foreign policy'. He claimed that anti-Communism was as destructive to democracy as Communism. As to America, she 'must work out her own fate. She has to go her own way. We Socialists know what the result will be. We know that in time there must be a great slump and a second New Deal, and that gradually America will work her way round to where the rest of the world is going.' Although Bevin was not seriously threatened, 122 Labour MPs abstained on the motion. Some rather rough things were said about the USA in the course of the debate. Norman Smith, the Labour member for Nottingham South, felt that our American friends were 'not grown up in their social economics', and Tom Driberg found it necessary to describe the United States as the only great nation in the world where it was not true to say that none of the ordinary people want war, and referred to 'the barbaric thugs of Detroit and the Mammon Imperialists of Washington and Wall Street'.

Fortunately it was those self-same Mammon Imperialists who came to the rescue. As Britain became ice-bound in the early part of 1947, Attlee and Bevin felt compelled to tell the new American Secretary of State, General George Marshall, that Britain no longer had the resources to shore up Greece and Turkey against Communist pressure. Truman persuaded Congress to shoulder the burden, a turning point in European history since it signalled the realization that if Russian imperialism was to be contained in Europe a massive degree of American involvement would be necessary. This was characteristically described by Laski as the biggest threat to peace since the rise of Hitler. Crossman, Foot and Mikardo continued to argue in their pamphlet of May 1947, *Keep Left*, that Britain

* *New Statesman and Nation*, 9 February 1946.

should head a 'third force' on the international scene based on Europe, which was still struggling to revive its war-shattered economies, and the Commonwealth, which neither was, nor would be, capable of concerted action. A month later Marshall's outline proposals for American aid to Europe were accepted by Bevin with alacrity and by Russia with a contemptuous rejection coupled with the formation of the Cominform. Warsaw radio told its listeners that the Marshall Plan meant slavery and un-employment. In Britain Roy Harrod wrote: 'One's first thought about Marshall Aid is its supreme generosity. . . . The quality of the statesmanship involved is the more remarkable in that the generous impulse had to overcome two barriers; a strong dis-taste for Socialism, whose hold the aid tends for the time being to sustain, and a cousinly irritation with the whole present outlook and temperament of the British.' US foreign aid in 1948 accounted for one-sixth of the US budget. Without it Britain would have had to endure over a million unemployed and subs-tantial further cuts in food rations. This did not prevent Sidney Silverman, MP for Nelson and Colne, describing the Americans in October 1947 as shabby moneylenders. He earned a massive and memorable rebuke from Churchill who reminded him that the Americans 'took little when they emigrated from Europe except what they stood up in and what they had in their souls. They came through, they tamed the wilderness, they became what old John Bright called a refuge for the oppressed from every land and clime.' By contrast, within six months the Communists had enslaved Czechoslovakia, their purpose, as Denis Healey pointed out, being the essentially Fascist one of protecting a ruling section of the state against the possibility of overthrow by a majority of the population. As *The Times* put it, the Commu-nists in Eastern Europe were eating up the Social Democrats as a boa-constrictor does creatures several times his own size. Even E. H. Carr, with his peculiar genius for meiotic determinism, admitted that the Russians had always shown an inclination 'to move unobtrusively forward into lands not effectively occupied by another strong power'.

The tonic effect on Europe of Marshall dollars, combined with much greater realism about Stalin's Russia, led succes-sively to the creation, in April 1948, of the Organization for European Economic Co-operation; NATO just one year later;

and the Council of Europe in May 1949. In parallel stages Russia strengthened her grip on her satellites, except for Yugoslavia which had to be expelled from the Cominform in June 1948. The yearlong Berlin blockade, starting on 24 June 1948, was particularly instrumental in effecting the eventual incorporation of West Germany into the Western alliance.

Bevin was thus right to proclaim in January 1948 that the time was ripe for a consolidation of Western Europe. But his preoccupations were not limited to Europe. He had no need to be unduly concerned when in January 1948 the Argentinian fleet put to sea with five admirals aboard, merely sending the cruiser HMS *Sheffield* to head them off the Falklands. But Palestine was a different matter, his handling of which aroused more criticism than it deserved at a time when people still entertained some hope that 'the problem of Palestine' could be peacefully solved.

The Labour Conference of 1944 had passed a resolution in favour of Palestine becoming a highly-populated Jewish national homeland. In office Bevin stood for compromise between the conflicting claims of Jews and Arabs which consistently eluded him. Between 1945 and 1947 the mandate cost £100 million pounds, to say nothing of the manpower drain involved in the maintenance of a large occupying force trying to cope with re-markably skilful terrorists. Bevin's rejection of Truman's suggestion of a large Jewish migration to Palestine, reiterated by an Anglo-American commission (of which Crossman, Bevin's arch-critic, was a member), led in particular to the blowing up of the King David Hotel in Jerusalem by Menachem Begin and his friends in July 1946. Concern to harvest the Jewish vote led Truman to continue supporting large-scale immigration and the partition of Palestine. With his engaging frankness he explained to a meeting of Arab ambassadors that, while he had hundreds of thousands of constituents who were enthusiastic Zionists, he did not have any countervailing Arabs. Bevin's advisers con-tinually reminded him of the strategic and commercial value of Arab friendship in the Middle East, and the Anglo-American Commission did little to alleviate his difficulties by suggesting vaguely that Palestine should be neither a Jewish nor an Arab state. Whatever the Americans might demand on the question of immigration, Attlee and Bevin took the not unreasonable view that nothing should be done until the illegal Jewish under-ground armies were eliminated. But Bevin did little to sweeten what was becoming a dangerous Anglo-American quarrel by suggesting that the Americans wanted more Jews in Palestine and fewer in New York. As a result he was pelted with eggs on a visit to New York in November 1946.

There seemed no way forward which would not inevitably alienate either the Arabs or the Jews. Military and economic considerations seemed to make it impossible to abandon all British influence in the Arab world. Failure to satisfy Jewish aspirations would lead to a bloodbath involving British soldiers on the ground. Bevin told Attlee that he was at the end of his tether, and so the British surrendered the mandate to the United Nations. On 14 May 1948 the army was withdrawn and the Jews proclaimed the state of Israel. Anarchy, chaos and bloodshed ensued, and Crossman was in a strong position to tell Bevin that his policy had been a tragic and dismal failure. And indeed it was, but the root causes lay further back in history, further even than the Balfour Declaration of 1917 or the White Paper of 1939; nor did it help Attlee and Bevin in trying to deal with the situation to be continually advised by their officials that if fighting broke out the Jews would infallibly be driven into the sea by the Arabs.

Attlee had devolved responsibility for Palestine largely to Bevin but himself assumed the awesome responsibility for planning the manufacture of a British atomic bomb, a decision taken in January 1947 at a time when Dalton and Cripps were clamorously demanding defence cuts. The bomb would cost £140 million over seven years but that was ingeniously con-cealed in the supply estimates. Attlee worked secretly in con-junction with the Chiefs of Staff and certain top grade civil servants, but there was no cabinet consultation and the House of Commons was not informed until eighteen months after the final decision had been made by Attlee and five of his ministers. The five were Bevin, Morrison, Alexander, Wilmot, the Minister of Supply, and the much trusted Addison, the leader in the Lords. Dalton and Cripps were conspicuous by their absence. By September 1949 the Russians too had their atom bomb.

The Prime Minister was the central figure in the ending of British rule in India and Burma, conventionally regarded as the outstanding feat of statesmanship during the lifetime of his government. The importance of his role is attested by the words of Mountbatten, who as the last Viceroy presided over the coming to independence of the Indian sub-continent on 15 August 1947: 'The man who made it possible was you yourself. Without your original guidance and your unwavering support nothing could have been accomplished here.' But the first Labour exercise in dismantling the Empire was not in India, but in Burma.

As late as May 1945 Churchill's coalition government issued a White Paper which stated unequivocally that Burma was not ready for self-government or even for elections before the end of 1948 and the Labour party supported this. However, in a short time, under intense pressure from the Burmese military leader Aung Sang, who had formerly collaborated with the Japanese, Attlee decided to hand over Burma on 17 October 1947 to the Burmese, who promptly left the Commonwealth. In applying the word 'scuttle' to these proceedings, Churchill observed that the British Empire seemed to be running off almost as fast as the American loan.

The truth underlying the transfer of power both in Burma, by way of dress rehearsal, and in Palestine and India, was that the resources simply did not exist which would enable the British to remain sufficiently long in their former dependencies to avoid the bloodstained consequences of their departure. The extent of the slaughter which did in fact ensue after Indian independence and saddened the negotiators had been predicted by long-serving members of the British Raj.

India had ended the war having suffered 180,000 casualties on behalf of the allies and acquired sterling balances of £1250 million. It had been frequently promised Dominion status, but its Congress leaders had long since deemed this to be an inadequate response to their demand for complete independence. Unfortunately for any prospect of a united India, the Muslim League under Jinnah was unshakeably determined to ensure that Muslim Indians would never be subordinated to Hindu government. By the time Labour came to office, any hope of the British transferring power to a united India had disappeared, though months of futile negotiation ensued. Field-Marshal Wavell, the Viceroy, increasingly turned his thoughts to how best to achieve British withdrawal in a dignified and orderly fashion. He was replaced by the dashing Mountbatten, whose advocacy of a rapidly accelerated grant of independence on the basis of an inevitable partition found favour with the government.

Mountbatten's attitude and negotiating technique are perfectly exemplified by the record of his conversation in May 1947 with the Prime Minister of Madras, who was arguing that the British had a moral responsibility to stay long after 1948: 'He said that I was the only person who could bring peace between the two Indias. I told him that was ridiculous. I said: "One can introduce a couple to each other and hope for the best. But if they take a violent dislike to one another it is no good tucking them up in bed and hoping that the honeymoon will be a great success. . . ." His Secretary then chipped in with the remark that the British had become very popular during the last year, and how sorry everybody was going to be to lose them. I replied: "Yes, now that the British are going, the only thing that kept the Hindus and Moslems together is being removed; since it was a common hatred of the British that prevented you hating each other, the fact that we are going now has left you nothing but to hate each other." '

Sir Cyril Radcliffe was dispatched to finalize the new boundaries and the deed was done on 15 August 1947, ten months ahead of the previously agreed date. India and Pakistan, its two halves separated by the thousand miles between Karachi and Dacca, came into being. The Indian princes bowed out of history, and the slaughter began. Churchill had told the Commons on 6 March: 'We must do our best in all these circumstances, and not exclude any expedient that may help to mitigate the ruin and disaster that will follow the disappearance of Britain from the East. But at least let us not add – by shameful flight, by a premature hurried scuttle – at least let us not add to the pangs of sorrow so many of us feel, the taint and smear of shame.' But Dr Dalton was of the opinion that not one in a hundred thousand in Britain cared tuppence about India as long as British people were not being mauled about there. In more elevated tones Stafford Cripps stated that the British hadn't left India because of 'circumstances outside our control, but because it is consistent with all that we hold to be just and right'.

· 4 ·
Running Out of Steam

'The state is expected nowadays to accomplish easily what nobody would expect from an individual. The dangerous incline leading down to mass psychology begins with this plausible thinking in big numbers and powerful organizations, where the individual dwindles away to mere nothingness. Yet everything that exceeds a certain human size evokes equally inhuman powers in man's unconscious.'   CARL JUNG

'There is no such thing as the state. There are only taxpayers and taxeaters – and politicians.'   DEAN INGE

THE FROZEN PIPES AND FLOODS of the winter of 1946–7 had engendered a growing scepticism about the government's competence and a revival of confidence among its critics. The following spring Professor Laski favoured Judge Frankfurter with some pen-portraits of Britain's rulers. Attlee 'is not a great PM, God knows' – timid, shy, resentful of opposition, more a chairman than a leader; Cripps good at things, but not people; Dalton a good minister but without deep convictions. Only Morrison passed muster, and his reputation among the party activists was soon to be at a low ebb for what was seen as a treacherous compromise over the nationalization of iron and steel. There was dissension in the cabinet about the size of the armed forces in relation to industrial manpower shortages. There were strikes. There was Mr Shinwell's penchant for off-the-cuff remarks calculated to inflame class-consciousness. There was the necessity to import coal, while the miners' working week was reduced. Not all critics were assuaged by an imposing programme of 'democratic' planning unveiled by Sir Stafford Cripps at the

Board of Trade, which was followed by alarming posters proclaiming: 'We're up against it. We Work or Want.' This injunction clearly failed to impress either the miners or the dockers, who did a good deal of striking that summer.

Abroad, the withdrawal from Greece had finally revealed the hollowness of any hopes that Britain would emerge in the post-war world with a foreign policy significantly independent of that of the USA. Dalton, as Chancellor of the Exchequer, found himself confronted with a worrying problem. The American loan, secured with considerable difficulty, as we have seen, by Keynes at a time when Congressman Short felt that not a dollar should go to Britain as long as the Crown jewels were in London, had uncomfortable strings attached to it. One of them was the restoration of sterling convertibility. The Treasury view was that the economy was thriving sufficiently for the pound to be once more convertible and it became so in the middle of July. Just over a month later, after an alarming run on sterling, this had to be rescinded. Even before that – on 6 August – the government announced an austerity programme involving cuts in food imports and the basic petrol ration. Behind the scenes and unknown to the public, some of the Labour overlords were busy trying to rid themselves of what Michael Foot described as Attlee's palsied leadership. On 5 September Cripps gave Morrison dinner and suggested that the two of them together with Dalton should ask Attlee to resign and give way to Bevin. The weakness of this project was not only that Morrison loathed Bevin, who tended to describe him as a scheming little bastard, but also that Bevin had no intention of knifing Attlee in the back. So Cripps went alone to see Attlee, who with his usual political skill immediately replaced Morrison as planning and economic overlord with Cripps himself. As Morrison's biographers wrote of Cripps: 'Only a high-minded and upper-class Christian from the moralizing and Marxist left of the socialist movement could get away with such blatant self-advancement.'

It was not a moment too soon for Attlee to take a firm grip, since the government was rent with dissension and the volume of informed criticism was steadily mounting. Labour, though very much a party of Christian names, tended under the stress of events to be also the party of unChristian feelings. Both Dalton and Morrison were prodigious intriguers. George Strauss, who became Minister of Supply in October 1947, recorded Dalton's habit of writing 'daily notes to the Prime Minister, making his comments about the activities of other ministers, usually very critical comments, a most peculiar thing to do'. Shinwell described Dalton as 'the most wicked man in politics I've ever known. Intrigue, conspiracy, always whispering about people. His whispers were very audible, they could be heard hundreds of yards away.'* Ian Mikardo said of Labour women that they were world-class haters, with Edith Summerskill as champion. Attlee condemned Morrison with the phrase – 'Herbert cannot distinguish between big things and little things,' whereas Bevin described him as nothing better than a policeman's nark. Foot characterized Strachey as 'writhing smoothly in endless, harmless evils, a cobra without a fang'; and Morrison as substituting 'for a guiding hand or a real grip a finger in every pie'. But for really scathing vituperation the palm rested with Crossman, who talked of Dalton having a cloven hoof in each camp and an unkind word for all except 'his own young men', and of Mrs Jean Mann as 'the sour little mamma from Glasgow'. A characteristic revelation in Crossman's diary was of an encounter with L. J. 'Stoker' Edwards, Civil Lord of the Admiralty, who told Crossman he was 'a dirty Communist who had done nothing but dirty Communist propaganda in the *Pictorial*'. 'I said he shouldn't talk like a shit, whereupon he called me a bastard and honours were even.' Fraternity is often more difficult to achieve in human affairs than Liberty and Equality.

Nor did the government behave in that difficult summer as a united and convincing administration. Morrison, instead of concentrating his mind on the critical economic issues of the moment, was much given to fussing over the details of the complicated Whitehall administrative machinery which had been developed for purposes of planning. In addition to the Economic Section of the Cabinet office and the Central Statistical Office, there were inter-departmental planning committees for manpower, materials, balance of payments and capital investment. There was the new Central Economic Planning Staff under its Chief Planning Officer, Sir Edwin Plowden. There was also a National Production Advisory Council on Industry and a National Joint Advisory Council under the Ministry of Labour

* Alan Thompson, *The Day Before Yesterday*, p. 53.

and below them a number of regional and local boards and a Capital Issues Committee, which had the effect of ensuring that new funds were not channelled into 'inessential' enterprises such as insurance, hire purchase, banking and entertainment. When, during the autumn crisis, Cripps was made Minister of Economic Affairs, Attlee told him that his position was to be 'one of co-ordination'. Mercifully, Dalton's notorious budget indiscretion led to his immediate resignation in favour of Cripps in November, so that one storey at least was removed from the planning edifice.

Apart from having lost his way in this economic labyrinth, Morrison, at the prompting of Attlee, became involved in the acrimonious struggle over the iron and steel industry. From the point of view of the party purists with their concern for securing the commanding heights of industry 'for the nation', iron and steel seemed a prime target. The industry was making healthy profits and had had no strikes for forty years. In other eyes there seemed much to be said for Churchill's view, that there was no point in transferring it from 'the list of our British profit-makers under private enterprise to the loss-makers' account'. The passionate concern of Labour back-benchers reached its zenith in a speech by S. N. Evans, MP for Wednesbury: 'Steel and insurance are the remaining citadels of twentieth-century privilege, and no society moving towards a socialist economy can afford a menace within its midst such as the Iron and Steel Federation. . . . The spectacle of "steel barons" peddling their armaments around the world is an affront to the Christian conscience and can no longer be tolerated.' Bevan, not to be outdone, told an audience at Hull: 'We shall nationalize the steel industry. It will not be left in the hands of those who have betrayed the nation's need.'

Although Bevan, Dalton and Cripps were for full nationalization, Attlee and Morrison were less than enthusiastic. Morrison and John Wilmot, the responsible minister, sought a compromise whereby the control of the industry should be shared between the employers and the government's Iron and Steel Control Board, with the government having reserve powers to take over inefficient firms. This was acceptable to Lincoln Evans but provoked a cabinet row in which Bevan threatened to resign. So the compromise disappeared and with it much of Morrison's popularity in the party. The unfortunate Wilmot, who in happier days had won the East Fulham by-election which had so shaken Stanley Baldwin's nerve, was sacked. The cabinet decided to introduce full nationalization in the 1948–9 session and ordered the new minister, the wealthy metal broker G. R. Strauss, to investigate the technicalities of the problem. By this time public support for nationalization was less than vociferous and many agreed with the view propounded in *The Times* on 5 September: 'Nationalization as a remedy for the basic malaise of the steel industry was and is an irrelevance.' Subsequent history might seem to endorse such a view. It is after all rather ironic to read the relevant section in *Let Us Face the Future*, which accused private enterprise of keeping 'inefficient high cost plants in existence'.

The word 'cuts' now began to assume an importance in the post-war political vocabulary of Britain which it was to retain for many years. Stafford Cripps, however, was an impressive expert at making a virtue of necessity. The first of his great exhortatory broadcasts was delivered on 15 September 1947: 'We can all help, every one of us, if only by being hopeful and cheerful, by being honourable in our dealings, by not encouraging black marketeers or spivs and by saving all we can from waste whether it is paper or bottles or foodstuffs or anything else. . . . I remember always a simple text inscribed on the wall of the class-room in which I sat when I first went to school. It was in the words of St Paul: "Quit you like men, be strong."' Earlier that summer Churchill had described him as an able and upright man, tortured and obsessed by his socialist tenets. His language as Chancellor of the Exchequer, earnestly voicing a tireless demand for production exports, technical efficiency and personal self-sacrifice, was to sound more like that of a Victorian entrepreneur than the dangerous radical who in 1937 had told the munition workers that the capitalists were in their hands. He would have earned the admiration of Samuel Smiles.

It was due to Cripps more than to any other single person that the fortunes of the Labour party began to mend noticeably during the comparatively mild winter of 1947–8. Indeed, without him the whole socialist enterprise might have foundered. As it turned out, the combination of leadership through austerity, Marshall Aid, and the co-operation Cripps secured from the Trade Union leaders in holding wages till 1950, began to produce remarkable results. The *Sunday Times* leading article of 15 February proclaimed: 'There is no escape from our insolvency unless our production can be driven up and our prices held down. That is the lesson which Sir Stafford Cripps is now trying to din into heads fuddled with contrary propaganda.' Much of the limited column space in the newspapers was devoted to periodic Reports to the Nation which spelt out the rudiments of economics and gloried in the virtues of the work ethic in language which owed more to Bunyan than to Keynes. Readers were confronted with a photograph of Harry Thomas, aged thirty-seven, who was in the habit of breaking over three tons of granite every hour at Shilton with a thirty-eight-pound hammer – the last of the British Stakhanovites. George Isaacs told the Burnley cotton-workers that Britain's bread hung on Lancashire thread. A stream of moral blackmail issued from the National Savings Committee, as for example: 'We make no apology for reminding you that the peace we are now working for was bought with the lives of men and women you knew and loved. It was understood that we should not let them down. There are signs that some people are forgetting this. With prosperity and security as yet only half won, there is a loosening of the purse-strings and a letting up on savings.'

One way and another the unpalatable medicine began to work. Production rose rapidly and exports spectacularly. The balance of payments swung into surplus. Cripps's budgets were deflationary and designed to increase industrial investment and stimulate exports. Government spending was reduced in some areas, notably in the building programme and on food subsidies. Both Cripps and Attlee talked honestly and realistically about inflation, Attlee warning the nation bluntly in February 1948 that 'if incomes go on rising, there must come a point at which the government cannot hold the cost of living at a reasonable level any longer.' His broadcast on 28 June after he had invoked the Emergency Powers Act to cope with the London dock strike was both explicit and peremptory as far as the dockers were concerned – 'your clear duty to yourselves, to your fellow citizens and to your country is to return to work.'

Britain had been living on tick since the war – £380 million in 1946; £675 million in 1947 and another £250 million in the first half of 1948 with, under Marshall Aid, the prospect of more by way of free gifts. But at any rate much of it was now being put to good use. Before the war we had exported 70,000 cars. The figure had now risen to 220,000 – three out of every four cars produced. A lady from Pennsylvania reported that in her old car she could not get her husband to go shopping with her. Now he wouldn't let her go alone. 'While I pick up my messages in the store he's out front, showing off our English car to the people who gather around.' Australia was importing 50,000 British cars a year. By the second quarter of 1948 our imports were 81 per cent of what they had been in 1938 while the volume of exports stood at 134 per cent. W. W. Rostow, the American economist, praised our production record as good and our trade recovery as unique. Geoffrey Crowther, editor of *The Economist* and previously a sharp critic of the government, summed matters up on 30 December: 'At the end of this year 1948 we can say that we are paying our way. That quite remarkable change in one year is due overwhelmingly to one man – the Chancellor of the Exchequer, Sir Stafford Cripps. . . . In 1948 he has in my opinion saved the country.' It might well have been argued that Cripps's well-earned encomium should have been shared with General Marshall, but few begrudged him a note of self-congratulation in a broadcast which ended: 'Well, how are we doing? Not so bad, and if we can keep it up and remember that our country's success depends upon our individual efforts, it ought to be all right in the end.' Moscow Radio celebrated the festive season by recalling that New Year's Eve in Britain is a time when hundreds of British children are begging in the streets. 'We are with you, little Comrades. The time will come when there will be a cele-bration in your street too.' Perhaps, after all, that time was not so far away, though not in the sense envisaged by the Kremlin.

It did not, however, escape the awareness of the government's critics that all these successes were not directly attributable to socialist orthodoxy. Thus the economist, Roy Harrod, pointed out at the beginning of 1949 that the trade recovery largely derived from the conversion of a big budget deficit into a sub-stantial surplus and cuts in government expenditure, thus enabling resources to be released for export. 'So long as we relied on controls only, as we did before the autumn of 1947, we got nowhere – indeed our balance of trade got worse and worse.'

An influential voice was that of another economist, Graham Hutton, who lost no opportunity to question the prevailing orthodoxies. He dug out from the Annual Abstract of Statistics the alarming fact that, in 1947, one out of every nine persons in civilian employment was a central or local government employee. He was not enthusiastic about the growing power of the trade unions and employers' associations vis-à-vis the nation's elected representatives – associations, as he described them, of lead-swingers, woolpullers and wirepullers. He preached perceptively the need to produce more capital, more productive apparatus, more tools and more machinery as opposed to consumable items, if we were to shore ourselves up against future competition. Nor did he feel it helpful for civil servants in the back streets of Whitehall to determine the number of nails to go in a boot – a decision better made at the point where the boot was manu-factured. He brought to economics something of the awkward fervour of the Old Testament prophet: 'Here and now, un-hesitatingly, I say that Britain will stumble and bump along the bottom for ever unless these out-of-date restrictive devices to "make work" or "stabilize profits" or stop "working a buddy out of a job" are removed. We are now in over-employment, not unemployment.'*

A more celebrated critic of the government's economic stance in 1947 was Professor Lionel Robbins of the London School of Economics, who called for a large budget surplus, a temporary check on home consumption to encourage exports, together with the elimination of subsidies, the restoration of incentives and the removal of price-fixing. From Cambridge, where support for the planned economy was notoriously strong, there were heretical noises from Denis Robertson, the Professor of Political Economy, and from a young lecturer, S. R. Dennison, who roundly declared that it was not the system of free enter-prise which had been rendered obsolete by the economic de-velopments of the last two centuries, but overall state planning, which belonged to an earlier and simpler world. He might have added that not even Colbert had made a success of it. However, the word profit continued to be used largely as a term of abuse, the tendency being to link it with the pejorative 'profiteer'.

* *The Listener*, 10 July 1947.

The *Sunday Times* under W. Hadley (and from 1950 Harry Hodson), the more popular of the two quality Sundays, was persistently critical of socialism. It employed in G. L. Schwarz a devastating commentator on the economic fallibility of the government. His method was to intersperse relatively abstruse economic analysis with satire a good deal sharper than was normal in a period where the polite conventions of wartime unity had not yet disappeared. Thus, when Cripps was appointed Minister of Economic Affairs while Dalton was still at the Exchequer, Schwarz suggested that the new arrangement conjured up a picture of the Chancellor trying to flog the bowling all round the ground with a good deal of vocal intimidation of the umpires, while Sir Stafford was held back to go in later to save the side. When Attlee made a broadcast appeal to people to ask themselves whether the job they were doing was useful as well as lucrative, he suggested that unilateral decisions of this sort could have curious consequences. It would for instance be gravely disconcerting for the Prime Minister if the Cabinet secretariat walked out in a body on the grounds that, though it might entail loss of income, they would be more usefully employed in agriculture. He invented what he called Neo-Micawberian economics of which the central principle was Income one pound; Expenditure twenty-one shillings . . . with predictable consequences. He persistently harped on the unaccountability of the nationalized industries. If you received a hundredweight of slate in your coal, if the 8.15 was invariably late, if the gas pressure was completely unreliable and you were still waiting for the telephone to be installed, all you would hear on complaining to the Minister was that he wished to do nothing which might impair the commercial freedom of the Board. Attacking the abuse of differentials, he told his readers that, when he was an economics lecturer, he always asked the undergraduates: 'Why does the fat lady at the fair earn £25 a week?' to which the answer was, 'Because of her scarcity.'

No single subject gave the critics more ammunition than the discovery of bureaucratic follies or planning disasters. Schwarz was an assiduous seeker out of the more lurid curiosities. His most gruesome discovery was culled from the *Board of Trade Journal* as late as 1952 and read as follows:

Purchase Tax 'D' Scheme
Corsets, Suspender Belts and Roll-on Elastic Belts

The following garments are not regarded as corsets and are outside the scope of Code No. W17 of Appendix A to Notice No. 78D.

Articles not exceeding 10 inches at the deepest part. (These are regarded as suspender belts under Code No. W18.)

Articles falling within the following definition (These are regarded as roll-on elastic belts under Code No. W18):

Belts which, apart from finishing at top or bottom or the addition of suspenders or crutch piece, are wholly made either:

a. from tubular knitted, netted or crocheted elastic material or

b. from one or more pieces of identical knitted, netted or crocheted elastic material sewn together in tubular form.

The addition of a crutch piece to a corset or a roll-on elastic belt would not cause such a garment to be classified as a pantee under Code No. W15.

Revelations of this sort tended to impugn the credibility of Morrison's assertions that Labour represented all the 'useful' people.

As the difficulties of the government mounted it became something of a national pastime to exchange examples of muddle and inertia perpetrated by the authorities. In order to start a housing scheme you needed to clear the purchase of your land with the District Valuer, the Ministry of Health, the Minister of Town and Country Planning, and the Ministry of Agriculture and Fisheries; the preparation of the lay-out required consultation with Town and Country Planning, with Transport and with Health; the design of the houses needed clearance from Health; the licensing of the necessary materials from Health and from Works; the acceptance of tenders from Health; the sanctioning of a loan from Health. Any weak link in this elaborate chain might send you back to your starting point and impose a lengthy delay. The elaborate timber controls were based on pre-war patterns, so that Scotland, now using much more timber than in 1939, had to acquire it from English quota-holders rather than buy it from timber-traders at Scottish ports. Hugh Gaitskell at the Ministry of Fuel and Power seriously considered controlling the price of logs till the Permanent Secretary persuaded him that it would not be easy with eighty thousand sellers and a flourishing black market. It was discovered that, whereas the Coalition government had spent £1,610,000 on paper in 1945, Labour had budgeted for nearly £6 million in 1946 and the Ministry of Works had used 120 tons more paper in 1946 than in 1936.

Instances of this sort of thing could be multiplied, exaggerated or even invented, but one way or another there developed a widespread tendency to question the efficacy and desirability of planning, the very idea of which had commanded so much enthusiasm two or three years previously. This even spread to supporters of the government. R. R. Stokes, a Labour MP and a junior minister, who was a heavy engineering manufacturer, opposed iron and steel nationalization in the House in September 1948, saying: 'We have all seen what has happened inside industry as a result of over-centralization of control. I find that departmental delays are quite intolerable.' After elaborating this at some length, he quaintly blamed the Tories for training a civil service with armies of people whose one idea was to pass the buck. This was hardly a convincing argument in view of the fact pointed out by Churchill in April 1947 that 450,000 additional civil servants had been taken from production and added to what he called the oppressive machinery of Government and control. A junior minister in Civil Aviation, Ivor Thomas, a Welshman with an Oxford First, who sat for Keighley, crossed the floor of the House and published in 1949 *The Socialist Tragedy*, a critique of Socialism which could hardly have been bettered by the Conservative Central Office.

The previous year had seen the publication of an even more influential book, *Ordeal by Planning* by John Jewkes, Professor of Political Economy at Manchester and formerly director of the Economic Section of the War Cabinet secretariat. Written in a combative fashion by an unashamed advocate of private enterprise, it contained a number of prophetic passages, as for example: 'There is a very serious danger that the second half of the twentieth century may be the age of inflation as the first half was the age of mass unemployment. We may, that is to say, jump from the frying pan into the fire. For the prevention of general unemployment calls for the maintenance of national expenditure up to, but not beyond, the critical point at which inflation runs.' The fulfilment of that prophecy lay ahead, but for the moment the popularity and impact of *Ordeal by Planning* derived from his vivid exposure of existing bureaucratic controls. There was the difficulty, for instance, of the market gardener who needed a new shaft for a wheelbarrow, a piece of wood costing about ninepence. For this a licence was required from the surveyor of the district council after the appropriate form had been submitted. This licence had to be registered and filed by the district surveyor and presented to, registered and filed by the timber merchant. Then there was the local roads authority, wishing to improve visibility at a dangerous road junction by substituting twenty yards of iron fence for the existing hedge. This process involved five large forms and nine maps, some of them coloured. Or again there was the provincial corn-merchant, who had to master the intricacies of fourteen licences and 160 fixed prices; or the owners of private gardens, who required a licence to sell bottled fruit to the public; or the retailers, who received a stern warning from the Board of Trade for embellishing utility furniture. A school in Sussex, Churcher's College, received a form from the Ministry of Fuel and Power to the effect that their previous allocation of coke had been cancelled and that their basic allocation for the twelve months to 30 April 1948 was nil tons, that it was possible only to allocate nil tons, divided as to nil tons a month in the summer and nil tons a month in the winter, with the name of the retailer provided. While in general the public undoubtedly approved of the government's desire to avoid the unjust and unfair free-for-all which had followed the previous war, it did seem as if controls were getting out of control. Jewkes described planning as an unscientific gamble with all the odds against success.

Unfortunately for the government, planning was not only acquiring a bad name at the grass roots (as in the case of Mrs Shenton, aged 79, who was fined £10 for growing too few potatoes when she had mistakenly responded to an official appeal to grow more wheat), but also on a much wider scale as a result of some unwise initiatives at ministerial level.

An ingenious Labour barrister, who became the first Lord Trefgarne, was put in charge of the Colonial Development Corporation. This body was supposed to create vast new markets and resources ranging from shark-fishing in the South Atlantic to a huge poultry farm in Gambia which, it was promised, would produce twenty million eggs a year. 'Expect nothing for two or three years,' said Lord Trefgarne. 'But by then we should be really under way, employing hundreds of thousands of young workers in the colonies.' There were to be no eggs from Gambia, the Dark Continent proving consistently impervious in this and all other respects to the new wave of British enterprise, however philanthropically conceived. But the fiasco of Gambia was as nothing to that of the Ministry of Food's scheme for the cultivation in Central Africa of 2,500,000 acres of what were invariably called groundnuts, to avoid the word peanuts, with its overtones of cheapness and prodigality. Not only would the scheme provide mass employment but it would also offset the world shortage of fats and so marvellously supplement the British housewife's exiguous margarine ration. The scheme was launched in 1946 and was eagerly espoused by John Strachey, the Minister of Food, as 'one of the most courageous, imaginative and well-judged acts of the Government for the sake of the world that has been taken in the life of this Parliament'. There were to be a hundred miles of railway, thousands of bulldozers (if available), new towns, new schools, new ports and Major-General Harrison of the Fourteenth Army to bring his long experience of Burma to the task in hand. *The Times*, commenting on the 1947 White Paper, *A Plan for the Mechanized Production of Groundnuts in East and Central Africa*, wrote: 'In its breadth of vision and the technical resourcefulness with which it plans to impose man's will on recalcitrant nature it invites comparison with the Tennessee Valley Authority and with the far-reaching development schemes of the Soviet Government. It offers, in fact, a stirring example of what science can do to make life worth living.'

The reality was somewhat different. The first report on the progress of the scheme had to point out that for 1947 it would be 94 per cent behind target, since it had turned out that 'the extensive, tough and pliable roots of the Kongwa thorns and the multiplicity of stumps have proved beyond the power of normal rooting machines.' Nature, apparently determined to be unhelpful, had also produced a drought and a great many baboons who ate the seeds. However it was confidently predicted that, at the end of 1948, 56,000 tons of shelled peanuts would be produced, rising to 609,000 tons annually, the minister suggesting in the spring of 1949 that the resultant revenue might well turn out to be twice the original estimate. In the end a total of just over 9,000 tons of shelled nuts, together with a little maize and millet, had been produced by 1951. When the enterprise finally petered out, £36,500,000 of taxpayers' money had been written off.

Even the most paralytic Parliamentary opposition could scarcely have failed to make some capital out of mistakes of this magnitude, and the Conservatives were now beginning to recover a measure of their old confidence. In the immediate aftermath of the electoral catastrophe, which had surprised so many of them in 1945, they acquired a valuable recruit in Fred Marquis, first Earl of Woolton. Woolton is a suburb of Liverpool, and it was from a Liverpool base that this ex-Fabian and warden of the university settlement developed a remarkable career in business and public administration. He had controlled the supply of blankets for the armies of the First World War and had completed the clothing of the British army in the Second World War between April and August 1939. Studiously nonpolitical, he had become a much admired national figure during the war as Minister of Food and skilful popularizer of near-inedible concoctions like Woolton pie, but had been somewhat too bland and anxious to please all parties as Minister of Reconstruction. He joined the Conservatives as the General Election results were coming through and the next year accepted Churchill's invitation to become party chairman, a role which he performed with remarkable success for nearly a decade. Beneath his bonhomous exterior lay a fierce determination to revive the fortunes of the party since, as he put it: 'However well-intentioned the other people now in office may be, if they pursue their policy to the end it will be disastrous for the economic life of this country and for personal freedom.' No more succinct statement of post-war Conservative philosophy was ever enunciated.

Woolton owed something to the work of his predecessor, Ralph Assheton, who revived the Research Department and the Young Conservatives, an organization which originated towards the end of the war and had 2375 branches by the end of 1949. Woolton's most celebrated constitutional reform, recommended also by another Liverpool politician, David Maxwell Fyfe, was to prevent Conservative candidates subscribing more than £25 to their local party funds. This had little effect in altering the social background of Conservative MPs, but had the most dynamic consequences in revitalizing the constituencies, where it was now necessary to maximize the number of small subscribers and to wear out the local doorsteps to that end. Woolton spent money lavishly on publicity of all sorts and, between 1947 and the summer of 1948, more than doubled the membership of the party (from 1,200,000 to 2,250,000). While the Labour ranks held firm at the by-elections, much to Herbert Morrison's satisfaction, there were occasional pointers calculated to encourage the Tory faithful, as for example the contest at Bexley in 1946 when a Labour majority fell from 11,763 to 1851 and a Gallup poll in November 1947 which gave the Tories a lead of eleven points, the best poll result they were to achieve before 1951. 1947 looked a promising year from the Conservative point of view with big gains in the municipal elections and favourable votes in both the Oxford and Cambridge unions.

Evelyn Waugh recorded gloomily in his diary in July 1945 that the Conservative benches would not only be empty but without talent – 'Chips Channon, William Teeling, Juby Lancaster etc.' All Lord Woolton's energy would have been wasted unless the Conservative politicians had been able to recover sufficiently to be able to present themselves and their programme as a credible alternative government. Churchill, for his part, found it difficult to conceal how much he missed the national unity of the war years, and contented himself largely with occupying the role of a world statesman without portfolio, only occasionally using his formidable powers of invective in debate. Anthony Eden finished the war with stomach ulcers and for a time considered becoming Secretary-General of the United Nations. He adopted a markedly bi-partisan approach towards the Russians with Bevin, who was accused of having dropped none of his predecessor's policies except the aitches. His relations with Churchill were far from harmonious and the issue of the succession a constant irritant because of the impossibility of discerning when, if ever, Churchill intended to retire. 'Winston is like a porpoise in the bath and one of uncertain moods,' wrote Eden in August 1946. Eden's stance on the Left of the party made less impact in the field of ideas than it might have done because of his rather desultory involvement in domestic policy. At the 1946 party conference he was enthusiastically applauded for a speech in which he harped on the theme of 'a nation-wide property-owning democracy', which can with hindsight be seen to have inaugurated a long ding-dong struggle in which the Conservatives have aimed to take the people out of council houses as quickly as the Socialists have tried to put them in. But for the most part his speeches were damned with faint praise, as by Colin Coote, the editor of the *Daily Telegraph* – 'his elegance was on a higher level than his eloquence, but he said what the average person was thinking quite competently.'

The ground thus vacated by Eden on the Left of the party was contested by Butler and Harold Macmillan, both described as neo-socialists by a disgruntled right-winger in the person of Brendan Bracken. At the 1947 Party Conference at Brighton, presided over by Macmillan, Eden proclaimed: 'We are not the party of unbridled, brutal capitalism and have never been.' The main difficulty confronting the party was the danger of appearing to repudiate what they had agreed to in principle during the Coalition. This, combined with the magnitude of their defeat at the General Election and their consistent lack of success in by-elections, tended to make them focus their opposition more on the practicability of the Government's plans than on their theoretic desirability. On 25 August 1945 an instructive little exchange took place in the House:

> Sir W. Darling (Edinburgh S.): 'Why this passion to do things?
> (An Hon. Member: 'We are sent here to do things.')

It was not going to be easy to turn or even stem the high tide of socialist activity. Churchill demanded to know, almost querulously: 'Could there be a worse occasion for deep-seated organic changes in the life of Britain than now, when she is exhausted and overburdened to a fearful degree?' Macmillan's response was to espouse the concept of the middle way. He advanced the view that Labour was sacrificing the practical and the empirical to the doctrinaire and the theoretical. 'No government of whatever complexion,' he told the House in November 1946, 'can disassociate itself from a large degree of intervention, and indeed management, in the economic life of the modern State. We can never return to the old classical laissez-faire. It is the Conservative party, at any rate, which has opposed that doctrine for a hundred years. The question is not, as I see it, whether the government should play a part in the economic life of the nation. The question is by what means, at what level and for what purpose.' He went on to explain, perhaps with an eye to his sceptical backbenchers, that 'a new monetary policy has been devised. It holds the field. Associated principally with the name of Lord Keynes, it was expanded and adapted by the general agreement of all parties in the last Coalition. It has not, I admit, been put to the test, but it is vital to strengthen and not to undermine the general belief in its efficiency.' Party lines were beginning to converge on the middle way, a point not lost on the astute Bevan, who observed unkindly that since the middle is always the point equidistant between two other points, Macmillan never knew what position he was to take up until his opponents had taken up theirs. Macmillan had after all advocated the nationalization of the mines before the war, although the exigencies of politics required him now to oppose it.

R. A. Butler, from his vantage point as Chairman of the Research Department, was the chief architect of Conservative re-thinking. Quintin Hogg wrote to him suggesting that what the party needed was a new Tamworth Manifesto. Overwhelming support for the idea was expressed at the 1946 conference at Blackpool and the end product was the *Industrial Charter* of 1947. An Industrial Policy Committee under Butler's chairmanship with Oliver Stanley, Oliver Lyttelton, Macmillan and Maxwell Fyfe, together with the Research Department and the Political Centre, comprised what Butler himself called a 'thinking machine which helped us to wrest from the Left much of the middle ground in the battle of ideas'. There was little to choose between the middle ground and the middle way. Butler took it as a compliment that when the *Industrial Charter* was published Lyttelton wrote to him *'il n'y a que le calme qui règne sur les âmes,'* a phrase which might well have been employed as a communiqué by General Gamelin from a headquarters in the Maginot Line. Its principal author has admitted that rarely in

the field of political pamphleteering can a document have been
written in so deliberately flat a tone. It was not well designed, he
tells us in *The Art of the Possible*, to captivate Churchill's attention. It is, however, only fair to add that Churchill himself had
forbidden the publication of specific electoral pledges. In
Butler's own words: 'The Charter was first and foremost an
assurance that, in the interests of efficiency, full employment and
social security, modern Conservatism would maintain strong
central guidance over the operation of the economy.' More and
more such charters emerged (including one for Wales written
almost single-handedly by Enoch Powell) culminating in *The
Right Road for Britain* in 1949. Although there were references
to concepts like mutual ownership and co-partnership, incentives, tax cuts, industrial research, reduction of physical controls, publicity about restrictive practices and other panaceas,
the general message was clear enough – full employment and the
Welfare State were safe with the Tories, who could now offer
the people everything the Socialists offered but with much more
efficiency and rather more humanity. Enterprise without selfish-
ness would be the order of the day. New Presbyter was to be old
Priest writ large. It was an intelligent gamble, likely to succeed,
provided, but only provided, the Socialists ran into further
trouble. But even Butler occasionally entertained doubts,
Malcolm Muggeridge recording a lunch with him in February
1948 at which he was pessimistic about the prospects of the
party, since the local associations always selected bad candidates.
'He thought that Labour won't last very long, and obviously
himself favoured coalition.'

The Labour government did in the event run into further
trouble towards the end of 1948. It had been a year in which
things had gone much better for them. Marshall Aid; the signing
in March of the Brussels treaty between Britain, France and the
Benelux countries providing for a fifty-year alliance and a programme of co-operation; the dramatic improvement in the
balance of payments and the export drive; the ending for good
or ill of the Palestine mandate; the renewed sense of national
unity engendered by the Berlin airlift; the end of bread rationing
and the restoration of ninety miles a month's worth of basic
petrol – all this seemed to presage a much better future than had
seemed possible in 1947. Although Bradman's Australians

trounced our cricketers, the Olympic games had been successfully completed in August, the *Sunday Times* commenting that
almost for the first time since Attic history there had been no
sort of international brawl. It had been a lovely summer and the
prudent had put away against the winter substantial stocks of
fuel, variously labelled unscreened coke breeze, washery slurry
or anthracite duff. It was the summer of the New Look (of which
more later) and of *Oklahoma!* The guardsmen were back in
scarlet for the Trooping of the Colour, it being discovered that
their waistlines were much smaller than they had been pre-war.
The Athenaeum and Boodle's were repainted, and Herbert
Morrison proclaimed that socialism was the only moral policy
since there was no profit in it. Then on 27 November things
began to go wrong as the country learned that the Prime Minister
had appointed a tribunal under Mr Justice Lynskey to investigate charges of corruption involving a junior minister and government officials.

The public hearing, conducted in an upstairs room in Church
Hall, Westminster, lasted five weeks. Starting with a buzz of
rumour and speculation which seemed to suggest the imminence
of a political scandal of Panama or at least Stavisky proportions,
it eventually settled down into something more like a long-
running comic serial. The principal members of the cast were
John Belcher, Parliamentary Secretary at the Board of Trade
under Harold Wilson; George Gibson, CH, a former Chairman
of the TUC, Director of the Bank of England and Chairman of
the North-West Region Electricity Board; and the *soi-disant*
Sidney Stanley, the 'Spider of Park Lane', contact man *par
excellence* and a personality whom Dickens at his most imaginatively fertile would have been hard stretched to invent. Stanley,
a Polish immigrant, was an undischarged bankrupt with a varie-
gated commercial career pursued under the successive names of
Solomon Kohsyzcky, Schlomo Rechtand, Sid Wulkan and
Blotts. Under fifteen hours cross-examination by the Attorney-
General, Sir Hartley Shawcross, he established himself as a
comic genius combining limitless ingenuity with wholly un-
convincing injured innocence, a cross between Fagin and Charlie
Chaplin. The salient facts of the matter amounted to relatively
little, a storm in a teacup rather than a Teapot Dome. In order to
promote the interests of his multifarious clients Stanley had

persuaded John Belcher to accept a gold cigarette case, the payment of a hotel bill at Margate for his wife and himself, and some suits; and the gifts accepted by Gibson were even more venial. No criminal charges were proceeded with. Belcher applied for the Chiltern Hundreds, Gibson resigned his offices, and Stanley sold his memoirs to *The People* and eventually made his way to Israel. No civil servants were involved. Justice had been done and seen to be done.

However, the effect of these bizarre proceedings on public opinion was considerable. On the one hand, here was Harry Thomas, slogging away at his granite with his famous thirty-eight-pound sledgehammer, and Mrs Thirkell's housewives struggling with their shopping baskets in the fish queue, and Sir Stafford Cripps and Mr Morrison propounding the virtues of austerity and the moral superiority of the government, while quite another world was being revealed in lurid limelight as the Lynskey Tribunal examined and cross-examined crowds of witnesses. Here was a director of the Bank of England playing solo-whist in the Manchester train with the dubious Mr Stanley, and a trade minister receiving small gifts from a whisky distiller called Sir Maurice Bloch. In a world of bouncing cheques and greasy palms, enterprising businessmen seemed to be continually trying to evade government regulations preventing them from promoting football pools or importing merry-go-rounds or exporting millions of cement bags. At one stage a piece of paper was produced, purporting implausibly to be a letter from the Chancellor of the Exchequer to Stanley, reading: 'Dear Stanley, We are very pleased with the way you are helping us in the government and the work you have done for the party. Yours sincerely, Stafford Cripps.' At another, Stanley, asked how so much money flowed through his bank account, explained that he regularly drew cash by cheque from the banks of the Greyhound Racing Association and, between then and the moment the cheques were presented to his own bank, had time enough to 'play about with the money'. All in all, the British public felt that a corner had been lifted of the hitherto impenetrable curtain, behind which everybody but themselves seemed to have access to whisky and nylons and bananas and steaks and petrol and foreign travel. And the two principal sufferers who had fallen from grace seemed all too representative of Britain's new rulers – Belcher, the junior minister who had been a Great Western Railway clerk, and Gibson, former errand-boy and asylum attendant who epitomized the successful trade union boss. Nothing in the story of the Lynskey Tribunal redounded to the credit of capitalism or private enterprise, but it had a considerable effect in confirming the mounting tide of criticism directed at the world of controls and rationing.

There were those too who linked what seemed to be going on in circles close to the government with a moment in the previous summer when Aneurin Bevan had indulged in some flamboyant oratory at Belle Vue, Manchester. He claimed for Britain the moral leadership of the world and in scarcely veiled terms attacked Morrison's enthusiasm for consolidation rather than for the onward march of nationalization, which could alone achieve the domination of the public sector over the economy as a whole. It was in this speech that Bevan, recalling his youth, talked of his deep, burning hatred of the Tory Party, ending with the phrase which history will record as the epitome of Welsh rhetoric out of control – 'so far as I am concerned they are lower than vermin. . . . I warn you, they have not changed – if they have, they are slightly worse than they were.' *The Observer* described these remarks as a crime against democratic society and they earned their perpetrator a stinging rebuke from the Prime Minister. The same speech contained the phrase: 'What is Toryism but organized spivvery?' While nobody knew how the arch-spiv Sidney Stanley voted, it seemed clear enough that he was in the habit of hobnobbing with persons other than Tories.

Thus, as the relatively triumphant year drew to a close, there were indications of trouble ahead. There was, for instance, Ivor Thomas's resignation over the Iron and Steel Bill which he described as dogma run mad. The bill itself announced the setting up of a public corporation to buy out and control the two thousand firms involved and compensate their shareholders, the vesting day to be 1 May 1950 or within eighteen months thereafter. Morrison's announcement that the guillotine would be used to expedite the passage of the bill produced much Conservative and Liberal uproar. It did not receive a good press, *The Economist* presenting its readers with what it saw as a rhetorical question – 'Do state officials run industries better than private individuals?' The Conservatives consistently linked Morrison's Parliament

Bill (eventually passed in 1949), which reduced the Lords' veto from two years to one, with their desire to minimize the Lords' likely opposition to the Iron and Steel Bill. A Gallup poll in November showed 44 per cent opposed to steel nationalization and only 22 per cent supporting it. Such considerations did nothing to deter Hugh Gaitskell, who told the House that same month: 'The case for nationalization of steel rests on its own merit; but the policy of nationalization pursued by this Government . . . is an integral part of the whole conception of socialist democracy in this country.' A Labour renegade, Alfred Edwards, the former MP for Middlesbrough who had been expelled from the party the previous May, claimed that the Government had only kept the bill in the programme to appease Bevan, who had threatened to resign, and stated that at a Middlesbrough meeting the bill had only found favour with one out of three hundred. Churchill described the bill as actuated entirely by 'squalid party motives', designed by Labour to show their supporters that they 'still hate and are trying to maul the other half of their fellow countrymen'. Small wonder that the Prime Minister retired to hospital with eczema and a duodenal ulcer.

Harold Wilson presided over a great bonfire of controls in November which got rid of 200,000 varied licences and permits, including those relating to hairnets, pine-oil and raw goatskins. This was seen by many as a step in the right direction (it was followed by the elimination of 930,000 more in March 1949), but it failed to stop the persistent grumbling. The *New Statesman* unhelpfully pointed out that at any medium restaurant in Munich one could now eat better and more copiously than in the best West End restaurants. There seemed no end in sight for National Service, given the need for 100,000 men to fight the Communist guerrillas in Malaya. The nation, as a whole, was still prepared 'to soldier on', but in a mood of ironic apathy rather than dedicated idealism.

The last year of the first post-war Labour government began auspiciously enough to all outward appearances. Marshall Aid was still underpinning the economy and Cripps's personal authority with the eminently biddable Trade Union leaders was such that a virtual wage freeze was in being. The remarkable fact in this connection was that, from 1948 till as late as August 1950, average weekly wages rose in real terms by only 5 per cent as against a rise in retail prices of eight per cent. It would not be long before the workers woke up to the truth of Professor Jewkes's dictum that inflation is the great confidence trick which the state plays upon the public, but for the moment what Crossman called the tiger of organized labour was still contained in his cage. However, for a government increasingly concerned with export competition it was awkward that the wages of the industrious Germans were 40 per cent lower.

It was becoming evident that Morrison's manpower projections were beginning to relate less and less to the true state of affairs. His targets had been badly missed in 1947 and now it was revealed in 1948 that instead of 32,000 additional miners there had only been 8000; 20,000 instead of 58,000 cotton workers; 36,000 instead of 55,000 agricultural workers. That sort of planning did not seem to be working, and indeed it became less and less credible that it conceivably could without direction of labour, for which the government had reserve powers which they were understandably reluctant to use. Nor did it seem particularly wise that, at a time of acute labour shortage in key industries, two million persons should be employed in national and local government.

Cripps was in fact moving from physical planning to economic management, a process which seemed to make state ownership irrelevant despite protestations to the contrary. For party purposes the Conservatives were continually encouraging his natural penchant for austerity. Thus in January 1949 Harold Macmillan warned the House against the dangers of telling the people that, so to speak, they had never had it so good: 'Any party or group of men which tries to tempt the electorate by bribes, or by holding out some agreeable picture of an automatically realizable Utopia, will incur more than ordinary guilt.... Anyone who paints a rosy picture will carry a very heavy responsibility.' Cripps obliged in his March budget which he described as a hold-fast operation. He introduced what was yet another austerity budget with what Eden called condensed and brilliant oratory. He had much on which to congratulate himself. Even clothes rationing had just been wound up. '1948 has been a year of great achievement by the British people,' he declared. Why then, *The Times* enquired tartly, did that seem to mean nothing except dearer food, dearer matches, dearer football pools, with the subjection of a third of National Insurance contributions to income tax, all of which was offset only by a penny off beer and two shillings off a bottle of *vin ordinaire*. For the Labour benches, it was uncomfortable to have to acquiesce in ceilings on food subsidies and social service expenditure. True, the tax on distributed profits was increased, but there was an even bigger remission on profits ploughed back into new plant. There was also a disturbing finality about the Chancellor's observation that the great and highly desirable redistribution of wealth had gone to the point 'where new wealth must be created for redistribution'. Cripps had for some time been in the habit of employing the uncomfortable metaphor of the national cake. Oliver Stanley, in a budget broadcast, felt that this was now the end of an era of Socialist policy and Socialist propaganda. Sir Richard Acland was alarmed to see the nation 'drifting into a thoroughly unhealthy attitude of "Good old 1938. Let us get back as quickly as we can." '

On April 12 the Labour party produced a new political pamphlet, *Labour Believes in Britain*, which had its genesis at a merrymaking at Shanklin, Isle of Wight, at which Morrison recited from the *Rubaiyat*, Laski sang *Poor Old Joe*, Tom Williams gave a rendering of *Ilkley Moor*, with A. V. Alexander providing the piano accompaniment. It included a phrase which stimulated a good deal of caustic linguistic analysis: 'Labour has set out to convert into practical reality the Socialist ideal that the best should be available to all.' The question now was – did Britain believe in Labour? The local government elections were not encouraging in that respect. In Herbert Morrison's LCC the solitary Liberal councillor held the balance between sixty-four Socialists and sixty-four Tories, till the Labour aldermen restored the balance. In Birmingham, scene of such exciting triumphs in 1945, there were now sixty-nine Tories and forty-nine Labour councillors. Industrial trouble seemed an awkward possibility when Mr Deakin told a press conference that he knew in considerable detail Cominform plans for an imminent assault on certain key industries. However, it was the warmest Easter of the century and – a straw to clutch at – two successive Gallup polls gave the party a one per cent lead over the Tories for the first time since January 1947.

As the party faithful at Blackpool in June heard Bevan

demanding more nationalization and Morrison stressing the need for more consolidation, they were evidently not aware of a massive economic crisis looming ahead. There was something of a recession in the United States, with four million unemployed and some talk of an over-valued pound making it difficult for Britain to earn sufficient dollars. Just a year earlier (6 May 1948) Cripps had magisterially rebuked the supporters of devaluation, which he said would mean 'that we should have to export much more and get very much less than we get today. To embark on such a programme would be the extreme of folly. This Government certainly have no intention of embarking on such a programme.' In December 1948, when a respected financial journalist raised the question of a possible devaluation at a press conference, Cripps told him crisply that the introduction of the subject was 'merely a piece of gratuitous offensiveness'. Although an alarming increase in what the Prime Minister called 'dollar trouble' took place in June, Cripps once again stated categorically in answer to a question on 6 July: 'His Majesty's Government have not the slightest intention of devaluing the pound,' and this despite being told by the American Secretary of State that British export prices were not competitive. Furthermore there were suddenly far fewer exports, since Arthur Deakin's Communists were busy in the docks and the nationalized railwaymen were also on strike, losing between them 265,000 working days. On 22 July George Isaacs deported two Americans and one Dutchman, and later Attlee ordered 30,000 copies of a speech by Bob Mellish on Communist infiltration to be distributed among the dockers. On 2 August the much respected economist J. E. Meade wrote to *The Times* on the dollar gap in language as worried as it was prophetic: 'We are still attempting to live beyond our means. The consequentially excessive domestic demand inflates our requirement for imports and restrains our manufacturers from vigorously searching for exports.' *The Times* by 12 August was taking the government to task for its evident unpreparedness, observing that, whenever there was a crisis in the economy or in industry, they behaved like the old-time Turks who were always surprised when winter came. The next day the sweet ration was re-introduced.

Meanwhile the Chancellor had gone into a Zürich clinic and the Prime Minister had been converted by Hugh Gaitskell and

Douglas Jay to the need for devaluation. They set in motion the necessary preparations for what was initially called Operation Caliban, and later Operation Rose. The Chancellor had no option but to fall in line and on 18 September the pound became worth only 2·8 dollars as opposed to 4·03, a devaluation of 30 per cent. That weekend Richard Crossman had succeeded in confusing the minds of the readers of his column in the *Sunday Pictorial* by telling them that, since devaluation meant unemployment, Sir Stafford Cripps had refused to countenance it. *The Times* felt that it would have been better if disinflation at home had preceded devaluation. Disinflation was duly announced by the Prime Minister on 26 October, after a series of cabinet meetings at which resignations were threatened from all directions and it became unhappily clear that Cripps himself was a sick man, his morale badly undermined by Churchill's attacks on his integrity, which he had of course put much at risk by his repeated denials of the intention to devalue. With a General Election not more than a year away, the programme of cuts was not calculated to enhance the party's confidence or please the back benches. Although it included defence cuts, it also increased food prices and reduced agricultural subsidies and the housing programme. A proposed shilling charge for NHS prescriptions (never in fact introduced by Labour) seemed to many the first step in a retreat from principle in the funding of the Welfare State.

Attlee sounded tired and querulous as he broadcast the bad news in his usual clipped military tones on 27 October: 'We are having to make some heavy reductions in expenditure. They amount to £250 million. This is a very large sum. . . . There will be some postponement of educational and other public works and a reduction in the housing programme, though care is being taken to see that municipal housing schemes are affected as little as possible. . . . There has been some excessive and unnecessary resort to doctors for prescriptions. A charge not exceeding one shilling for each prescription will now be imposed. . . . There are workers who only do the minimum, who don't care, who take days off. . . . The welfare state can only endure when it is built on a sound economic foundation.' *Figaro* observed that Mr Attlee addressed himself to public opinion in the language of a worthy administrator. To others it sounded more like the language of an elderly headmaster whose school was getting out of control. It was certainly not the sort of language which could be said to echo Bevan's rallying cry only a few months earlier at the Blackpool conference – 'This great movement has the right to raise its head high and look at the stars.'

Attlee hammered out a decision to go to the country in February 1950, strongly urged thereto by Cripps who had no stomach for another budget before an Election. There was a final settlement of the inter-related disputes over the Steel Bill and the limiting of the Lords' veto. The latter became law before the end of the year and the Minister of Supply, G. R. Strauss, the object of over-audible contempt on the part of Dalton, agreed to postpone steel nationalization till after the Election. Steel denationalization would thus become a prominent electoral issue, though less attention was paid to Bevan's demands for the nationalization of ICI and the Prudential Assurance Company, Morrison pointing out in his tiresomely practical way that he did not wish 'the man from the Pru' to act as a Tory agent on the nation's doorstep. However, before the Election took place, the party produced a pamphlet advocating the nationalization of sugar, cement, wholesale meat distribution, water supply, cold storage plants, 'all suitable minerals', marginal food-producing land not fully used, 'appropriate' sections of the chemical industry and industrial assurance which was to be 'mutualized'. As Morrison had explained: 'You must expect the new programme to be of a somewhat different character and a somewhat different tempo from the last.'

If Morrison was lukewarm about the new nationalization proposals, Dalton went further and described them as a dog's dinner. Many of the workers in the industries involved were opposed to them and, if Dalton is to be believed, the great majority of Labour candidates were not briefed to argue the case for them. Tate and Lyle launched a vigorous propaganda campaign against the plan for nationalizing beet sugar manufacture and sugar refining and their campaign mascot 'Mr Cube' seemed to many to symbolize a whole breed of sturdy little Britons standing up for their rights against the oppressive weight of unpopular nationalization.

Despite the difficulties experienced during the summer and

autumn of 1949, the Cabinet had some reason for the optimism with which they regarded the outcome of the election. The party had not lost a single seat in thirty-five by-elections. Churchill seemed to be banking once again more on his prestige as a world statesman than on any policy initiatives, and Eden hardly talked about anything except foreign affairs. Relations between the government and the unions were still close, and at the beginning of the year the TUC endorsed the wages freeze, if only by 657,000 out of 8 million votes*. The *Financial Times* listed as the main issues: 1. The cost of living; 2. Housing; 3. The future of subsidies; 4. High taxation; 5. Full employment. On the first four Labour could be seen as being to some extent vulnerable, but Churchill in the campaign called the prevention of mass unemployment 'the most solid duty of government' and the maintenance of full employment was invariably seen as particularly the province of Labour. The Labour Manifesto *Let Us Win Through Together* proudly proclaimed: 'Today destitution has been banished.' Priestley was recruited for a party political broadcast, which he proudly announced was not paid for either by the party or the BBC so that he could characteristically term it 'summat for nowt'. In it he explained that it was important to vote for the Labour party as it was broad-based, had an ethic and was not governed by cynical expediency.

The Conservative manifesto *This is the Road* was, however, a skilful document which reflected the increased sophistication of Central Office thinking on the post-war political scene. It pointed out, what even Labour admitted, that full employment was a result of Marshall Aid. While there was much emphasis on individual freedom and initiative, there was a clear commitment to the Welfare State and a modest programme of denationalization limited to road transport and iron and steel. There was also the following significant statement: 'They have put more money into circulation, but it has bought less and less. The value of every pound earned or saved or paid in pensions or social services has been cut by 3s 8d since they took office. It's not a pound but 16s 4d.' The Gallup poll, which failed to dismay the confident Bevan, showed the Tories with a one per cent lead.

The General Election of 23 February 1950 was preceded by a campaign which Churchill, enjoying his thirteenth General

* As opposed to votes of 5,421,000 to 2,032,000 in 1948.

Election (to say nothing of some momentous by-elections), described as 'demure'. However, the electorate was far from apathetic, as is indicated by an 89·3 per cent turn-out. The minor parties made strenuous efforts to make an impact on the voters. The Liberals ran 475 candidates, of whom 319 lost their deposits and only 9 were elected, but with 9 per cent of the vote. The Communists fielded exactly a hundred candidates, none of whom was successful. Most of them were party officials, paid from the war chest, but there were three research scientists, one doctor, nine teachers, one Old Etonian and two Old Marlburians. There was some hilarity at Bethnal Green, where the Tory candidate was a painter and decorator's wife called Mrs Welfare and the Communist a bricklayer who had been wounded in the Spanish Civil War and was called Mildwater. Overnight, after the polls closed, the Labour pundits were prophesying a majority of about a hundred. By 4.45 p.m. on the 24th Labour was one seat ahead; at 4.46 the parties were level. In the final count Labour had 315 seats, the Conservatives 298 and the remainder twelve, giving Labour an overall majority of six. The swing to the Conservatives was less than 3 per cent and the Birmingham results disappointed them. On the other hand the swing in Middlesex was large, nearly 9 per cent. Whereas all thirty-seven candidates sponsored by the National Union of Mineworkers were safely returned, the suburbs were evidently slipping away from Labour, and the new Tory intake included many bright young men, often with impressive war records – Heath, Macleod, Powell, Maudling, Soames – who seemed likely to revivify the 'old gang'.

It was all a rather disappointing outcome for Labour, which had seen itself as the greatest reforming government of all time. Morrison, it is true, consoled himself with the reflection that 'the British people are wonderful. They didn't mean to chuck us out, only to give us a sharp kick in the pants.' His colleagues were less philosophical. Had there perhaps been too much whittling away of full-blooded Socialism? Bevan had told a percipient journalist just before the Election that he was not interested in the return of another Labour government, but in the election of a government that 'will make Britain a Socialist country'. But, by way of contrast, the rising young Minister of Fuel and Power, Hugh Gaitskell, himself very much an idealist according to his own lights, was intensely concerned with the realities of responsible government and already confiding to his diary such thoughts as: 'When the Election is over the Government ought really to face up to the issue of Power Station strikes and decide whether they can afford to treat them as ordinary industrial disputes. In my view they cannot.' There were in fact a number of reasons which could be advanced to explain Labour's comparative discomfiture – the redistribution of parliamentary seats; the unwillingness of the middle classes to appreciate high taxation and to enthuse about further redistribution of wealth; and, most familiar of all, since it crops up after most elections, the party's alleged failure to get across its message to the voters, who were thus left in partial ignorance of the blinding truth.

While Labour had held on to its working class vote, the evidence from several Gallup polls that there was much less enthusiasm for doctrinal as opposed to pragmatic socialism seemed to have been borne out on the hustings. Furthermore, in one significant respect Labour had lost one of its important theoretical assets. Nobody now talked of the supreme benefits conferred by the state socialism of the Soviet Union on its own inhabitants and on the outside world. Orwell's *Nineteen Eighty-Four* (published in 1949) seemed to be much more of a talking point than the celebrations attendant on the seventieth birthday of Stalin, described by *Pravda* as 'the bearer of the name most beloved and cherished by the workers of the whole world'. The publication of *The God That Failed*, a group of six essays by party renegades like Koestler, Gide and Silone, with an introduction by Crossman, represented for many disillusioned intellectuals the death-knell of the high hopes which they had once entertained for the regeneration of the human race. In the concluding essay Stephen Spender recorded how Rákosi, the Hungarian deputy Prime Minister, told him that the British Labour government was Fascist because it had not filled the army with Socialist generals or taken over Scotland Yard. This was not quite the post-war world which Spender had anticipated when instructing his comrades in the Holland Park Avenue fire station during the war on the virtues of collectivism.

It was the clash of rival ideologies on the international scene which largely destroyed any hope of Labour recovering throughout the Fifties from the setback encountered at the polls in February 1950. But in addition there was something of a failure

154

of political nerve. As compared with what was to happen in 1974, the assumption that a single figure majority was unworkable and must soon lead to another dissolution seems on the face of it surprising. However, not only was that the received political wisdom of the period, but the Labour leaders were beginning to break down under the prodigious strains of office. Cripps had to yield the Exchequer to Gaitskell in October 1950 and died in April 1952 at the age of sixty-two. Bevin relinquished the Foreign Office in March 1951 and died a few weeks later. Just before his death the entire Foreign Office staff, from the Permanent Under Secretary to the messenger boys, had attended his seventieth birthday party, all having contributed sixpence a head. Attlee was now nearly seventy and suffering from ulcers, sciatica and lumbago; Addison, the leader in the House of Lords, was eighty-one; Chuter Ede, leader in the Commons, was sixty-eight; and Morrison's wife was dying. Laski died in March 1950. The future seemed increasingly to rest on the shoulders of Gaitskell and Bevan, whose relations at this juncture were no more harmonious than those which had existed between Bevin and Morrison.

There were initially some mildly encouraging portents for Labour in the months immediately after the election. The gold and dollar reserves were improving. The potential threat of industrial conscription was removed with the abolition of the Control of Engagement order. Points rationing went, the price of fish was de-controlled and the absurd five shilling limit on restaurant meals ended. Even clotted cream reappeared, although Maurice Webb at the Ministry of Food had recently prohibited the import of Irish cream on the grounds that it would become a high-priced luxury food, leading to the irritation of housewives, a curious argument in terms of a nation at that time spending £1600 million on drinks. Cripps's last budget seemed almost deliberately uncontroversial, though a promising maiden speech by the young Anthony Crosland criticized it for imperilling the wage freeze by inadequate concessions to the workers. But the clouds began to gather as the Fuchs trial was followed by the announcement by the Russians that they had successfully manufactured an atomic bomb and the London dockers went on strike again between 19 April and 7 May, the third strike within twelve months and described by George

155

Isaacs as 'clearly Communist inspired' (as was a bus strike later that year). And as the wet, cold summer of 1950 unfolded, the news from abroad became even more menacing.

The Korean War which started on 25 June 1950, and which was ended by an armistice only in 1953, effectively extinguished any prospect of Labour recovering its fortunes as a consequence of the financial and ideological turmoil it engendered. By the end of 1952 more than a million Chinese and North Korean Communists were deployed in Korea with tanks, artillery and two thousand aeroplanes. As the Communist MP Willie Gallacher had observed in the House: 'The Chinese people, who have been liberated, are on the march and are holding high the blood-red banner of Socialism.' To assist General MacArthur to resist the Chinese onslaught fifteen other nations provided a small measure of assistance, with the Commonwealth division from Britain, Canada, Australia and New Zealand in the van. By the middle of July the Americans were locked in battle. Here was a war of international implications in the new atomic age, ushered in at Hiroshima. Could it be effectively localized and would the atomic arsenals he brought into action? Although the Russians were in possession of a small number of atomic bombs, their capacity to deliver them at long ranges was still far short of that of the USA. Might the Russians be tempted to capitalize on American and United Nations involvement in Korea to blackmail Europe into submission by one means or another? The Russians could have put into a European theatre of war eighty infantry divisions and twenty-five armoured divisions against twelve and less than two respectively. Some anxiety was discernible in Attlee's broadcast of 31 July: 'If the aggressor gets away with it, aggressors all over the world will be encouraged. The same results which led to the Second World War will follow; and another world war may result. That is why what is happening in Korea is of such importance to you. The fire that has been started in distant Korea may burn down your house.' In a recruiting speech the following week, he added: 'I would ask you all to be on your guard against the enemy within. There are those who would stop at nothing to injure our economy and our defence.'

A number of consequences followed for Britain. National Service was extended to two years and a rearmament programme

156

set in motion which would cost £3600 million over three years, £830 million of which would have to be found in 1951–2 by Gaitskell. The £3600 million was increased to £4700 million in January 1951, in what Gaitskell recorded in his diary as an atmosphere approaching panic following MacArthur's spectacular loss of Seoul and Inchon. The economic consequences of this, combined with a high rise in the cost of imports as a result of world-wide stockpiling, was to alter a £300 million surplus balance of payments into a £403 million deficit in the space of a year. The statesmanship of Harry Truman removed from the scene in due course both General MacArthur and the imminent threat of nuclear war. In this he was assisted to some extent by Attlee, who on returning from a visit to Washington, in which he failed to secure an absolute British veto on the use of the bomb, described himself and Truman as 'really very representative of ordinary people'. But the fact remained that rearmament on the scale deemed necessary could only be paid for by measures which would destroy the unity of the Labour party.

At the beginning of 1951 the Gallup poll showed the Tories enjoying a 13 per cent lead and the National Coal Board was importing coal from America, India and Nigeria. Had it not been a very wet rather than a cold winter it might have been 1947 all over again. Stocks of meat were low and the Argentinians were so clamorously demanding excessive prices for bulk purchase that Maurice Webb was constrained to observe that Britain was a great and proud country which he was sure was prepared to stand up against Argentina. By the end of 1950 it was internationally agreed that the nation was solvent, though it was as well not to forget Marshall and Commonwealth aid amounting to 2694 million dollars. So, as Marshall Aid ended, two things became alarmingly clear to the government – first that rearmament could only be paid for by considerable belt-tightening and, secondly, that the wage freeze was not holding and would not hold.

The death knell of the wages freeze was sounded at the 1951 TUC Congress. The vital resolution – 'This Congress, recognizing the inconsistency of supporting a planned economy on the one hand and of insisting on an unplanned wages sector on the other, calls on the General Council to examine the possibilities of formulating a planned wages policy' – was heavily defeated.

It was an important moment in British post-war history. The Conservatives were able to put at the forefront of their election manifesto – 'The greatest national misfortune which we now endure is the ever falling value of our money.' The statistical descent in the purchasing power of the pound was beginning to look disturbing:

1914	100
1938	64·16
1946	37·91
1950	31·25
1951	28·75

It is unlikely that even George Schwarz would have predicted that the relevant figure thirty years later would be 4·16.

In February 1951 Aneurin Bevan made one of his most effective speeches in support of the government's rearmament programme, which doubled defence expenditure from what it had been before the crisis and indeed involved some 14 per cent of the national income. 'We shall carry out our defence programme,' he said. 'We shall fulfil our obligations to our friends and allies.' The President of the Board of Trade, Harold Wilson, knew, however, that the proposed expenditure was unrealistic since, apart from anything else, the necessary raw materials were not available. When Gaitskell presented his belt-tightening budget he introduced his celebrated proposals to add charges for false teeth and spectacles to the existing authorization of a shilling prescription charge, if found necessary, put through the House earlier by Bevan himself. Bevan, attacking the steelmasters, once used a Biblical phrase – 'Act so that thy enemy shall be aware of thee.' On this occasion he made perfectly clear that Gaitskell was his political enemy. Recent events had run awry for Aneurin Bevan. Attlee had decided that Britain could not afford him as either Chancellor of the Exchequer or Foreign Secretary*, and he had been passed over for both posts in favour of Gaitskell in the one instance, and Morrison in the other. He had had to accept 'with a shrug and a curse' the Ministry of Labour†. He now

* Kenneth Harris advances the view that Bevan did not want the Foreign Office on the basis of a 1962 *Observer* article by Attlee.

† We are indebted to K. O. Morgan for emphasizing the extent to which Bevan in his three months at the Ministry before his resignation was embroiled in uncongenial difficulties over strikes and the wage freeze.

resigned on the issue of teeth and spectacles, having made a speech at Bermondsey to the effect that he would never be a member of a government which made charges on the National Health Service for patients. His earlier compliance with the one shilling prescription charge he explained away by saying that he knew all along that any such charge was impracticable. The *Daily Herald*, reminding Bevan of one of his most celebrated definitions of Socialism, commented: 'Priorities are no longer Mr Bevan's creed. He appoints himself instead the idol of the Wishful Thinkers, who look upon socialism not as an orderly and responsible way of life, a religion of priorities, but as a device for getting everything for nothing.' If we are to believe Dalton, Bevan exhibited during this period 'unbearable conceit, crass obstinacy and a totalitarian streak'. Be that as it may, it was not helpful for the Labour party to have to listen to one of its own cabinet ministers describing the budget as remarkable, 'in that it united the City, satisfied the opposition and disunited the Labour party'. The Labour party being prone to disunity, Harold Wilson also resigned for reasons best known to that inscrutable politician, as did John Freeman, the Parliamentary Secretary to the Ministry of Supply, who became assistant editor of the *New Statesman*. *Tribune* likened Gaitskell's budget to that of Philip Snowden in 1931. Any mention of Snowden is the height of obloquy as between one Labour man and another. The unfortunate Prime Minister had to follow these proceedings from St Mary's Hospital, where his troublesome duodenal ulcer was being nursed.

Although he soon returned to politics, Attlee's troubles were far from over. The last great nationalization measure was not working out particularly well. The Iron and Steel Corporation came into being on 15 February 1951. Only one of its members came from the industry. The government had wanted as Chairman a South African steel magnate called Dr Van Der Bijl but he had declined the offer, so they had had to choose S. J. L. Hardie, Chairman of British Oxygen. Lincoln Evans refused to join and no other trade unionist was asked. *Iron and Steel*, the industry's journal, stated in March 1951 that the existing controllers would continue to run the industry, 'while the members of the newly constituted Steel Corporation are learning the difference between steel and slag'. People in all walks of life were beginning to take the government a little less than seriously.

Nor were there any compensatory triumphs as a result of Attlee's misguided substitution of Morrison for Bevin at the Foreign Office. During his seven months as Foreign Secretary Morrison gave the impression of floundering from crisis to crisis. He should never have accepted the office, but with his eye on the succession to the leadership of the party he could not afford to turn it down, having wisely kept himself out of contention for the Chancellorship. Like his predecessor, he was unable to pronounce foreign place-names, limiting for example, the word Euphrates to two syllables, but unlike Bevin he tended not to know where the places in question were. Nor were Foreign Office officials impressed by his habit of ostentatiously carrying around with him Guedalla's life of Palmerston. In general, he preferred to take questions on his other principal preoccupation, the Festival of Britain, leaving the intricacies of foreign affairs to his deputy, Kenneth Younger.

This was the period when Labour's lukewarm attitude to European integration began to emerge. Bevin in January 1948 had said: 'the free nations of Europe must now draw closely together. . . . Britain cannot stand outside Europe and regard her problems as quite separate from those of her European neighbours.' Yet he turned down participation in a Consultative Assembly and in September 1948 told the Commons that the roof could not be built before the house. Both Bevin and Attlee were concerned at the consequences of any form of association which might appear to threaten ties with the Commonwealth. Both major parties tended to feel more at home trying to strengthen ties with the Commonwealth than in the pursuit of European co-operation with its uncharted perils. Labour in particular entertained the most extravagant hopes for the Commonwealth, as exemplified by Patrick Gordon Walker: 'I am more deeply convinced than ever of the future greatness of the British Commonwealth, and of the nobility of the conception and practice of the Commonwealth. There is no higher cause that any of us can ask to serve in the world today.' This contrasted with Churchill (or for that matter Smuts), whose commitment to Europe, if never very precise, was comparatively enthusiastic, as when he spoke at Zürich in 1946 of a 'kind of United States of Europe', and when he chaired the United Europe Committee set up in London in 1947 and the Hague Conference on European unity in 1948. Labour's attitude to efforts of this sort was indicated clearly enough when the NEC wrote to forty Labour MPs who planned to go to The Hague, warning them that the concept of European unity 'might be corrupted in the hands of reaction'. The Brussels Treaty, NATO, the Council of Europe and the OEEC all represented substantial advances, but any closer integration ran the risk of subordinating British socialism to an unacceptable degree of potential dilution. So when Robert Schuman put forward his proposals for a European Coal and Steel Community in the spring of 1950, Morrison, as acting Prime Minister, scotched the possibility of British involvement with, according to his biographer, the revealing phrase: 'It's no good, we cannot do it, the Durham miners won't wear it.' Cripps told the Commons that there could be no full and final integration of European economy except on the basis of common economic politics and planned social democracy.

So Morrison began his tenure of the Foreign Office by sharply distancing himself from his colleagues on the Committee of Ministers of the Council of Europe by opposing their desire to discuss defence. The European Coal and Steel Community went ahead without Britain. Shortly afterwards came the escape of Burgess and Maclean and the nationalization of the Anglo-Iranian oil-fields by Dr Moussadegh of Iran, an event which provoked Morrison unwisely to talk of 'sharp and forceful action' in Palmerstonian vein. He ordered a naval demonstration in the Persian Gulf while at the same time accusing the Tories of imperialism. Eden observed of Morrison's speech during the emergency debate on Iran, 'there never has been in my judgement a speech more unworthy of the office.' By the beginning of October Attlee removed the problem from the excitable hands of Morrison and Shinwell, the Minister of Defence, by handing it over to the United Nations. The *Sunday Times* was exaggerating when it described this unhappy affair as 'the worst defeat suffered by Great Britain during the present century in the field of foreign affairs', but Morrison's inept handling of both this and an outbreak of Egyptian hostility over the Canal and Sudan was highly damaging to the government's prestige.

The sands were running out. There was a huge trade gap and current-account deficit; and since 1950 prices of imports had risen 42 per cent as against a price rise of 18 per cent in exports. Now, in addition, there was the added cost of replacing the Iranian oil supplies. Yet the imposition of tough measures, including especially import controls, might well have enabled Labour to ride the immediate crisis and retain its hold on office, albeit with its tiny majority, had the will been really there. Had Gaitskell and Bevan, to say nothing of Attlee and Morrison, known that they would never again enjoy the fruits of office they might well have stiffened their resolution. But Labour was now a divided party. The art of governing competently and soberly, which appealed well enough to Attlee and Gaitskell, as it had to Cripps, held little appeal for those concerned primarily with a drastic reordering of society. As a consequence, it would be the Conservatives who on taking office immediately scaled down rearmament and tackled the balance of payments and so reaped the fruits of austerity to which Labour felt itself entitled.

It mattered, of course, a good deal how you happened to view austerity. A comparison of the weekly food ration in July 1945 with that prevailing in October 1951, as the election was about to take place, was decidedly revealing:

	July 1945	October 1951
Butter	2 oz	3 oz
Bacon and Ham	3 oz	3 oz
Cheese	2 oz	$1\frac{1}{2}$ oz
Margarine	4 oz	4 oz
Cooking fat	1 oz	2 oz
Tea	2 oz	2 oz
Sugar	8 oz	10 oz

There was slightly less meat on the ration in 1951.

The 1951 Labour manifesto contained no mention of either socialism or socialists. That of the Tories proclaimed their intention to change the whole climate of opinion towards enterprise and hard work. The Labour manifesto promised 'to maintain the present rate of 200,000 new houses a year'; the Tories promised (and achieved) 300,000. The Tories emphasized the steep rise in the cost of living, which according to Gallup, was the main concern of 56 per cent of the voters; Labour, much aided by the *Daily Mirror*, paraded the alleged bellicosity of the Tories,

Dr Somerville Hastings telling his electors: 'Vote Tory and reach for a rifle. Vote Labour and reach old age.' In general, it was another quiet election, *The Times* commenting that the Tories seemed 'to be campaigning to avoid losing votes rather than riding out to win them'. But the same newspaper headed its election leader 'Time for a Change', and this was reflected in a narrow outcome on October 25 whereby the Tories gained twenty seats from Labour and three from the Liberals, with Scotland evenly balanced at thirty-five Labour seats, thirty-five Conservatives and one Liberal. Despite the Conservative majority Labour secured a higher percentage of the total vote – 48·8 per cent to 48·0 per cent Conservative. This time there were only ten Communist candidates, all of whom lost their deposits; and the Liberals, who indirectly assisted the Conservatives by fielding only 109 candidates, were reduced to six seats. The placards proclaimed in large letters: 'Churchill Wins'. The Attlee years were over. Attlee's former public relations adviser, Francis Williams, had seemed to pronounce their epitaph in the summer of 1950: 'In the last ten years the proportion of the national income distributed in wages has risen sharply. That going in profits has fallen considerably. And that going in salaries has remained fairly stable. In fact, it is now almost certainly true that this process of redistribution has gone as far as it can.' As an explanation this would not, however, have remotely satisfied D. N. Pritt, who considered that Attlee's government had betrayed everything for which it stood, leaving class relations, capitalist power and working-class conditions scarcely altered in five years of full power and six of government. Nor was Crossman happy as he confided to his diary what it was no longer easy to conceal: 'Already there is an enormous amount of concealed unemployment, with millions of people working on short time.'

As in politics, so among the higher reaches of the opinion formers, there were signs that the easy dominance of the Left was being eroded. Reviewing a new edition of the collected works of Lytton Strachey in 1949, the young Noel Annan complained that intellectuals 'prefer fashionable irrationalism and believe in original sin'. You were liable, he felt, to be distrusted and despised in the world of ideas if you believed that you could make people better by appealing to their reason. However, there were many who felt that the origins and conduct of the Second World War were scarcely a vindication of human rationality. In the light of such an experience, T. S. Eliot in *Four Quartets* had a receptive audience for ideas owing nothing to visions of a brave new world, such as: 'The only wisdom we can hope to acquire is the wisdom of humility.' Jung was beginning to rival Freud, and Barth's black pessimism about the human situation became more fashionable than the social gospel of William Temple. The Professor of Physical Chemistry at Manchester University, Michael Polanyi, was calling for 'a new enlightenment to re-assert the spiritual life of man and to reinterpret it in spiritual terms'. The popularity of *Brideshead Revisited* was a curious tribute to a writer to whom most post-war values were actively repugnant. There were no reassuring sounds from W. H. Auden and in Orwell, to progressive eyes, there was something of a Janus quality. Cyril Connolly came to the conclusion that 'the sole outstanding Socialist writer remains J. B. Priestley,' and Malcolm Muggeridge's diary entry for 6 July 1950 reads: 'It is encouraging that nowadays one finds the adventurous, alive, young men on the right rather than on the left.' Even the despised Victorians, buried deeply and without ceremony by Lytton Strachey, made a surprise comeback in a prolonged radio series called *Ideas and Beliefs of the Victorians* on the Third Programme, the BBC's cultural waveband. In one of his contributions to the series, Harold Laski saw the Victorian era as a 'natural prelude to the swifter and more massive collectivism which, with its socialist emphasis, is the foundation of our own social effort', a striking example of the Whig interpretation of history. But the general tone of the series could be described as one of puzzled admiration. An enthusiast for all things Victorian was a youngish poet with a growing coterie, John Betjeman. He countered Le Corbusier's *Perspectives Humaines* with its brave new world outlook, with irreverent mockery, as in *The Planster's Vision*:

> I have a Vision of the Future, chum,
> The workers' flats in fields of soya beans
> Tower up like silver pencils, score on score;
> And Singing Millions hear the Challenge come
> From microphones in communal canteens
> 'No Right! No Wrong! All's perfect, evermore.'

If the new architecture was to be taken as illustrative of the planned society, then opinions differed. Peter Shepheard, one prominent architect, proclaimed a renaissance of English architecture to be at hand in 1950, while another, W. G. Holford, thought that the majority of the post-war structures were 'heavy examples of overbuilding, forever unlovely and unlovable'. If Le Corbusier was right in describing town planning as 'the social matrix *par excellence* . . . the true expression of the material and spiritual conditions of an epoch', then many took alarm at what they saw going on around or, more precisely, above them. It was not only in Middlesbrough that there was a gap between promise and performance.

Gone too was the 'committed' theatre of the late Thirties, the era of *Trial of a Judge* and *The Dance of Death*. A surfeit of revivals was punctuated by the striking emergence of two Christian and conservative dramatists, writing their plays in verse – Christopher Fry and T. S. Eliot. 'The enterprise,' says Private Meadows in Fry's *A Sleep of Prisoners*, 'is exploration into God.'* ; and Eliot's psychiatrist in *The Cocktail Party* tells his friends that 'only by acceptance of the past will you alter its meaning.' The exuberance of Fry's verbosity had about it a pyrotechnic quality which dazzled more than it endured, but Eliot, who received both a Nobel prize and the Order of Merit in 1948, was now enjoying unrivalled prestige in literary circles on both sides of the Atlantic. He had little to say in praise of social democracy and its idealisms. In *Notes Towards the Definition of Culture* (1948) in particular Eliot directed shafts of irony at a number of beliefs which were the accepted wisdom of the day. In discussing equality of opportunity in education, he pointed out that for every mute inglorious Milton, overlooked by the system, we may have saved ourselves from several Cromwells *guilty* of their country's blood. If you are serious about equality of opportunity you must ensure that no family fortune, no advantages due to the foresight, self-sacrifice or ambition of parents, are allowed to affect the educational process. The editor of *The Times Educational Supplement*, H. C. Dent, had written

* Fry explained his revulsion from 'realism' in the theatre clearly enough in his preface to *The Lady's Not For Burning*: 'Reality? We don't perhaps bark our shins against solid furniture as it is possible to do in many plays of our time, but even furniture has an atomic dance of its own, as true, in its way, as the solidity.'

in *A New Order in English Education* that 'our ideal is a full democracy.' Eliot quietly commented: 'Full democracy is not defined; and if full democracy is attained, we should like to know what is to be our next ideal for education after this ideal has been realized.'

The popularity of an even more celebrated Nobel prize-winner than Eliot suffered something of a diminution. When the news of Bernard Shaw's death in 1950 at the age of ninety-four reached India, Nehru adjourned a cabinet meeting; but the reputation in Britain of the most spectacular of all the Fabians soon sank into a scarcely respectful oblivion which would not have been thought possible before the war.

As the schools settled down after the wartime upheavals, the only issue which aroused much passion was an ill-judged attempt by George Tomlinson to prevent any child being entered for O-level before the age of fifteen, so that the grammar school high-fliers should not steal a march on the others. In the universities, however, a number of searching questions were being asked about the nature and purpose of higher education. Walter Moberley, in *The Crisis in the University*, expressed alarm about the atomization of the old culture consequent upon the ever increasing numbers of new specialisms. Professor Blackett, then at Manchester University, came out in favour of vocational training for students, but Professor Michael Oakeshott, who succeeded Laski at the London School of Economics, took a robustly traditional view: 'The pursuit of learning, like every other great activity, is unavoidably conservative. A university is not like a dinghy which can be juggled about to catch every transient wind. . . . A university needs to beware of the patronage of this world or it will find that it has sold its birthright for a mess of pottage.' On the other hand Mr Roger Wilson, head of the department of Social Studies at the University College of Hull, urged the universities to share the moral responsibility of statutory officials and voluntary workers. They should desire to solve problems and not only to study them. He need not have worried. The day of the worldly academic had arrived with a vengeance. Provincial railway platforms, airport lounges and broadcasting studios were thronged with bustling academics, profitably released from their cloisters and eager to lecture on the problems of the day, if not necessarily to solve them. As Roy

Lewis and Angus Maude commented in *Professional People* (1952): 'Even the natives of Melanesia are left temporarily in peace, so that anthropologists can be mustered for the really vital jobs, such as mapping the social behaviour patterns of Devonshire villages and discovering whether the public house or the Ebenezer Chapel is the focal centre of an east-end slum.' The students, freed after two years from patrolling the jungles of Malaya or filling sandbags in Korea, were glad to get back to their books and for the most part worked away quietly at their studies.

Manners and morals were beginning to alter perceptibly as the age of Crippsian austerity was visibly on the wane, despite the unwelcome renewal of national belt-tightening in 1951. 1948, as we have seen, was a good year. Mr Wilson at the Board of Trade promised slightly bigger newspapers for 1949; the shops were once again allowed to hold sales; and although a lack of confidence on the part of the tobacconists still tended to keep cigarettes under the counter, 1600 million went in to the shops each week, appreciably more than in 1939. Guinness was back to its wartime strength, although you were still not allowed a full bottle of the official SDI (Soft Drinks Industry) squash unless you returned an empty one. At the luxury end of the market Sotheby's had what was called an 'exceptional sale', a 'Self-Portrait' by Rembrandt, belonging to Lord de L'Isle, going for the gigantic sum of £13,500. The National Savings Committee was still nagging the nation in the spring with the admonition: 'Nobody can compel us to save, but we ought to be clear about the fact that if we refuse to do so we are admitting that we are not to be trusted with the freedom we cherish.' But suddenly the women of Britain decided that instead of saving they would go on a bit of a spending spree.

The New Look had its effective origins in Monsieur Dior's summer collection of 1947 and the desire of innumerable women to emancipate themselves from the far from flattering sartorial severity which was a legacy of the war years. By 1948 the so-called New Look was all the rage, despite the concern, economic rather than moral, of Sir Stafford Cripps who urged the British Guild of Creative Designers to do their best to keep skirts short. Mrs Braddock, never herself the rose of fashion, was hostile to the idea of anybody bothering their heads about longer skirts, and Mrs Ridealgh, a grandmotherly Socialist who represented Ilford, went so far as to broadcast to America: 'The New Look is dead. British women deplore it.' But they were no more effective than Mrs Partington with her mop. Pearson Phillips, writing in *The Age of Austerity*, claims to have found a civil servant, called Carruthers, who finally hauled down the colours of the Board of Trade by declaring that they were unable to dictate to women the length of their skirts.

By the summer of 1948 the *Sunday Times* reported that the average length of skirts left them twelve inches off the ground and commented favourably on the Dior winged-silhouette style with top coats of 'the swinging tent type'. Harold Hobson broadcast gloomily that, 'with tent-like coats that hang from the shoulders and don't fit anywhere, blouses that bulge at the back, and dresses that look as if they are slipping down, it is obvious that this summer Britain is going to be drabber and shabbier than ever. Still, we stood bombs and we can stand fashion.' Frilled petticoats and pencil-thin umbrellas were essential accessories. Had there been much more cloth to go round, Britain might have enjoyed a sartorial extravaganza comparable to that of the Directory. The New Look was, in part, a short-lived exercise in nostalgia, and in part a protest against 25,000 controls and the ethical rigours of the National Savings movement. As such, it did an enormous amount of good for the national morale.

All wars engender mass promiscuity, but by 1948 there were no signs of post-war hedonism on the scale notorious in the Twenties. However, a considerable cultural shock was administered to the nation by the publication and mass circulation in 1948 of Kinsey's *Report on the Sexual Behaviour of the Human Male*. At once it was noticeable that the popular press adopted a markedly more explicit editorial attitude and vocabulary in the public discussion of a wide range of sexual 'problems'. It was not till 1951 that the 'X' certificate 'liberalized' the cinema, but before that a number of continental films were depicting human passions in a style markedly different from the prevalent Hollywood formulae. When *A Streetcar Named Desire* was produced on stage in 1949 with Vivien Leigh and Paul Muni, a number of susceptible occupants of the stalls required medical attention to offset their shock at what was presumed to be going on behind the curtain. *Per contra*, nobody's susceptibilities were harmed by American theatrical imports like *Oklahoma!* and *Annie Get Your Gun*, both of which were produced within two months in the spring of 1948. They were immensely popular, and more than compensated for the demise of the traditional British music hall.

Ninety per cent of British homes had a radio, although Rowntree and Lavers found in the course of their enquiries that they 'rarely met persons of the lower middle or working classes who recognized that a radio set is a device for listening to selected programmes'. George Orwell in a *Tribune* article in 1946 considered that the essential ingredients of a pleasurable existence for the masses, as encountered for instance in a Lyons Corner House, were that one should never be alone, nor do anything for oneself, nor ever be within sight of wild vegetation or natural objects, nor ever out of the sound of music. 'The music – and if possible it should be the same music for everybody – is the most important ingredient. Its function is to prevent thought and conversation, and to shut out any natural sound, such as the song of birds or the whistling of the wind, that might otherwise intrude. . . . In very many English homes the radio is literally never turned off, though it is manipulated from time to time so as to make sure that only light music will come out of it.' The Third Programme, launched in 1946 with the object of encouraging what Matthew Arnold would have described as high seriousness among the listening public, had by the end of its first year attracted one per cent of its potential audience, despite the excellence of the musical programmes on offer. The programme makers' enthusiasm for Oxford philosophers and Scottish theologians was evidently not shared by the generality of listeners, and a series of fifty unrelievedly erudite talks in celebration of Goethe's bicentenary was widely felt to be overdoing it.

The Home Service of the BBC was a more middle-brow affair, strong on current affairs and drama, generally informative and not without a hint of the moral uplift associated with the era of Sir John Reith, especially on Sundays. The Light Programme, with no cultural pretensions whatever, saw as its mission the painless entertainment of the masses. The great wartime favourite *Itma*, with Tommy Handley, survived for some years, the *Radio Times* proclaiming in 1947: 'For all the fame his sublime tomfoolery has brought him, Handley is still One of Us.' Its popularity was soon rivalled by entertainments in the same genre, like *Much-Binding-in-the-Marsh* with Richard Murdoch and Kenneth Horne or the long-running *A Visit to Water-Logged Spa at Sinking-in-the-Ooze, a Laughter Resort for All.* Three to four million women listened to *Woman's Hour* between two and three o'clock in the afternoon, absorbing perhaps with only half an ear information on subjects like 'A new hat for the New Year', 'The older woman – other people's stories', 'Beginners in the kitchen – what's gone wrong?' or 'Setting up house in Labrador'. For those who preferred a more narrative approach there was always *Mrs Dale's Diary*, of which a characteristic synopsis reads: 'Last week Sally drove down to Gimlet Green to see Francis Austin. He told her he had become engaged to Miss Pink but that they were not announcing their engagement until his mother's ring had been altered. Tony was still worrying Sally and when Dr and Mrs Dale, Bob and Mrs Freeman went to lunch with her they thought she was looking very unhappy and worried.' A rival programme called *The Robinsons*, an *Everyday Story of Everyday People*, never quite caught on. What was known as 'the younger listener of all ages' would await avidly the next instalment of *Dick Barton, Special Agent* – 'iron-fisted Dick is already part of the life of the nation.' By 1947 gardening was safe in the hands of Fred Streeter, who, although he had worked in turn for Lord Curzon, Lord Boston, Lady Henry Somerset and Lord Leconfield 'talks to millions as if he were addressing a handful of cronies in the Pied Bull'.*

Occasionally, the Light Programme would dramatize a well-known novel such as *Beau Geste* or slip in a short story (one of which was called 'Alice gets the Gastric'), but, as Orwell observed, its prime function was to provide a continuous flow of unexacting music. There was *Music While You Work, Melody Express, Family Favourites, Tango Time, Music Funfare, Rocky Mountain Rhythm* (with titles like 'The Old Cowpuncher' and 'The Yodelling Buckaroo'). There were frequent military bands and for the dancers the seductive strains of Victor Silvester and his Ballroom Orchestra (with ten-minute instructional interludes). But above all, there was the BBC theatre organ in the hands of performers like Sandy Macpherson, Robinson Cleaver and Reginald Foorte, who could be relied on to fill any gap in the

* *Radio Times*, 25 April 1947.

day's programme with Ketelby's *Sanctuary of the Heart* or the Grand March from *Tannhäuser* or, in more playful mood, *Fairy Tiptoe* or *The Wee MacGregor* or *L'Amour, Toujours L'Amour*. A particular favourite (at any rate with the organists) was the aptly named *Consoling the Console*.

By 1950 it is possible to discern the beginnings of a more sophisticated approach to popular broadcasting. That summer there was an enterprising programme in which Wynford Vaughan Thomas conducted listeners along Watling Street from Rochester to Canterbury 'linking the sights and sounds of today with the echoes of history', a process which found Richard Dimbleby in the the Royal Marine Barracks, Chatham; Raymond Baxter on the roof of a paper factory; Brian Johnston in a cherry tree; and John Arlott at a game of Bat and Trap. Relatively serious plays were now to be heard on the Light Programme as well as on the Home Service. *A Book at Bedtime* featured *Animal Farm* read by Leonard Sachs, and Richard Dimbleby won the *Daily Mail* award as 'Voice of the Year', observing: 'I enjoy it all, but between you and me, my idea of heaven is to run a little dairy farm.'

A programme called *Round Britain Quiz* was to set a style of entertainment which was to be remorselessly reduplicated through subsequent decades. It was instrumental also in creating the first really popular folk hero of post-war radio (and later television) in Gilbert Harding. Erratic, psychologically insecure and frequently inebriated, he was less obviously donnish than the giants of the wartime Brains Trusts like C. E. M. Joad, Julian Huxley or Kingsley Martin, purveying something of what we might today call pop culture. He was often a great conveyor of the contemporary cant, as when he referred to the Indian Civil Service as chinless idiots and the British Empire as an evil thing.

One of the more lively young Labour members, Woodrow Wyatt, frequently urged the government to accelerate the development of television. He pointed out that this was yet another example of the Americans enjoying the fruits of British technological invention, which we seemed powerless to exploit. By early 1948 there were 45,564 television licences; a year later this figure had risen to 188,356, as opposed to three million in the USA. Answering a question in the House, C. R. Hobson, the

Assistant Postmaster General, said that further development had to be subordinated to the export drive, which tended to be all too frequently a stock answer on the part of the government if anybody urged modernization. In 1950 the energetic BBC controller Norman Collins resigned in order to start the battle for commercial television. At a time when television was sweeping the USA, Drew Middleton was amused to hear a characteristically British upper-class reaction: 'We have one for Nanny and the children, but we never watch it. Frightfully tedious most of it.' However, the largest and most advanced transmitter in the world was now in service at Sutton Coldfield and by 1951 5 per cent of the population were enabled to watch in their parlour the reassuring features of Viscount Samuel making the first televised election address (on behalf of the Liberals), or the extremely elderly comedian Jack Hulbert performing, in *The Golden Years*, the first musical comedy written for television. By the time the Conservatives were in office television was taking off, even Scotland having its own transmitter at Kirk o'Shotts.

The circumambient gloom of post-war Britain was lightened symbolically in 1949 when on 4 April Mr Shinwell restored display and floodlighting by turning on a switch at Tooting and declaring: 'Let the lights of London remain for all time.' It was a long and beautiful summer preceded by the warmest Easter of the century. The Easter parade in Hyde Park was the first since the end of clothes rationing and heavily attended. It was described as informal, though 'hardly a woman in the Park wore slacks or sandals'. In May six hundred debutantes were presented at court, of which a third came from the Dominions. It was the year when the whole nation was humming the Harry Lime theme from *The Third Man,* and you could see the first performance since the war of *The Ring* with Kirsten Flagstad. It was also the year of *Nineteen Eighty-Four* and *Love in a Cold Climate.* In the autumn Clement Attlee laid the foundation stone of the Festival Hall, burying under it a copy of *The Times,* some coins and a copy of the score of Britten's *Amo Ergo Sum,* a cantata written for the wedding of the Earl of Harewood and the future Mrs Jeremy Thorpe.

It was in December 1947 that Herbert Morrison put an end to much speculation by announcing the government's intention to go ahead with the plan to stage a centenary exhibition in 1951 on twenty-seven acres of the South Bank. In the unpropitious circumstances of 1943 the Royal Society of Arts had drawn attention to the forthcoming centenary of the Great Exhibition, but a letter to *The Times* from John Gloag, shortly followed by an open letter to Cripps from Gerald Barry, set the ball rolling properly in 1945. Barry was a New Statesmanlike figure who had invented the famous 'This England' column and had edited *The Weekend Review* before it was subsumed in the *New Statesman*. A gregarious man who married four times, he was something of a hero in Fleet Street and the intellectual clubs as a result of having emerged creditably from a public row with Lord Beaverbrook. He was a good choice as Director of the Festival which, as Michael Frayn wittily demonstrates in *The Age of Austerity*, was essentially a concept of the radical middle classes. Nobody took very seriously the jolly populism of the claim put forward by Barry and the other organizers: 'We envisage this as the people's show, not organized arbitrarily for them to enjoy, but put on largely by them, by us all, as an expression of a way of life in which we believe.' The Festival was the extension and visible expression of the wartime Army Bureau of Current Affairs series called *The British Way and Purpose*. The organizers, particularly Hugh Casson, the architectural director, overcame appalling difficulties – erratic financing, shortage of essential materials and sustained vituperation in the Beaverbrook press – with remarkable persistence and ingenuity. The South Bank site was virtually completed on time for the official opening on 3 May after the wettest spring since 1870, an achievement the rarity value of which was to become all too clear in the decades which lay ahead. Even the Pleasure Gardens and Fun Fair in Battersea Park were only three weeks late. It was all to be seen as 'a challenge to the sloughs of the present and a shaft of confidence cast forth against the future'; or, as Noël Coward put it less imposingly in the *Lyric Revue*:

> Clear the national decks, my lads,
> Everyone of us counts,
> Grab the travellers' cheques, my lads,
> And pray that none of them bounce.
> Face the future undismayed
> Pray for further Marshall Aid

And have the toast from *Cavalcade*
Drastically rewritten.

On the whole the cynics were confounded. Professor Albert
Richardson's prediction that large numbers of visitors would be
drowned in the Thames was falsified and nobody paid attention
to him when he talked of the festering, as opposed to the Festival
of Britain. More and more visitors enjoyed the originality of
design and lay-out, the bright primary colours and skilful vistas.
In Frayn's phrase, the dominant impression was one of 'pre-
stressed concrete *élan*', but there was much ingenious contri-
vance in glass, aluminium, plastic, canvas and wood. To be
found everywhere were striped umbrellas and open air cafés,
dispensing the most fearful food. There were real huskies in the
Polar Theatre, and in the Lion and Unicorn Pavilion, designed
to portray what was called 'The British Character', you were
confronted by the two heraldic beasts, constructed in plaited
straw, pulling a rope which opened a cage which emitted white
plaster doves. Less abstruse symbolism was to be found in
Battersea Park, where there was a Guinness clock and an Emmett
railway of the type now seen on British Airways murals, as well
as young ladies, dressed like Nell Gwynn, selling oranges. The
Arts Council, the descendant of Keynes's wartime Council for
the Encouragement of Music and the Arts, allowed itself a great
surge of patronage in connection with the Festival. It commissioned work from twenty-four sculptors, including Jacob Ep-
stein, Barbara Hepworth and Henry Moore, and sixty painters,
including Graham Sutherland and John Piper, as well as Lucien
Freud, Ivon Hitchens and Claude Rogers, who were each commissioned to produce paintings of at least forty-five by sixty
inches. Choral music was commissioned from Dyson, Bax and
Rawsthorne, and opera was to be represented by Benjamin
Britten and five other composers. Subsidized performances of
Fry's *A Sleep of Prisoners* took place in churches up and down
the country, and Laurence Olivier and Vivien Leigh appeared
not only in *Antony and Cleopatra*, but also in *Caesar and
Cleopatra*. The BBC, not to be outdone, devoted 2700 programmes to the subject of the Festival. By 1 October when the
proceedings finally closed with community singing led by Gracie
Fields, 8,455,863 people had visited the South Bank. Then

suddenly the cloud-capped Skylon, the gorgeous Dome, the whole insubstantial pageant was dissolved, leaving not a rack behind, except the Festival Hall and the Battersea Fun Fair.

In July 1948 an act was passed which aroused little or no interest as compared with the Berlin blockade started by the Russians the same week, yet which may be seen by future historians as being more influential in changing British society than any other measure enacted during the lifetime of the Labour government. This was the British Nationality Act, which replaced the phrase 'British subject' by 'citizen of the United Kingdom and the colonies'. Had it been realized that as soon as 1961 nearly a quarter of the citizens of Kensington and Paddington would have been born abroad, the matter might have been handled more cautiously. George Orwell, writing in *Tribune* in November 1946 on the subject of the immigration of foreign (not coloured) labour into Britain, complained that the government was not telling people with sufficient clarity, 'what is happening, and why, and what may be expected to happen in the near future. . . . The fact is that there is a strong popular feeling in this country against foreign immigration.' The Trade Union movement was overtly hostile to the importation of Italian miners or the employment of Poles in the mines or on the land, on the other hand it was opposed to any form of colour bar. By 1949 it was calculated that the coloured population, overwhelmingly at this stage West Indian by origin, was only 25,000, of which 7000 were in Cardiff and 8000 in Liverpool*; and by 1951 the figure had only risen slightly and included few women. But even on this scale, the new arrivals were an object of curiosity and some apprehension, given the fact that a wartime survey had shown that 95 per cent of the population had no first-hand knowledge of coloured people. A careful study of West Indian workers in Liverpool between 1941 and 1951, carried out by A. H. Richmond, concluded somewhat bleakly: 'Whatever the results of further research may be, the present study conclusively proves that there is widespread colour prejudice in Britain.' Riots in Liverpool over the August Bank Holiday weekend in 1948 had ended in court cases, in which the police had not come out particularly well. Four years later two Jamaicans, Dr

* In both Cardiff and Liverpool there was a long-established black population, mainly descended from sailors who had jumped ship.

Clarence Senior and Dr Douglas Manley, produced an official report on Jamaican immigration to Britain, in which they concluded that one-third of the British population was tolerant of coloured people, one-third mildly prejudiced and one-third extremely prejudiced. A problem lay ahead, calling, like many others which would confront the incoming Conservatives, for a far-sighted solution.

· 5 ·
Tory Men and Whig Measures

'But meanwhile all these Treasury Knights and Knights-to-be stood in purposive array on my chess-board ready to move against our economic problems – as only such pieces are permitted to move – in more than one direction.' R. A. BUTLER

'This goes ill. The water looks cold to some of them. They prefer a genteel bankruptcy, *force majeure* being the plea. Yours sincerely, Micawber.'
OLIVER LYTTELTON TO R. A. BUTLER, FEBRUARY 1952

'Political necessities sometimes turn out to be political mistakes.' GEORGE BERNARD SHAW

AFTER THE CONSERVATIVES' NARROW VICTORY at the polls, *The Times* commented: 'Precisely because their majority is so small Mr Churchill and his ministers must see themselves less as a party than as a national Government.' It was an attitude which exactly mirrored the convictions of the leading Conservative politicians as they charted a course which was to give them a longer period in office than they had enjoyed since the days of Lord Liverpool. Out of office, Churchill had continuously criticized what he regarded as the divisive social policies of Labour, whom he accused of imperilling the organic unity of the nation. He was always at pains to emphasize his oneness with the British working man, notably in a speech at Woodford Green in 1948 when he said: 'I have always been a firm supporter of British trade unionism,' or, again, at Wanstead in 1951: 'Let the Socialists dismiss from their minds these malicious tales that a Conservative government would be hostile to the mining community. I have always affirmed that those who work in these hard and dangerous conditions, far from the light of the sun, have the right to receive exceptional benefits from the nation which they serve.' Almost immediately after the election, Churchill told the House that what the nation needed was several years of quiet, steady administration, 'if only to allow socialist legislation to reach its full fruition'. This attitude derived not only from his personal vision of his own role as being largely above party politics, but also from a belief, not justified in the event, that the economic situation was precarious to the point of being virtually irredeemable. On taking office, he told Lyttelton, Salisbury and Macmillan that he had seen a Treasury minute to the effect that the position was almost out of control and that the country had lost its way. Destiny seemed to have called him back to save the country once again, as in 1940. But he was now nearly seventy-seven, had had two minor strokes and was increasingly deaf. Lyttelton described him as having the tired look of a trawler captain who has got into harbour after a buffeting. There seemed to him no point in exacerbating the difficulties of his situation by the adoption of radical or provocative policies. His unfulfilled ambition was to mastermind one more great summit which would reconcile the two super-powers, so that the great war-leader at the end of his long course might receive the supreme accolade of the master architect of the peace. In this role he could hope to transcend party. This aspiration appeared to be amply justified in 1953 and again in 1954 on the occasion of succeeding visits to the USA. In 1953 Tom O'Brien, a Labour member and president of the TUC, was publicly upbraided by his General Council for sending Churchill a message to the effect that he carried with him the goodwill of the workers of Britain in his 'courageous mission'; and in 1954 David Logan, member for a Liverpool slum constituency, who was eighty-two and had been in the House for twenty-five years, said: 'I do not know any leader – and I have read a lot of history and have never found one – who is so prominent and whose word will count so much in the bringing of peace to the world as the present Prime Minister.'

In an attempt to recreate the cohesive and politically neutral spirit of wartime government one of Churchill's first acts was to institute a system of 'overlords', or ministers co-ordinating several departments, his choice falling on old colleagues of those years like Lords Woolton, Leathers and Cherwell and Sir John Anderson (who refused), none of whom had been career politicians in the accepted sense. Similarly, when Churchill found the Defence portfolio too much to carry in addition to his other duties, he summoned Field Marshal Lord Alexander of Tunis from Canada, who proved to be as uncontroversial as he was ineffective. Another prominent soldier, Lord Ismay, was for a short time Commonwealth Secretary. No aspect of the 'overlord' arrangement, which Attlee had briefly considered and rejected, was a success and it had to be abandoned by September 1953.

Given the philosophy and predilections of its most prominent members, there was no danger of the government proving anything but conciliatory and pragmatic in outlook, as anxious as Herbert Morrison himself to dig in and consolidate. Anthony Eden's reputation, with Suez still in the future, stood high both nationally and in Parliament. Uniquely knowledgeable about foreign affairs, industrious and patriotic, his stance, in so far as he had one, on domestic affairs was that of a moderate on the far left of the party, a proponent, like Macmillan and Butler, of the 'middle way'. Broadcasting in his pleasant, cultured voice to what he always called 'my friends', he had an almost unique capacity for avoiding the memorable. For six months in 1953 Eden was *hors de combat* with three major stomach operations, a circumstance which, for the second time (the first being the death of George VI in February 1952), encouraged Churchill to continue as Prime Minister, even after he himself had had a major stroke in the summer of 1953. Neither Churchill in the final, nor Eden in the penultimate phase of their careers were concerned with upsetting what was rapidly becoming something very like a post-war political consensus.

In no way was this more evident than in another of Churchill's surprise 'non-political' appointments – that of Sir Walter Monckton to be Minister of Labour. It had been widely expected that this key post would go to Sir David Maxwell Fyfe, a Scots lawyer of prodigious industry and a photographic memory who had made a great reputation for himself as deputy to his former pupil, Sir Hartley Shawcross, at the Nuremberg trials, where he had dominated even Goering. He had shown himself to be an astonishing master of the minutiae of Parliamen-

tary business, having made 178 speeches in six months in connection with Labour's Transport Bill. In a Party Political
Broadcast he had firmly proclaimed Conservative opposition to
the closed shop and the political levy, but had generally pledged
the party to a policy of co-operation with the unions. In a
subsequent broadcast he went even further than this in saying
that a Conservative government would introduce no trade union
legislation without prior trade union agreement. This was glee-
fully seized on by Herbert Morrison and triggered off much
argument and uproar over the principles involved, thus rein-
forcing Churchill's conviction that any form of confrontation
with the unions would be awkward and uncomfortable. A more
sure-footed figure would be needed at the Ministry of Labour,
so Maxwell Fyfe became Home Secretary and in 1954 Lord
Chancellor. Thus, yet another non-political appointment was
made, with momentous consequences both for the party and the
nation. During a sea voyage to New York in 1946 Lawther and
Deakin had twitted Churchill about the insuperable difficulty he
would find in choosing among his colleagues a Minister of Labour
who could expect to command the respect of the trade unions as
Bevin had during the war. 'I think I know a man I can persuade,'
said Churchill. He had in mind a very different sort of barrister
from Maxwell Fyfe in the person of Sir Walter Monckton, who
at the age of sixty had just entered the House at a February 1951
by-election necessitated by the death of Oliver Stanley. Monckton, one of a brilliant generation of Edwardian undergraduates
at Balliol, had served with distinction in the Great War, despite,
or perhaps because of, wearing a monocle in the front-line
trenches, and thereafter had acted as confidant and adviser to
Edward VIII during the Abdication crisis and to the Nizam of
Hyderabad. An Anglican and a friend of Stafford Cripps, he
combined a high concern for good causes with a lucrative practice and an expensive life-style. His role in public life was essentially that of a conciliator, somewhat akin, *ceteris paribus*, to that
of Lord Goodman in our own day. It was noted with approval
that he always took his hat off to the cleaning ladies, and even if
the middle way were a tightrope he could be guaranteed to walk
it. Muggeridge labelled him as belonging essentially to 'the
Duke of Windsor – personal contacts, let's try and understand
the other fellow's point of view school, now totally obsolete';

and the former Tory Chief Whip, David Margesson, wrote to his successor James Stuart – 'What are you doing with that old oil-can in the Cabinet?' When summoned by Churchill, Monckton expected to be offered a Law office. Instead, Churchill said: 'Oh, my dear, I can't spare you for that. I have the worst job in the cabinet for you.' So Walter Monckton became Minister of Labour and National Service, the Prime Minister explaining that he had been selected because he had no political past and Monckton observing ruefully that he evidently had no political future either. His biographer held that, throughout his four years at the Ministry, he was in a state of chronic and self-consuming anxiety. He told his Parliamentary Private Secretary, C. I. Orr Ewing (a Harrovian, like both Churchill and Monckton), when the latter reported for duty, that they were there purely to conciliate and keep the peace. He was understandably immensely popular with Trade Union leaders, whom he used to entertain at the Aperitif Grill in Jermyn Street. Arthur Deakin told a delegate conference in 1953 that 'we have been able to do things which were difficult to do when our own people were at the Ministry.'

Labour's Ministry of Local Government and Planning was significantly renamed by Churchill the Ministry of Housing and Local Government, so as to emphasize the importance of Housing and diminish that of Planning. Whatever else happened, it was essential to meet the electoral pledge of 300,000 houses a year, housing being, as the 1951 election manifesto had put it, the 'first of the social services'. It was an inspired choice on Churchill's part to put Harold Macmillan in charge. It was a gamble with his career and the gamble came off, since on 1 December 1953 Macmillan was able to announce that the magic target had been reached. This achievement owed much to his ability to mastermind the legislative programme and his flair for public relations, but also to an able team of subordinates, such as Ernest Marples and Dame Evelyn Sharp. Macmillan had not particularly shone in Opposition, but from now on his rise to a position of supremacy in the Party became increasingly predictable. The political popularity of the housing drive was palpable, and altogether obscured the relative paucity of industrial building and the disastrous, long-term consequences of a continued failure of nerve over rent restriction.

Another successful appointment was that of Churchill's old friend, Oliver Lyttelton, who had hoped for the Treasury, to the Colonial Office. No great parliamentarian and greatly disliked by many on the Opposition benches, Lyttelton was something of a wit and cynic and an expert mimic of the staider members of his party, such as Lord Woolton. But he was forceful and able, with a good record behind him in the wartime coalition and possessed of first-hand knowledge of business and industry. As such, he seemed to Butler the obvious candidate for the Chancellorship instead of himself. Lyttelton, like so many of Churchill's associates, had strayed into politics more from a sense of duty (both he and Monckton suffered considerable financial loss by so doing) than by way of vocation. He was anxious to slip out of harness as soon as he could, but in his three years of office achieved more than most of his colleagues. He was a robust and convinced Conservative and as such readily distinguishable from many of his colleagues.

Another revealing example of Churchill's desire to transcend conventional party allegiances in forming his last government was his plan to make Clement Davies, leader of the six strong Liberal rump in the House, Minister of Education. That would not have been a good appointment because of Clement Davies's drinking habits, but in any case the Liberal party refused to let him off the leash. Churchill consequently substituted a rather severe spinster lady called Florence Horsburgh. Miss Horsburgh had earned some notoriety before the war in her constituency in Dundee by trying to prevent the drinking of methylated spirits and suggesting that, if food were short, people could always boil up bones for soup and then hand them on to the next door house. With the brilliant Sir John Maud as Permanent Secretary and Kenneth Pickthorn, a peculiarly astringent Cambridge don, as her parliamentary deputy, Florence Horsburgh suffered from a good many odious comparisons before being replaced by Sir David Eccles in 1954. She was not allowed into the Cabinet until 1953, becoming then the first woman to be a Conservative cabinet minister, only just over twenty years before the first woman became prime minister. She was to spend most of her time trying to accommodate a huge bulge of postwar babies in overcrowded primary schools, while Pickthorn gloomily concerned himself with Wales and cases arising from teachers' misconduct.

Churchill's original cabinet was far from youthful, having an average age of fifty-nine, with Peter Thorneycroft at the Board of Trade the youngest at forty-two, and the new Lord Chancellor, Viscount Simonds, touching seventy. Of the younger generation of Conservatives knocking at the door, Iain Macleod succeeded Crookshank at the Ministry of Health in 1952 after a brilliant debating foray against Bevan; Reginald Maudling became Economic Secretary to the Treasury in the same year; David Eccles, Duncan Sandys and Alan Lennox-Boyd were all promoted in 1954; and Edward Heath became a Junior Lord of the Treasury in 1955. To outward seeming, there was still an observable aura of pre-war Conservative politics among the survivors of the 'old gang' with their black coats, striped trousers and discreet gold watch-chains. But it was no accident on Churchill's part that key positions were held by men on the far left of the party – Eden, Macmillan, and the enigmatic Chancellor of the Exchequer, R. A. Butler.

When Churchill offered Butler the Chancellorship he told him that Eden and he had thought the matter over carefully and concluded that Butler would be best at handling the Commons – 'in this crisis of our island life, when the cottage homes could so easily be engulfed in penury and want, we must not allow class or party to be needlessly inflamed. . . . It's no great matter that you are not an economist. I wasn't either.' Churchill was not entirely confident on this last point, presumably recalling that his own tenure of the Exchequer had not been the most distinguished phase of his career. Consequently he saddled Butler with a so-called Minister of State for Economic Affairs in the person of Sir Arthur Salter, an elderly economist who had been an early convert to Keynesianism and had sat for many years as Independent MP for Oxford University. Salter bombarded Butler for thirteen months with memoranda written in green ink, after which time his services were dispensed with. The new Chancellor considered himself better served by his phalanx of Treasury Knights headed by Sir Edward Bridges, Sir Robert Hall and, until 1953, the arch-planner Sir Edwin Plowden.

The only specific economic pledge to which the Conservatives had committed themselves at the election was once again a striking example of the acute sensibility which Churchill and Eden felt about maintaining national unity at all costs. An Excess

Profits Levy was to be introduced, so as to ensure that there would be no talk of hard-faced capitalists profiting from the rearmament programme necessitated by the Korean War. Whatever the merits of such a measure, it was not of any significance in averting ruin from 'the cottage homes'. They, as well as the rest of the country, were believed to be in imminent peril from the currently large balance of payments deficit, there being nothing more calculated to disturb Treasury equanimity than a balance of payments deficit. Butler recorded that, at his first encounter as Chancellor with Bridges and his new Private Secretary, William Armstrong, in the gruelling circumstances of a rationed lunch at the Athenaeum, their talk was of 'blood draining from the system and a collapse graver than had been foretold in 1931'. Butler picked up the metaphor in a broadcast early in 1952: 'The crisis is the one you would be in, if you went on spending more than you were earning. We really are up against it. Our life-blood is draining away and we have got to stop it.' Things were beginning to look black again. Macabre recipes were once more the vogue, such as sheep's head, 'Poor Man's Goose' (half a sheep's liver, some bacon, powdered sage and boiled onion), and prune mould. If you tired of 'Poor Man's Goose' you could try 'Savoury Duck', of which the main constituents were $1\frac{1}{2}$ pounds of sheep's fry, $\frac{3}{4}$ of a pound of lights and 3 onions. Austerity threatened to be the permanent condition of the nation.

Christopher Hollis, a notably independent backbencher, complained in September 1952 that 'in all essential matters the two parties are the same. Mr Butler's financial policies are the same as those of Sir Stafford Cripps.' Labour and Conservatives alike, he felt, were 'like two old sieves arguing which of them has the most holes, or two lunatics trying to settle which of them really is Napoleon'. But precisely as he spoke, the age of austerity was coming to and end and the British, or at any rate the greater part of them, were about to experience an atmosphere of unaccustomed affluence.

The fact was that the Conservatives inherited a deficit of £700 million on the balance of payments, which, thirteen years later when they left office, amounted to £750 million. The deficit was predominantly due to the unrealistically large rearmament programme and a large overall worsening of the terms of trade between 1950 and 1951 of twelve per cent, with import prices rising 33 per cent. The rearmament programme was cut, as Harold Wilson had said it would have to be, and then miraculously, as it seemed, the terms of trade improved by 6 per cent between 1951 and 1952 and by another 6 per cent the following year. From early in 1952 to the latter part of 1954 the trend of import prices was so generally favourable that the country had £400 million available to spend abroad without raising a finger. By the end of 1952 there was already a surplus on the balance of payments of £300 million.

Given the complexities of international finance, it was not altogether surprising that the credit for this happy state of affairs largely accrued in the eyes of the man in the street to the evidently ingenious Chancellor of the Exchequer, whose successive budgets between 1952 and 1954 were introduced with an effective combination of almost impenetrable economic density and a wealth of homely metaphor (mostly meteorological). On assuming office he began by imposing import controls, cutting food subsidies, restricting hire purchase, slashing foreign travel allowances and increasing the bank rate from 2 to 2½ per cent, which was the first time it had been increased since before the war (there would be twenty-six more changes in the next twelve years). By 1953 the outlook seemed to have improved so much that his April budget was the first since the end of the war to contain neither proposals for new taxes nor increases in existing ones. Not unnaturally, the government captured Sunderland from Labour in a by-election the following month. Nobody much bothered by then that it was proving necessary to import large quantities of coal from the Saar and Lorraine, although in some sections of the press this was likened to England having to hire foreigners to complete a cricket team against Australia, a practice which would not then have been condoned.

Indeed, in June 1954 Butler went so far as to speculate in public: 'Why should we not aim to double our standard of living in the next twenty-five years and still have our money as valuable then as now?' That neither of these aspirations was to be realized was a consequence of the largely bi-partisan system of economic management described by *The Economist* as Butskellism. Since, far earlier than might have been expected, Britain was able to enjoy a return to prosperity under the shelter of a world economy undergoing a steady and unprecedented expansion, it was irresistibly tempting to postpone politically difficult decisions. In a leading article the day after the coronation of Elizabeth II, entitled 'And After', *The Times* commented prophetically that present ease was being subsidized by future penury and that neither political party was facing up to the gravity of rampant restrictive practices and the widespread disinclination for hard work, which seemed increasingly to characterize what Lord Nuffield called a nation in semi-retirement. American visitors had no difficulty in detecting what was wrong. M. J. Wiener, in his *English Culture and the Decline of the Industrial Spirit 1850–1980*, quotes the Minister for Economic Affairs at the US Embassy in 1950 as noting 'a sense of doubt concerning the social utility of industry and the legitimacy of profit, a sort of industrial inferiority complex suffered by business leaders themselves.... In the extreme, some British industrialists seem almost ashamed of their vocation.' Others noted with amazement the prevalence of price-fixing and identical tendering, and the extent to which even the most inefficient firms were guaranteed easy profit-margins. A survey in the Fifties showed that 40 per cent of British managers had only worked in one firm and 30 per cent had only made one change. A great many firms were deficient in technical skills at the managerial level, as exemplified by the fact that in 1952 only 20 per cent of directors in the engineering industry had any technical qualifications and the great majority were not even graduates.

The attitude of many recruits to business was typified by the young graduate, who told his potential business employer at interview that his first choice had been the Foreign Office, his second UNESCO, his third the BBC; this only left teaching and business and, since he hated little boys, he had finally chosen business. Nor was organized labour in much better shape to face up to a competitive world. No legislation on monopolies remotely affected trade union restrictive practices, and too many of the veteran trade union leaders continued to regard profits as merely a device for lining the bosses' pockets and new machines as a threat to job security. The workers' attitude to nationalization increasingly resembled a syndicalist conspiracy of producers against consumers. Hardly a voice was heard which cast any doubt on the permanency, let alone the desirability, of full employment, though a notable exception was Professor Arthur Lewis, Stanley Jevons Professor of Political Economy at Manchester, who warned in May 1950: 'In this respect we are living in a fool's paradise. All our political parties, for example, have sworn to guarantee full employment. Whereas the truth is that neither I nor anybody else in the world really knows how to prevent unemployment in this country. I very much doubt whether such unemployment can be prevented if there is a slump in America.' Professor F. W. Paish was considered dangerously eccentric as a result of the unfashionable frequency with which he linked full employment with inflation. The editor of *The Economist*, Geoffrey Crowther, who observed in 1950 that the British economy was beginning to resemble the brontosaurus in its inability to adapt to new conditions, called for some sort of penalty for inefficiency if we were ever to restore efficiency, but nobody could see what that might be. It was noted widely how difficult it was to get good foremen, as their differentials were eroded and their status lowered. The future lay with the sterile concept of the struggle on the shopfloor with the employer.

R. A. Butler was, of course, far too percipient not to be aware of the dangers Britain faced as first Germany and then Japan began to re-enter world markets. Although we were still dis-mantling German factories as late as 1950, the Germans and their European partners were taking off at a prodigious speed. In the period between 1950 and 1954 British exports increased 6 per cent, while those of the EEC countries increased 76 per cent. Indeed in 1952 exports, especially in terms of the rapidly declining textile industry, actually fell, but since raw material prices were also falling and stockpiling levelled off, the balance of payments looked healthy enough. Butler's first two attempts to get at the root causes of the nation's problems both resulted in frustrating defeats, which strikingly illustrate the lack of realism with which he had to contend. Convinced by the argu-ments of Leslie Rowan, one of the ablest of the Treasury civil servants, he proposed to abolish exchange controls and let the pound find its true value on the open market. Operation Robot, as it was called, had the wholehearted support of Oliver Lyttelton and of the Governor of the Bank of England, Lord Cobbold, and evoked some sympathy from Churchill, but was effectively quashed by Eden, together with veterans like Salter,

Lord Swinton, the Chancellor of the Duchy of Lancaster, and Lord Cherwell, the Paymaster-General. It was a measure, the merits of which were open to dispute, but the known opposition to it of the Shadow Chancellor, Gaitskell, and the Labour party, meant that its implementation would have threatened the relatively comfortable consensus which endured till 1955. Gaitskell's biographer makes it clear that the matter of exchange controls was one of the most significant differences between Gaitskell and Butler. The collapse of Operation Robot underlined the disinclination of the government to kick up political dust. As Gaitskell wrote: 'Butler is on the extreme left of the Tory Party and is shrewd enough to understand that they have got to . . . live down. . . . the reputation inherited from . . . the Thirties . . . to be able to say to the electorate when the election comes "no war; no unemployment; no cuts in social services. Just good government." If I am right about this they will want to stay in power for three or four years, and I don't really see why they should not.'

Butler was similarly frustrated by the trade unions, the Conservative attitude to which was described by Crosland as almost deferential. He proposed in May 1952 that the unions should draw up with the government certain rules to regulate the national wage bill so that it would not outstrip national production. This again represented a virtually bi-partisan approach, since Bevan was advocating in the same year some sort of national wages policy as an inevitable corollary of full employment, 'if we are not to be engulfed by inflation'. But of course nothing came of Butler's tentative *démarche*. Even as far back as 1946, the *New Statesman* had observed that the General Council of the TUC had developed a habit of snorting like an old war-horse when it heard the words national wage policy. In any case, Sir Walter Monckton's handling of labour relations, which commanded the full support of the Prime Minister, ensured that no attempt by the Chancellor or anybody else to retard the onward march of the unions could possibly succeed. Nor, in this respect, was the Opposition in any better shape, Bevan writing in 1954 to a Barrow councillor: 'We have actually reached the position where it would be true to say that the leaders of the Transport and General Workers' Union and the Municipal and General Workers' Union decide the policy of the Labour Party.'

Butler made no further attempt to tackle the country's underlying problems and, though he makes much play of his so-called expansionist policies in his autobiography, there is more than a grain of truth in Crossman's observation in 1955 that, however much the Conservatives talked about their belief in the virtues of free enterprise, the government had done little to stimulate it since 1951. It was true that, with the easing of supply conditions, most surviving controls were abolished rapidly and government trading restored to the private sector. In 1954 Butler was entitled to boast that 'in the past three years we have burned our identity cards, torn up our ration books, halved the number of snoopers [the derogatory term for government inspectors], decimated the number of forms and said good riddance to nearly two-thirds of the remaining wartime regulations.' Furthermore, almost everybody felt a lot better. At one level a great stock exchange boom meant that huge tax-free capital gains were realizable; at another the proportion of those receiving after-tax income of £500–£2000 rose in the period 1949–59 from 11 per cent to 47 per cent. It seemed a good world for the skilled workers and the huge army of junior clerical workers. All would undoubtedly go well enough as long as boom conditions lasted. But the stop-go alternation in economic policy which, as will be seen, was dramatically demonstrated in Butler's last year as Chancellor, was no substitute for a thoroughgoing reappraisal of the nation's fundamental economic weaknesses. Butler himself knew this well enough, as is clear from what he said in February 1954: 'The renewal and modernization of industrial plant in the United States and Germany, their volume of savings, and the rate of increase of their production, make uncomfortable comparisons with our own.'

Houses built to Aneurin Bevan's specifications had two lavatories (as yet the word toilet was confined to the would-be genteel lower-middle classes). Dalton, who succeeded Bevan for a short period, economized by having only one installed, as did Harold Macmillan. Macmillan council houses, while not markedly commodious, were declared by *The Times* to be emphatically not rabbit-hutches, and, as we have seen, the number of houses of all types increased with spectacular and well publicized rapidity. In 1951 195,000 were completed; in 1952 240,000; in 1953 300,000; and in 1954 347,000. 12 per cent were being built privately in 1951, 26 per cent in 1954. In

November 1954 the building licence system was finally wound up. It was noted, too, how many of the new houses of all sorts sported television aerials, Mrs Braddock observing in her down-to-earth manner that the basic insecurity now felt by the workers was the fear of a van drawing up to take the television away. The concept of a property-owning democracy was becoming rather more than a gleam in Anthony Eden's eye. In May 1953 the London County Council levied a record rate, twice that of any-where in the country, and the leader of the Conservatives on the Finance Committee suggested that economies could be made by the sale of council houses. Even the fourteen New Towns were coming on rather faster, although by the end of 1954 only 25,000 houses and a hundred new factories had been built and the more Utopian prospects originally held out for them were tacitly forgotten. The architectural critic Robert Furneaux-Jones gloomily observed in 1952 that: 'There are signs that some of the new towns, as they emerge from their seas of mud, may be just super housing-estates, pre-war sprawls with some modernis-tic detail to rub in the irony of it.' The same year saw a start at Gatwick and the first plans on the drawing board for the Barbican and Crystal Palace. A pointer to the prevailing architec-tural fashion was the award in 1953 of the Royal Institute of British Architects' Gold Medal to Le Corbusier, whose well-known enthusiasm for vertical communities still evoked the adulation of the critics.

Other aspects of the building record were less satisfactory. The rate of industrial building, so astonishing in Germany, was actually lower in Britain between 1952 and 1954 than it had been in 1951. Again, the 1951 census showed 4,500,000 households of more than one person with no fixed bath, nearly a million with no indoor lavatory and 690,000 without piped water. But as soon as slums were cleared in the early Fifties, more were created by the constant tide of disrepair as the new government followed its pre-decessors in failing to tackle the problem of the landlords and their controlled rents. As Disraeli told Queen Victoria in 1875: 'Unfortunately there is much in the relations between landlord and tenant in this country which is unsatisfactory and anomalous.

In the other area of social policy with which Bevan had been concerned – Health – it was the policy of the government to demonstrate above all else that the National Health Service was safe in their hands. In 1951 and 1952 the minister was Harry Crookshank, who combined the Ministry of Health with the leadership of the House, sensibly sloughed off by Eden to whom it had originally been assigned. Crookshank was a devoted servant of the state both in peace and war, as befitted the son of an inspector-general of Egyptian prisons, and a formidable debater whose technique was well described by his colleague Oliver Lyttelton: 'He liked to point out a thread showing in the lapel of an opponent's coat and pull it out. It could then be seen that the thread ran up the lapel into the shoulder, the shoulder into the sleeve, and suddenly the whole garment looked thread-bare.' Apart from introducing a few additional charges, such as that for dental treatment, over and above those which had aroused such discussion in the Labour party, Crookshank was deliberately uncontroversial and awarded the doctors a large, and at that time overdue, pay increase. But the two combined posts involved him in excessive work, and in 1952 he relinquished the Ministry of Health to Iain Macleod. Whereas Crookshank came demonstrably from the old patrician wing of the party with a red carnation, a Rolls-Royce and a house in Pont Street, Macleod was in many respects the standard-bearer in the Commons of the predominantly middle-class young veterans of the Second World War, and had served notably with others like him in the Research Department under Butler. Apart from his impressive gifts of character and intellect, Macleod seemed especially well equipped for his new post, as he had specialized in exploring the complexities of the Health Service in great depth while head of the Home Affairs section in the Research Department. Furthermore, in conjunction with Enoch Powell, he had produced a study called *Social Services: Needs and Means*, published in 1952, whose conclusion, as summarized in *The Times*, suggested that, as far as the Welfare State was concerned, the vital question was not 'should a means test be applied to a social service?' but rather 'why should any social service be provided without a means test?' Was it possible under this energetic and well-briefed young minister, recruited straight from the back benches, that a radical re-examination of NHS financing might lead to a change of direction in the consensus? The Macleod-Powell study had, after all, envisaged the possibility of charges for prescriptions and hospital beds.

The outcome, as John Vaizey has perceptively analyzed it in his essay on Macleod in *In Breach of Promise*, was all too predictable. Macleod appointed in 1953 a somewhat pedestrian economics don, C. W. Guillebaud, to head a committee to report on the administration of the National Health Service and to determine whether any economies could be effected. This overdue enquiry led Bevan to accuse Macleod of seeking another instrument to 'mutilate the National Health Service'. He had no need to worry. Guillebaud had available to him the advice not only of Richard Titmuss, Professor of Social Administration at the LSE, who was increasingly assumed to be about to don the prophetic mantle of Tawney, but also of the young sociologist Brian Abel-Smith, who would one day succeed to Titmuss's chair. Neither of them was in the business of cutting the costs of the welfare state, Abel-Smith in particular being dedicated to the cause of finally eliminating the idea that state intervention should only serve as a safety-net, the legacy, as he described it, of 'mutton-eating Beatrice Webb and the Poor Law'. Abel-Smith was not particularly interested in whether the Health Service was or was not extravagant and how it might best be financed, but was able to demonstrate from his researches that the proportion of the national income devoted to it had barely increased. It was to be an influential begging of an important question, since in the event the Guillebaud Report laid effectively to rest the last chance of a fundamental revision of health service financing for the discernible future. Instead, Macleod concentrated on a large hospital building programme and, as his only piece of legislation, a bill which enabled dental assistants to scale teeth and facilitated the recruitment of foreign dentists.

Winston Churchill's personal experiences in youth and early manhood had not induced in him any conviction that institutional education was an essential prerequisite to the good life; and even Butler's description of his 1944 Education Act as a giant umbrella under which all sorts of experiments could flourish hardly suggested a coherent Conservative policy for education. Miss Horsburgh was, as we have seen, rather pointedly kept out of the Cabinet until 1953, and Butler was not disposed to increase the financial resources available, which were far from generous as compared with other areas of public expenditure. Such new schools as were built were cheaply, if often imaginatively, designed, but the older inner city schools, especially the secondary moderns, became more and more dingy and dilapidated. The general neglect of the secondary moderns, often small schools doing a remarkably good and highly personalized job with the less able children, was to have momentous consequences. David Eccles, Miss Horsburgh's markedly more dynamic successor, promised soon after his appointment in 1954: 'My colleagues and I will never agree to the assassination of the grammar schools. We want you to continue and flourish.' A pledge the non-fulfilment of which was only surpassed by Harold Wilson's later assertion that the grammar schools would only be destroyed over his dead body. But in any case the survival of the grammar schools could only be ensured if the secondary moderns were given encouragement, status and financial support, so as to represent an acceptable alternative to parents. In fact, they were starved and neglected.

The agitation for comprehensivization was already under way. A motion deploring any tinkering about with the tripartite system was passed by the Conservative party conference in 1952 with only one dissentient, being countered by a Labour pledge the next year to abolish eleven-plus selection. Selection at eleven was, of course, too unscientific to be easily defensible and was a consequence of a disastrous failure to think the matter through properly in the drafting of the 1944 Act. Many local authorities in the early Fifties were working on flexible modifications of the selection procedure and by 1955 only twenty-three out of 146 local education authorities proposed any measure of comprehensivization with London, Staffordshire and Coventry in the van. Once the idea caught on, the administrative advantages of building one *omnium gatherum* educational emporium as against a grammar school and a cluster of secondary moderns became decisively seductive. An opinion on the comprehensive school, still shared at that time by many, even in left-wing circles, was that succinctly expressed by the notably progressive High Master of Manchester Grammar School, Eric James: 'Unless they are of enormous size they can provide neither the variety nor the standard of work found in the grammar school. Their spread will mean the wasting, for reasons of doctrinaire equalitarianism, of that most precious asset, the gifted child.' Miss Horsburgh, to her credit, refused to allow Bec School to be converted from a five hundred place grammar school into a two thousand place comprehensive. But, in general, as in Health, so in Education, the consensus was holding for the moment. As *The Times* put it in 1953, 'except for some egalitarian and extra-ordinarily expensive adjustments wished for by Labour there is little to divide the two parties.' In May 1954 the government announced the first step towards the introduction of equal pay, at a time when male teachers over thirty were getting on average 20 per cent more than females of the same age and grade – an overdue social reform, but not one which could have had more than a marginal effect on the supply and quality of female teachers who comprised 60 per cent of the profession. It was a considerable vote-winner.

As has been seen, Sir Walter Monckton, on assuming office as Minister of Labour and National Service, had it made abundantly clear to him by the Prime Minister just what his role was to be in the strategic plans of the government. 'Winston's riding orders to me,' he said, 'were that the Labour party had foretold grave industrial troubles if the Conservatives were elected, and he looked to me to do my best to preserve industrial peace.' Given the strategy of appeasement, Monckton was assuredly the right man. Even Bevan admitted that the new Minister became such a personal friend that he found it difficult 'to knock him about'. The more militant unions suffered no such inhibition. There were a number of contributory factors – the cost of living-wages spiral had taken off, though the end of the Korean War in 1953 temporarily halted the rise in the cost of living; much of industry was making a belated effort to modernize itself under trans-atlantic promptings, a process originating in the Anglo-American Productivity Council of 1948; and there were the Communists. The twenty-third Congress of the Communist Party of Great Britain in April 1954 was able to congratulate itself that its central executive committee included the General Secretary of the Foundry Workers, the assistant General Secretary of the Electrical Trade Union, the General Secretary of the Fire Brigades Union and the General Secretary and two area presidents of the National Union of Miners. Delegates included more than a hundred members of the AEU, to say nothing of a large throng of members of constituency Labour parties.

The first sign of trouble was in the summer of 1952, when

Monckton had the temerity to refer back a number of pay awards proposed by the Wages Councils which had been set up during the war by Ernest Bevin. The TUC Economic Committee disapproved of this and demanded an interview with the Prime Minister. Monckton promised not to offend again. Between October 1950 and May 1952 prices had risen by 17 per cent but wages by only 16 per cent. The engineers and shipbuilders, having got rises in 1951 and 1952, put in for 15 per cent in 1953. Strikes developed, and after what could be called hard bargaining by the standards of the government, they got 6 per cent for skilled and 5 per cent for unskilled workers. The Communist-led electricians in August 1953 started a selective strike, an ingenious device calculated to produce the maximum of dislocation and to cost the minimum in strike pay. Even more instructive for the future was the railway strike of July 1953, which involved the three unions NUR, ASLEF and the Transport Salaried Staff Association, who put forward a 15 per cent claim, which would have cost British Rail £50 million pounds. The claim went to arbitration. A four shillings a week award was not met with approbation by the railwaymen. The government instructed British Rail to add to this a promise of a review in order to break off the strike. In February 1954 an offer of 6 per cent all round was accepted; this narrowed differentials and put British Rail in the red, in violation of its constitution, which optimistically had required it to be self-supporting. When Butler went to his office the following morning Churchill sent for him and told him: 'Never mind, old cock, Walter and I settled the rail strike last night without deciding to keep you up – on their terms.' *The Economist* commented: 'The railway rumpus was handled with sympathy, patience and funk. In the particular circumstances of this particular case these may have been the right qualities to show. But as Sir Walter Monckton surveys the wreckage this weekend – the award of a duly authorized tribunal thrown over, the accounts of a public corporation unbalanced, and a fluttering standard of inflation run up before the militant trade unionists elsewhere – he should not forget the truth behind the applause that his skill in negotiation has earned. His triumph is really one more retreat from reality.' *The Times* saw it as 'a turning point in the course of labour relations since the war. Until now arbitration has ruled.' Labour MPs crossed the floor of the House to pat the Minister on the back.

In November 1954 the railwaymen returned to the attack. *The Economist* described clearly enough what everybody knew then and has known ever since: 'The pay-roll is still far too big. If the staffs were cut by one-fifth, the wages of the remainder could be made really economic, and the railways could be made to pay. Everybody knows it; but nobody dares to say it in public.' Monckton set up a Court of Enquiry, which told British Rail to pay 'a fair and adequate wage', even if they went into the red. In January 1955 a new award was made to the lower paid. ASLEF naturally objected. Their objection was overruled. ASLEF called a strike. Efforts were made to avert the strike.* A familiar scene ensued, with members of the NUR, ASLEF and the TUC in separate rooms while Monckton paced up and down his office with what was reported as 'a haggard expression'. On 28 May ASLEF proceeded with their strike. Eden made a broadcast suggesting that ASLEF and the NUR should come together, which was like suggesting that Medea and Jason should settle down to a happy retirement in a Black Sea dacha. On 31 May there was a state of emergency, and the strike ended on 14 June with the ASLEF senior drivers (but not the firemen) getting nearly all they wanted. The electricians' selective strike went on till March 1954 and in the early part of the year they were joined by miners, engineers, dockers, foundry-workers and film technicians. October, too, was a bad month with two hundred ships in London and Merseyside idle and 44,000 dockers out.

Early in 1955 a committee of enquiry into the railway dispute stated emphatically that the Transport Commission had been wrong in assuming that wage claims could not be met because of its financial obligations under the 1947 Act. 'Having willed the end, the nation must will the means. This implies that the employees of such a service should receive a fair and adequate wage.' Sir Brian Robertson, the one-time administrative genius of the Eighth Army and now Chairman of the Transport Commission, contented himself, as a man of few words, with the observation: 'The settlement will, of course, cost a great deal of money, and that may well have to be found somewhere.' It was, however, officially suggested, after *The Times* had thrown into the arena emotive terms like 'feather-bedding' and demarcation,

* 'Avert' is a word which would henceforth enjoy a greatly enhanced currency.

that a searching and detailed examination should be conducted of just how the railways really worked. Two days later it was announced that the railway unions objected to that and so the proposal was dropped. Wage settlements throughout the country stood at £100 million pounds for the first quarter compared with £180 million for the whole of 1954. That spring, perhaps not unconnected with an imminent General Election, there were strikes of Yorkshire miners, busmen, tugmen, bargemen and of course ASLEF. An awareness was beginning to dawn that there could be some connection between full employment and a tendency to go on strike. As the newly knighted Sir Lincoln Evans put it in a speech in January 1953: 'It is with our political smart Alecs that the difficulty lies. They want to carry the political battle on to the floor of industry. They forget that political beliefs are not a condition of trade union membership.' A radical solution to that particular problem was suggested by Mr Andrew Caird in a letter to *The Times* on 16 March 1953: 'Our rulers might consider whether it would be possible to enact that secret ballots should be the rule for trade unions. I believe it is the fear of criticism by their fellow workers which induces so many men to vote for strike or no work in the show of hands. Let them have the secret ballot as a right.'

The nation's brief love affair with the nationalized industries had already, as we have seen, lost much, if not all, of its initial rapture and the government earned little unpopularity, apart from routine demonstrations in the House, when it fulfilled its election pledges to denationalize road haulage and iron and steel in 1953. But the problems of the mining industry remained as intractable as ever. Things had clearly come to something of a pass when the MP for Caerphilly (of all places) Ness Edwards, a former miner himself, could make a speech (February 1953), in which he said: 'In spite of all that has been done to secure material improvement, a minority still play the fool, disregarding their social and moral obligations.' Hugh Gaitskell pointed out in a speech at Swansea that a good Socialist in a nationalized industry works for the community not the government. Whoever the miners were working for (or in some cases not working for) it was all too clear that they were uninterested in assuming any sort of participatory responsibility for the higher management of their industry. Arthur Deakin told the Labour party conference at Margate in 1953 that it had proved virtually impossible to get the miners to represent their interests on the National Coal Board, as they were not prepared to accept responsibility. He was in fact highlighting the general lack of enthusiasm felt by orthodox trade unionists for effective worker participation in management. For many, it seemed best to regard nationalization as a guarantee of full employment, leaving everyone free to acquire more money for doing the same job. The results certainly bore this out. The National Coal Board's report of May 1953 stated that in the previous year average earnings were up 12 per cent; that there was a minute increase in production, altogether failing to match an increase in the number of miners; and that there was an increase in absenteeism. The report predicted a fall in output in 1953 as a result of an extra week's paid holiday. There had been a fall in output in both Scotland and Wales. Fortunately the need to import coal was offset by an encouraging upturn in tourism and the export of whisky. The export potential of the motor-car industry was offset by a damaging strike at Austin's in 1953, an ominous precedent in an increasingly competitive market.

Despite all these problems the government after 1952 was never more than three points behind Labour in the Gallup polls (except in August and September 1954) because of the cumulative popularity it earned in the process of dismantling the rationing system. The responsible Minister, Major Gwilym Lloyd-George, was a popular, if rather easy-going figure, and the driving force behind what was by no means a simple operation was Dr Charles Hill, who had a facial resemblance to Billy Bunter and had originally made his name discoursing on the radio about constipation, a subject of absorbing national interest at that period. Derationing was a bolder enterprise than might be imagined in retrospect. Three-quarters of the nation's imported food was being purchased in bulk by the government in 1951 and there were potentially alarming problems in ensuring supplies adequate to ensure that prices remained reasonably stable, and in reviving some sort of competitive spirit in the food industry, which had hardly needed to think for itself since 1939. Even Churchill's nerve faltered from time to time, although he never wavered in his conviction that the English achieved little without meat, his most celebrated memorandum on the subject reading:

'Would it be possible to make a plan to deration pork and let it rip?' The job was tackled piecemeal, which served to enhance the public interest. A sound psychological start was made with tea in 1952 and sugar and even cream followed in 1953, which also saw the end of controls on the price and meat content of sausages, the decontrolling of eggs and the end of sweet rationing. In 1954 the process was completed with butter, cheese, margarine, cooking fats and meat finally freed. An Osbert Lancaster cartoon in the *Daily Express* depicted a spiv exhorting his equally repulsive son to disregard the gloomy headline 'all rationing to end' – 'My boy, I want you to regard this not as a set-back but as a challenge – go right out and start creating shortages.' In the general rejoicing, Labour did nothing to enhance its popularity by dividing the house on each derationing order. During the Election campaign of 1955 Conservative supporters tried to lumber Labour candidates with bogus ration books until very properly rebuked on the television by James Callaghan. However, the state was still paying out £330 million in food subsidies in 1955.

Much less publicized was the government's programme for reducing controls in trade and industry. There were, of course, strict limits as to what could be achieved by way of 'freeing' the economy, if full employment and the welfare state continued sacrosanct and nothing was to be done which might prove unacceptable to the trade union leadership. Labour's initial enthusiasm for planning had in any case appreciably diminished during their years in office. The Korean War had, however, led to the creation under Richard Stokes of a Ministry of Materials in July 1951 to co-ordinate the control of raw materials. This was eventually wound up in 1954 by Woolton, the third Conservative minister to hold the office. Commodities such as wood, zinc, aluminium, copper and hemp were returned piecemeal to private traders, often less than enthusiastic to accept the responsibility. The London Metal Market returned to the scene, as did the Liverpool Cotton Exchange (closed down by Labour after the war). Import quotas and price controls were largely eliminated and there was a notable diminution in Conservative enthusiasm for the old-fashioned theory of imperial preference, so beloved of Lord Beaverbrook, in favour of the more widely based General Agreement on Tariffs and Trade. R. A. Butler was well satisfied with what had been achieved by 1954. In the speech at Gloucester in July which has already been quoted, he proclaimed: 'Within the limits of law and social justice, our aim is freedom for every man and woman to live their own lives in their own way and not have their lives lived for them by an overweening state.' The Chancellor's reference to social justice was a striking indication of how skilfully the Tories were beginning to steal the Whig clothing. A concomitant of the new 'Conservative freedom' from which the party's more traditional supporters derived understandable satisfaction was a large boom in equities. Between the summer of 1952 and that of 1955 the *Financial Times* index of industrial ordinary shares rose from 103 to 224.

The Labour Manifesto of 1951 contained the phrase: 'The Tory still thinks in terms of Victorian imperialism and colonial exploitation.' In Oliver Lyttelton, the descendant of a family which had produced one governor of South Carolina, two governors of Jamaica, the founder of Canterbury, New Zealand, and the Secretary of State for the Colonies in 1903, Churchill might seem to have put colonial affairs into the hands of just such an atavistic Tory. Confronted with an acutely critical situation in Malaya, Lyttelton in fact showed a combination of firmness and imagination in preparing the way for early independence which contrasted favourably with the maladroit record of the French and Dutch in dealing with the difficult legacy left by the Japanese occupation. In the aftermath of the precipitate Japanese withdrawal after Hiroshima, Communist guerrillas had initiated a terrorist campaign which by 1948 had become open warfare, culminating, just as Labour left office, in the murder of the High Commissioner, Sir Henry Gurney. Within three years the guerrillas were routed and the war was over. This was partly due to Lyttelton's inspired appointment to the combined post of Commander-in-Chief and High Commissioner of Sir Gerald Templer, a soldier of consuming nervous energy and high intelligence. Nothing, however, could have been achieved but for the sensitive and even-handed treatment of the different races involved – Malays, Chinese and Indians – so that the tide of popular opinion turned against the Communists. By the end a quarter of a million British and Gurkha soldiers were engaged in the conflict, but its successful outcome meant that the world-wide demand for Malayan rubber and tin could be met to the great advantage of a sterling area avid for dollars. In 1955 elections took place for a new legislative council, which prepared the way for full independence two years later.

In Africa Britain was still responsible for no fewer than fifteen territories in different stages of development. In one of them, Kenya, the Churchill government found itself confronted with a sinister and bloodthirsty insurrection, the Mau Mau rebellion, at its height between 1952 and 1955. Nearly a hundred Europeans and 13,000 Africans lost their lives. It was not an easy moment to persuade 50,000 comfortable white settlers to come to terms about power-sharing with six million Africans, many of whom were both land-hungry and politically self-conscious. Despite this, Lyttelton managed to establish a multi-racial government in 1954. The Central African Federation of 1953, comprising what we now call Zimbabwe, Zambia and Malawi, was a less happy attempt at power-sharing between black and white which the Tories took over from Labour and which persisted uneasily until 1953. The conflict of interests and races which plagued the Federation was not in evidence in the Gold Coast, which was rapidly metamorphosed into Kwame Nkrumah's Ghana and served as a pace-setter for other emergent African nation states. Despite Labour fears, Victorian imperialism seemed to have had its day. The Colonial Development Corporation, largely forgotten since the heady days of the Gambia egg saga, was allowed to fade gently into oblivion.

British foreign policy under Churchill and the vastly experienced Eden, who had first been Foreign Secretary sixteen years previously, seemed, after the unhappy Morrison interlude, to be both firm and flexible. Eden had an easy command of the dispatch box and, in the light of his subsequent debacle, a surprisingly high reputation among his political opponents, as Crossman's diary testifies. The *Annual Register* for 1954 expressed a general view that 'not since the Locarno days (1925) had the reputation of a British Foreign Secretary stood so high'. That the truth was rather less rosy was largely attributable to the curious relationships that existed between Eden and Churchill and between Eden and successive US Secretaries of State, Dean Acheson and John Foster Dulles; and indeed to Eden's strange personality, so devastatingly captured by William Coldstream's portrait in Christ Church, Oxford.

While Eden never quite shoook himself free of the post-war illusion which saw Britain as a Third Force intermediary between East and West and between America and Europe, Churchill had by now largely lost interest in Europe and longed to relive the vanished world of wartime summits based on the Anglo/US special relationship. He was seeking, as he put it characteristically in his election campaign, 'some more exalted and august foundation for our safety than this grim and sombre balancing power of the bomb'. In a speech at Plymouth just before the election, with his mind full of the prospect of another meeting with Stalin, he said: 'If I remain in public life it is because, rightly or wrongly but sincerely, I believe that I may be able to make an important contribution to the prevention of a third world war. . . . It is the last prize I seek to win.' The extent to which he clung to this increasingly chimerical vision is attested by his extraordinary behaviour in July 1954 when, during a trans-atlantic crossing with Eden, he sent Molotov a message suggesting a Moscow visit without consulting either the Americans or the cabinet. Eden preferred to think in terms of 'spheres of influence' (from some of which the Americans might be politely excluded), and told his private secretary Evelyn Shuckburgh, to whom he was far from being a hero, 'I am inside right, the Americans outside right, Molotov is inside left, China outside left,' a diplomatic line-up which curiously omitted the centre forward. The Americans and notably President Eisenhower enjoyed humouring Churchill, though they were realistically aware that he was no longer the leonine hero of the war years. They found Eden, on the other hand, discouragingly tepid about any form of ideological crusade and his personality difficult to relate to any known American life-style. Dean Acheson agreed with Lester Pearson, the Canadian, that it was preferable to be called 'my boy' by Ernie Bevin than to be called 'my dear' by Anthony Eden. The mutual antipathy between Dulles and Eden, although probably not so consistently bad as made out retrospectively by Eden after Suez, might certainly be described as the wrong sort of special relationship.

These tensions and disagreements broke out again and again on the international plane between 1952 and 1955 – in Iran, in Egypt, in Western Europe and in the Far East. It will be recalled that the lachrymose Dr Moussadegh of Iran had much plagued

Herbert Morrison by expropriating (or nationalizing, according to one's point of view) the Anglo-Iranian oil company. It may be thought that his reasons for so doing were not wholly blameworthy, since the company paid remarkably low dividends with the result that the Iranians were only drawing 1·50 dollars for each ton of oil produced, whereas the Saudi Arabians and the Iraqis were doing a great deal better. Neither Churchill nor Eden held the Iranian character in high regard, the former professing to believe that the crisis would never have occurred had we employed 'a splutter of musketry', and the latter informally referring to the Iranians as rug merchants. Acheson in the summer of 1952 suggested that matters would be improved by a little dollar diplomacy by which Iran would seek international arbitration on the appropriate rate of compensation for the nationalization. Eden's reaction was to insist that there first had to be arbitration as to whether nationalization was even legal, and relations became decidedly acrimonious. The overthrow of Moussadegh with CIA assistance in 1954 led to a settlement whereby eight companies formed a consortium to produce and market oil, 50 per cent of the capital being British and 40 per cent American. The Iranians were to get 32 per cent of the profits and the other members of the consortium would compensate the British to the tune of £25 million for their partial loss of capital. The whole episode illustrated diverging British and American interests in the area, the British concerned primarily for the protection of their remaining foreign investments, the Americans keen to support emergent nationalisms in the Middle East as a bar to Soviet influence, while by no means unconcerned with the advancement of their own commercial interests. If Eden appeared in the short run to have achieved a diplomatically creditable settlement of the oil crisis, Iran had now effectively become an American as opposed to a British sphere of interest.

Churchill's attitude to Egypt and the Sudan oscillated bewilderingly from Eden's point of view. As a survivor of the battle of Omdurman he was understandably loath to see British influence diminished in the Sudan and anxious to use the special relationship to bring US troops into the defence of the Suez Canal. As a Zionist himself he was concerned at the potential threat to Israel represented by the new rulers of Egypt. At the same time he had no illusions about the Suez Canal being any longer strategically essential, given Indian independence. On 17 January 1952 he told Congress: 'We do not seek to be masters of Egypt. We are there only as servants and guardians of the commerce of the world. It would enormously aid us in our task if even token forces of other partners were stationed in the Canal Zone as a symbol of the unity of purpose which inspires us.' There was not a ripple of applause. Instead Acheson urged Eden to acquiesce in the Egyptian repudiation of the 1936 treaty, which gave Britain the right to a military presence in the Canal Zone, and to abandon Anglo-Egyptian condominium in the Sudan, which had originated in 1899. Anti-British riots in January and the overthrow of the Egyptian monarchy by General Neguib and Colonel Nasser in July exacerbated the situation. As Eden was negotiating with Egypt's new nationalist leaders for full elections in the Sudan, Churchill was fulminating that he had never known before that Munich was situated on the Nile. The veteran Conservative, L. S. Amery, wrote presciently to *The Times* urging the desirability of not abandoning the Canal Zone because of the awesome consequences of 'a second round' between the Arabs and Israel – 'the Suez Canal offers the only adequate base for the defence of the Middle East.' Nevertheless the Sudanese acquired their independence in 1956. Negotiations about the Canal Zone were interrupted in the summer of 1953 when both Churchill and Eden were out of action owing to illness, but in October 1954, much to Churchill's chagrin, Eden agreed with Nasser, who was now effectively dictator of Egypt, that with certain safeguards the Canal Zone would be evacuated within twenty months. It would not be the last the British would hear of Colonel Nasser.

Eden, struggling with ill-health and irritated and frustrated by a deteriorating relationship with Churchill, had other pre-occupations all over the world from Cyprus to the Falkland Islands, where, when Britain submitted the dispute to the International Court, President Peron significantly failed to file counter-claims. Such matters were, however, relatively trivial compared with the difficulties with which the Anglo-American alliance was confronted by Moscow in Western Europe and Peking in the Far East.

It will be recalled that Labour's attitude to the emergence of European co-operation had been unenthusiastic. As a NEC pamphlet had put it in 1950, 'many European governments have not yet shown either the will or the ability to plan their own economies,' a somewhat narrow and sectarian point of view considering that economic planning in Europe was to prove markedly more effective than anything achieved by Labour in its first or subsequent terms of office. Churchill in opposition, on the other hand, had gone out of his way to proclaim himself a good European, and important members of the cabinet in Maxwell Fyfe and Macmillan were known to favour closer relations. The Americans, for their part, were consistently impatient to see a united Europe, with Britain playing a leading or, at least, a prominent role. Eden was concerned not to see his position as a world statesman unnecessarily circumscribed by too close a link with Europe. A few months after taking office in January 1952 he went out of his way to tell his audience at a Columbia University degree ceremony that 'forming a European federation is something that we know in our bones we cannot do'. Nobody was in fact asking him to join a federation, the issue on the *tapis* at that moment being British membership of the European Defence Community, a joint international force into which West German units would be incorporated. Churchill at Strasbourg in 1950 had appeared to give the idea its first impetus by talking of 'the immediate creation of a European army under a unified command'. Once in office, Churchill showed himself to be more interested in a prolonged tussle on the question of whether the NATO fleet should have a British or an American commander, although Britannia was manifestly no longer ruling the waves. Eden made it clear that Britain would not join the EDC, but suggested vaguely that 'there might be some other form of association'. His acceptance in principle of an Anglo-American treaty of guarantee for the EDC did little to diminish his unpopularity as the spokesman of *perfide Albion* with active Europeans like Jean Monnet in France or Paul Spaak in Belgium. The French parliamentarians became less and less enthusiastic about the EDC and finally rejected it in August 1954. The Americans were very angry, and since only the previous year Dulles had threatened his famous 'agonizing reappraisal' of US foreign policy if the EDC did not eventuate, there was much diplomatic confusion. Eden, as a consequence, enjoyed a triumph by working closely with Dulles at a nine power conference in

London which led to the inclusion of a fully sovereign West Germany and Italy in NATO and a British pledge to maintain four divisions and the Tactical Air Force on the continent. Eden acquired great public respect for this achievement, although Churchill was unimpressed, taking the view that we would never have withdrawn our troops anyway. Eden was made a Knight of the Garter and early in the New Year entertained the low-born Colonel Nasser to dinner in the Embassy in Cairo. The Russians formed the Warsaw Pact and the battle lines of the Cold War in Europe were drawn up.

In the Far East the special relationship was also subjected to a good deal of tension from 1952 onwards. Eden and Acheson had sharp differences of opinion about the American failure to consult Britain before the bombing of power stations on the Yalu river in the concluding stages of the Korean War; as also about a diplomatic initiative by India in the matter of the repatriation of prisoners of war unwilling to return to Communist China, on which Eden took a markedly more humanitarian line than he had in 1944 over a similar issue. The Korean War out of the way, the focus of attention shifted to the death throes of French imperial power in Indo-China, where a war which was to last for seventeen years had been started by the remarkable Communist guerilla leader Ho Chi Minh in 1946. By 1954 his Viet Minh nationalists aided by Communist China were evidently on the point of defeating the French, who were heavily subsidized by the Americans, intent on containing what they saw as militant Communism on the march. The key fortress of Dien Bien Phu fell on VE day (8 May) 1954, with 7000 French casualties and 11,000 prisoners. The decision arrived at during the subsequent Geneva conference to partition Indo-China along the seventeenth parallel was widely regarded as yet another triumph in what was being increasingly seen as Eden's *annus mirabilis*. He certainly made it as clear to Dulles as diplomatic techniques permitted that Britain would have nothing to do with the American suggestion that international armed force should be actively brought to bear in the area. We can see in retrospect that Ho Chi Minh could have been dealt with in one of two ways, either of which might have avoided the disasters of the nineteen-sixties. Either he could have been regarded as a sort of Far East Tito or he could have been halted in his tracks.

As it was, he was left in undisputed possession of North Vietnam with the prestige enjoyed by a nationalist war hero, while the Americans were freed to fill the vacuum in the South created by the withdrawal of the bitterly humiliated French. That Dulles tended to feel he had been double-crossed by Eden, with momentous consequences at Suez in 1956, is not altogether surprising, given the frequency with which Eden had spoken in the past of the need to resist Communist advance and infiltration.

Despite an unkind caricature in *Punch*, then edited by Malcolm Muggeridge, of Eden returning from the Geneva conference accoutred with an unmistakably Munichois umbrella, his reputation was at its zenith. Appropriately enough, he was about to achieve his long-frustrated desire to be Prime Minister. Churchill had resolutely clung to his belief (fortified by the death of Stalin in March 1953) in the possibility of a summit and obstinately remained in office. After his major stroke on 23 June 1953, even he thought that he would retire in the autumn as soon as Eden had recovered sufficiently from his own illness to take over. But a successful return to the political battlefield at the Margate party conference seemed to reanimate him. He became convinced that the death of Stalin and the emergence of the hydrogen bomb opened new opportunities for old-fashioned summitry. By March 1955 he was still capable of making an impressive speech in the defence debate, which he claimed had taken him twenty-eight hours to prepare. Although Harold Nicolson prepared a television obituary of Churchill in August 1953 it was not to be transmitted till January 1965. Throughout 1954 there was constant communing among his colleagues how best to engineer the old man's retirement, particularly after he had performed lamentably in a debate on the hydrogen bomb in April. Enquirers were firmly told: 'I will not retire until I meet Malenkov.' The imminence of a General Election made 1955 obviously a time for decision, yet at a cabinet meeting on 15 December 1954 Churchill announced: 'I know you are trying to get rid of me and it is up to me to go to the Queen and hand her my resignation and yours – but I won't do it.' But go he eventually did on April 5 and was succeeded by Eden the next day. Although a General Election could have been postponed for up to eighteen months Eden chose to ask for a new mandate for the Conservative Party on 26 May.

In that month the Gallup poll figures read as follows:

Conservative	43
Labour	40
Liberal	2
Other	1
Don't Know	14

To far-sighted observers it might have seemed that R. A. Butler had accurately described the performance of the government as he drove Harold Nicolson home exactly three years previously: 'Winston is so brave in war and so cowardly in peace; the Tory government ought to convey the impression of people who are absolutely certain of themselves; as it is, they convey the impression of a wobble.' The electorate's judgement was to prove more indulgent. In April Butler had produced what was to become all too well-known in subsequent years as a pre-election budget. He 'gave back' half his surplus, taking sixpence off the income-tax and raising personal allowances, to the extent of taking nearly 2,500,000 people out of the tax bracket. He had just raised the bank rate from $3\frac{1}{2}$ to $4\frac{1}{2}$ per cent in February because of the evident danger of inflation. He was to have cause to regret and retract his generosity within a few months, but for the moment it enhanced the government's popularity. As *The Economist* commented, there was a distinct flavour of optimism about the calculation. That the same was true of the government's electoral prospects was partly due to a factor analysed by Christopher Mayhew in *Party Games*: 'We believed that after their election victory in 1951 they would put the clock back; in fact, however, they doubled expenditure on the welfare state and increased public as against private expenditure.' The Conservatives' prospects were also, however, enhanced by the fact that the Labour party was in considerable disarray in terms both of doctrine and of political unity.

When lecturing to the Fabian Society, Dick Crossman tended to abandon the role of vindictive opportunist revealed in his diaries and assume the mantle of political philosopher and prophet. For him, the Labour defeat in 1951 had been a deliverance from an indecision about the objectives of the party which would have crippled its power of action in a further period of office. If there was to be any reconciliation between the right of the party, advocating consolidation, and the left, demanding more socialism, a necessary pre-condition for coherent politics, certain fundamental questions could no longer go unanswered. Did democratic socialism, for instance, involve the permanence of a mixed economy? And if so, should profit-making in the private sector be encouraged or limited? If, under socialism, it is right for people to receive spectacles and dentures free, then is it logical to have to pay to travel on nationalized railways? If quite so many people seemed to feel secure and contented under welfare capitalism, how could they be persuaded to opt for more socialism? Had nationalization done any more than concentrate power in the hands of a small managerial elite, which would not be altogether surprising since 'the first stage of socialism was executed primarily by anti-socialist managers and neutral civil servants'? Could it be said that the post-war Labour government had even begun to distribute responsibility among the people? Might not a true historical perspective suggest that Labour's real achievement was the culmination of a century of social reform rather than the provision of a springboard for a new epoch? Until some or all of these questions were answered democratic socialism would lack a firm base for action, because as Aneurin Bevan said, its natural tendency was to vacillate since 'it must achieve passion in action in the pursuit of qualified judgements.'

The Churchill years saw the high tide of the dissident Bevanites and with it a remarkable measure of acrimony within the party. Ian Mikardo, the erstwhile hero of the fateful party conference of 1944, published an article in *Tribune* at the end of October 1952. In it he recorded that he and his associates had been called a little band of splenetic furies (by George Brown); parlour revolutionaries and other mischief-makers (by Morrison); extreme Left-wingers . . . some with outlooks soured and warped by disappointment of personal ambitions, some highbrows educated beyond their capacity (by Sir Hartley Shawcross); an uneasy coalition of well-meaning emotionalists, frustrates, crackpots and fellow-travellers making Fred Karno's army look like the Brigade of Guards (by Stanley Evans); and a group of frustrated journalists exercising mob rule (by Gaitskell). Attlee, determined to hang on as leader until it would be finally too late for Morrison to succeed him, was much exercised to maintain a semblance of peace. He was assisted in doing so by the fact that Bevanite activity was consistently leaked to Dalton by Desmond Donnelly, a future Labour party defector. The trouble began with the defence debate of 5 March 1952 when Bevan and fifty-six other MPs divided the House, ignoring the party instruction to abstain. Deakin demanded recantation on pain of expulsion, but this was considered to be going too far, and instead the PLP's standing orders, in abeyance since 1945, which required all members to abide by majority party decisions or lose the whip, were revived. The next month saw the publication of Bevan's *In Place of Fear*, which emphasized what its author saw as the absolute necessity of keeping the nationalization pot boiling and called Morrison's boards 'a constitutional outrage'. The highly unfraternal bawling and brawling at the 1952 party conference at Morecambe was matched only by the ferocity of the seaside weather. The constituency section of the NEC was spectacularly captured by the dissidents, Bevan, Barbara Castle, the sinister Driberg, Wilson, Mikardo and Crossman being elected in that order with Jim Griffiths fourth. Morrison and Dalton were both ousted. Deakin, who attended the conference wearing a cloth cap jammed flat on his head, felt constrained to make a speech in which he warned: 'There is no decision that you can take here as a party which will commit the Trade Union movement to industrial action for political purposes.' This must have come as something of a disappointment to the Far Left infiltrators, whom the observant Attlee noticed among the constituency delegations and who were much given to what Deakin called the antics of disruption. As it was, 1,728,000 votes were cast for industrial action to bring the government down. Gaitskell, who was much more of a fighter than Muggeridge's description of him as resembling a certain type of High Church clergyman with a slum parish might suggest, claimed immediately after Morecambe that it was 'time to restore the authority and leadership of the solid, sound, sensible majority of the movement'. As a start towards achieving this laudable aim Attlee disbanded all unofficial groups within the party and forbade all personal attacks.

This ensured something of a truce. In the balmier air of Margate the 1953 conference was relatively uneventful, although

Morrison's failure to fight for the Treasurership at the behest of the Trade Union leaders was symptomatic of his declining political nerve. Even so, he was able to ward off a challenge for the deputy leadership from Bevan by 181 votes to 76 in the PLP. A policy document, *Challenge to Britain*, published in 1953, ritually proclaimed the need to nationalize the chemical, electrical and machine-tool industries, and advocated the abolition of all health charges and the phasing out of the public schools, a cause particularly dear to the many left-wingers who had been educated at them. One such, J. P. W. Mallalieu, started up the Bevanite battle again by accusing the Shadow Cabinet of preaching socialism in the constituencies and consolidation behind closed doors at party meetings. By 1954 the issue of German rearmament intensified party disunity. Bevan, five months before the Korean War broke out, had described German rearmament as unthinkable and in that regard had an unexpected ally in Dalton, a First World War veteran, who loudly intoned the refrain: 'No guns for the Huns.' Morrison and Gaitskell on the other hand were in Crossman's view more enthusiastic about rearming the Germans than Eden himself. The extent to which the issue divided the party was revealed when an amendment opposing it put forward by Harold Wilson was only defeated by 113 votes to 104. Bevan also succeeded in convincing himself in April 1954 that the South-East Asia Treaty Organization, a rather shadowy defence grouping, which Dulles and Eden proposed in the aftermath of Dien Bien Phu, was a form of neo-colonialism. He worked himself up to a high pitch of criticism against his own party leaders.

Just as Bevan's resignation had inconveniently preceded the General Election of 1951, so his near expulsion from the party preceded that of 1955. The prospect of German rearmament continued to vex him. To avoid it, he pressed for a summit meeting which would link it with the threat posed by the hydrogen bomb, the British manufacture of which was announced by Churchill in February with one of his more tortuous metaphors – 'Safety will be the sturdy child of terror and survival the twin brother of annihilation.' In the ensuing debate in March Bevan openly criticized his own party leadership and led sixty-two Labour MPs in abstaining on an innocuous amendment which Attlee had moved. The only members of the Shadow Cabinet to vote against recommending the PLP to withdraw the whip from Bevan were Wilson, Alf Robens, Dalton and Griffiths. By the time the PLP met in Committee Room 14 the battle lines had been clearly drawn by Gaitskell in a speech at Doncaster when he talked of 'a direct challenge to the elected leader of our party'. Gaitskell, Morrison and Deakin hoped that that the NEC would expel Bevan from the party altogether; Attlee felt that withdrawal of the whip was sufficient, and that was decided by 141 to 112. The struggle then moved to the NEC on 23 March where, just as Morrison and Gaitskell looked like winning the day, Attlee stopped doodling and with the support of Griffiths proposed that a special committee should interview Bevan and secure assurances of good behaviour. This was passed by fourteen votes to thirteen and within weeks, as the Election loomed nearer, the whip was restored. The country was largely unaware of the details of this remarkable episode because of the newspaper strike engineered by the ETU Communists which started almost immediately after the NEC vote and which kept the dailies off the streets for nearly four weeks. Even so a Gallup poll just before the election indicated that 27 per cent of Labour voters would be lost if Bevan were to become party leader.

On 5 April Churchill resigned, and just over a month later another chapter ended when West Germany was admitted to NATO. The election campaign in May saw evident advantages to the Conservatives as it progressed. Eden, markedly lukewarm about summits when he was merely Foreign Secretary, managed to arrange one just in time for the election. A party poster with a picture of the Prime Minister captioned 'Working for Peace' seemed to be helpfully authenticated by the news of the signing of the Austrian Treaty. There was much talk of foreign policy, since this was both the new Prime Minister's forte and the main area of disunity in the ranks of the Opposition. The new Foreign Secretary, Harold Macmillan, appeared on television, but had not yet acquired his consummate mastery of the medium, to judge by the *Annual Register*, which commented that he would have won the approval of John Wesley, who used to read his sermons to an illiterate servant girl to find out whether they were suitable for an average congregation. Percy Cudlipp, recently editor of the *Daily Herald*, interviewed the seventy-two-year-old Attlee and his wife in their chintzy drawing room at Cherry

Cottage. Philip Fothergill for the Liberals inveighed accurately enough against 'the curse of a pound sterling that is worth less and less every year'. But everyone remarked that it was a singularly quiet campaign.

This was exemplified by a final turn-out of only 76·7 per cent of the electorate as compared with 82·5 in 1951. The Conservatives won 344 seats with 49·7 per cent of the total votes cast; Labour 277 with 46·6 per cent; and the Liberals six with 2·7 per cent. It was the first time a government in power had increased its majority since the days of Palmerston and Russell. The Labour vote had significantly declined by 1,500,000, but the Conservatives too received 42,000 fewer votes. Labour was still strong in London with twenty-seven seats out of forty-two, although it had lost two at the election; the Conservatives gained four in the Midlands, and six in the North. The party balance in Scotland – thirty-six Conservative, thirty-four Labour and one Liberal – was very different from what it would become in the years after 1959, 50 per cent voting Conservative to 46·7 per cent Labour. It was observable that right-wing Labour candidates did better than their left-wing rivals. The reformist, as opposed to the socialist wing, of the party noted the bad results at Middlesbrough and Cleveland (where the majority dropped from 5481 to 181), which suggested that workers in the chemical industry were less than enthusiastic about nationalization. As the results were analysed, commentators agreed that the depression and dole queues of the Thirties were now a remote historical memory as compared with their relevance to the 1945 vote. Hugh Gaitskell concluded after the campaign that, whereas the middle classes generally feared a Labour victory, there was no corresponding worry about a Conservative victory among many working-class voters. Butler and Monckton had seen to that. In their social origin the Conservatives in the new House would be little changed (although it was noted that fifty of them were Redbrick graduates), but they had not and would not, in the foreseeable future, contemplate unemployment or undermine the welfare state, which in 1954 was costing £1327 million. The consensus was holding and the affluent society beckoned.

The last months of the post-war decade were marked by changes in the political leadership of the country and storm signals for the triumphant Conservatives both in their economic and their foreign policy. Arthur Deakin died while addressing a May Day rally in Leicester. His union, the TGWU, had by now 1,300,000 members and during his ten years of dominance in the movement as a whole eleven union general secretaries had been knighted. For the moment there appeared to be no great change in the right wing orientation of the leadership. The most prominent figure in the next biggest union, the Amalgamated Engineers, Bill Carron, indeed acquired some notoriety by describing the Communists as werewolves rushing madly towards industrial ruin and howling delightedly at the foam on their muzzles which they accept as their guiding light. However, by 1956 the TGWU would be in the hands of an astute left-winger in the person of Frank Cousins. Stoppages would mount steadily year by year, those in the crucial motor-car industry reaching seven times the national average. Demarcation disputes in particular became endemic, important export contracts, for example, being held up for six months at Cammell Laird's while Merseyside wood-workers and sheet metal workers argued over who did what. The peculiarities of full employment were highlighted in October by Norman Dodds, the Labour member for Erith and Crayford, who informed the nation that he had been watching employees of the London Electricity Board for a week from his window in Dartford, during which time they did practically no work at all. The chairman of the Board pointed out that six men were sometimes sent out to perform a simple task which could be comfortably completed by two men, 'a procedure imposed on us by the unions concerned and we have no option but to accept it'. The National Coal Board put its prices up by 18 per cent, their biggest single rise so far.

Churchill's resignation was followed at a decent interval by that of the seventy-two-year-old Attlee, who after leading his party for twenty years made a resignation speech in December lasting under a minute. Although the Trade Union leaders still wished Herbert Morrison to be his successor, Attlee knew well that he had scuppered that possibility by his continuance in office through and beyond the election. Morrison's last conceivable chance vanished during a disastrous speech over Butler's autumn budget. Nor were Bevan's prospects enhanced when, just before the party conference at Margate, Attlee made a speech in which he pointed out that: 'Labour has nothing to gain by dwelling in the past. Nor do I think we can impress the nation by adopting a futile left-wingism. . . . It is no use asking what Keir Hardie would have done.' At the Conference itself Gaitskell skilfully, if also sincerely, exposed his much impugned socialist credentials in an emotional peroration – 'I became a Socialist quite candidly not so much because I was a passionate advocate of public ownership but because at a very early age I came to hate and loathe social injustice, because I distrusted the class structure of our society, because I could not tolerate the indefensible differences of status and income which disfigure our society.' Immediately before the conference a Gallup poll showed Morrison and Gaitskell as equally acceptable to the electorate with Bevan well behind. As Morrison began to look more and more like a loser, Gaitskell decided to stand. His prospects were considerably enhanced by an unedifying last-minute coalition between Morrison and Bevan, with the end result that Gaitskell secured 157 votes to 70 for Bevan and 40 for Morrison. The new leader told the runner-up: 'Nye, we haven't got on in the past, but if you will accept this vote, as I would have had to accept it if it had gone the other way, I promise you I will not be outdone in generosity.' Crossman anticipated rightly that in the end Bevan would accept the situation – 'After all, he is on the Front Bench, collaborating happily under Attlee, for whom he has a supreme contempt.' He was right, for after some sulking, Bevan closed ranks and the Labour Party enjoyed some years of uncharacteristic unity.

There was some concurrent political manoeuvre in the Conservative party, where the post-election honeymoon was unusually shortlived. After passing over the claims of the obvious candidate for the Foreign Office, Lord Salisbury, Eden appointed Harold Macmillan, far from being one of his closest associates. It was an uneasy relationship and was terminated by Macmillan going to the Treasury in December. His short tenure of the Foreign Office was rendered memorable by his reply to the insistent probing of Marcus Lipton from the Opposition benches about a hitherto unpublicized member of the Security Service: 'I have no reason to conclude that Mr. Philby has at any time betrayed the interests of this country.' His elevation to the Treasury owed much to the sudden discomfiture of R. A. Butler, but at last he was in effective charge of a great department of state, instead of being subordinate to Churchill as Minister of Defence at the end of the previous government and to Eden as Foreign Secretary in the existing one. His star was in the ascendant.

By contrast, Butler's mastery of the art of the possible was now seen to have deserted him at the time of the pre-election budget in terms at any rate of economic prudence. Apart from the consequences of the previous year's highly inflationary wage settlements and sharply deteriorating trade figures, a decision to restore convertibility without allowing the pound to float threatened a run against the pound. So on 26 October Butler introduced an 'emergency' autumn budget (a technique to which the tax-payer was not yet hardened), after having been refused permission to cut the bread subsidies. The £110 million concessions to individual taxpayers in April were now to be taken back but in indirect taxation, including increased purchase tax on psychologically sensitive commodities like household pots and pans. Postal charges were raised and expenditure cuts imposed on the nationalized industries and local government. The contrast between April and October was so evident that, as Crossman put it, there was a general sense of swindle and deception. Gaitskell had, as it happened, foretold in the spring exactly what was to happen in the autumn and so had a parliamentary field day: 'He has persistently and wilfully misled the public about the economic situation and he has done it for electoral reasons. . . . Having bought his votes with a bribe, the Chancellor is forced – as he knew he would be – to dishonour the cheque.' These were strong words and uttered at a time when the British people had not become quite so inured to the relationship between budgets and elections. There was a dawning awareness that doubling the standard of living in twenty years belonged more to the realm of political rhetoric than to that of scientific prediction, though the stop–go metaphor had not yet passed into the national vocabulary. All in all, it is not surprising that the episode was given less than prominent treatment in the Butler memoirs.

Eden's good fortune in foreign relations also ran out after the election. Ill feeling and mutual recriminations arose between him and Dulles over the so-called Baghdad pact, the Americans claiming that Eden had deceived them by including the British client state of Iraq in a Middle East alliance, which they understood would be restricted to states contiguous with the USSR. Step by step the likelihood of Britain sustaining its traditional role in the Middle East seemed to be ebbing away. As the British forces streamed out of the Canal Zone, Cyprus, the alternative bastion, which a junior member of the government, Henry Hopkinson, had rashly asserted would never be independent, was in the grip of the EOKA terrorists demanding union with Greece. Finally, on 28 September, Colonel Nasser concluded an arms deal with Czechoslovakia. 1956 opened with an article in the *Daily Telegraph* by its deputy editor, Donald Maclachlan, which contained the sentence: 'There's a favourite gesture with the Prime Minister. To emphasize a point, he will clench one fist to smash the open palm of the other hand, but the smash is seldom heard.' It was the year of Suez.

· 6 ·
The Mood of the Mid-Fifties

AN INSTITUTION MUCH SCRUTINIZED by Mass Observation and other analysts of the English social scene was the monarchy. Although there were pockets of republicanism, and Willie Hamilton, its champion, had represented his Fife constituency since 1950, the bulk of the nation was either enthusiastically or latently monarchical, the latent element coming to the fore on the great royal occasions – weddings, funerals or a coronation. The national unity which Churchill tried so hard to re-animate in the post-war years surfaced again on such occasions with an epidemic fervour which astonished and impressed foreign visitors.

The King and the Royal Family had earned much admiration during the war for their unwavering application to duty, and a celebrated photograph of the King in a relaxed and friendly pose with the new cabinet ministers and chiefs of staff after the 1945 election afforded a comforting sense of uninterrupted constitutional propriety. There was some criticism, given the austere and arctic conditions of 1947, about the royal trip to South Africa on the grounds of unjustifiable expense. The King even considered coming home so that he could share the blizzards with his subjects. Attlee having dissuaded him, he continued the tour, during which he handed over President Kruger's Bible, captured in the Boer War, to Field-Marshal Smuts in Cecil Rhodes's house. Princess Elizabeth, celebrating her twenty-first birthday in Cape Town, informed her listeners on the radio that: 'Everywhere I have travelled in these lovely lands of South Africa and Rhodesia, my parents, my sister and I have been taken to the heart of the people, and made to feel that we are just as much at home here as if we had lived among them all our lives.'

In November of that year she was married, Archbishop Garbett striking a popular note by pointing out that this sumptuous affair, described in a provincial newspaper as 'England's answer to *Oklahoma!*' was 'in all essentials exactly the same as it would be for any cottager who might be married this afternoon in some small country church in a remote village in the dales'. The silver wedding of King George and Queen Elizabeth was celebrated in April 1948 with a state drive in brilliant weather, but the King's days were now numbered. In September 1951 a chilling bulletin announced: 'The King underwent an operation for lung resection this morning. Whilst anxiety must remain for some days, His Majesty's immediate post-operative condition is satisfactory.' What were to be his last days were cheered by a message in October from President Truman who reported: 'We've just had a visit from a lovely young lady and her personable husband. They went to the hearts of all the citizens of the United States . . . as one father to another, we can be proud of our daughters.' The shocked reaction to the news that George VI had died in his sleep in the early hours of 6 February is extensively documented in Philip Ziegler's *Crown and People*, which draws on the files of Mass Observation. A characteristic comment was that of a Durham pit-head worker: 'I mean, he's special, isn't he? I mean, he's the King. It's different when the King dies, isn't it?'; while a forty-year-old woman in a country village reported that on hearing the news: 'my husband poured himself out a brandy and I said pour one out for me. You really felt as though you wanted it, it was such a shock. All I can say is, thank goodness we've still got Churchill.' At the end of March 1953, and only ten weeks before the coronation, old Queen Mary died at the age of eighty-five, Chips Channon observing quaintly: 'Everyone, Socialists, policemen, everyone seemed deeply moved and sad.'

The weeks leading up to the Coronation were characterized by such over-exposure in the press that it became fashionable in all sections of society to affect a mood of boredom and disillusionment, and the anticipated expense inevitably prompted the *News Chronicle* to suggest that the money would be better spent on education and welfare. Mass Observation found a fireman who was suspicious that the whole thing was being financed out of post-war credits, the payment of which seemed to be indefinitely deferred; and Mr Shinwell complained that the standard-bearers were all to be aristocrats or military men and suggested that room should be made as well for some eminent scientists, doctors, nurses, miners, farm workers, steel workers and railwaymen 'who were the salt of the earth'. But as the imposing London decorations appeared in all their tinsel glory and the bunting was hung out of the back street windows of provincial towns and on the new housing estates, the mood of scepticism rapidly waned and was succeeded by a general euphoria and a roaring trade in coronation mugs.

The attitude of the aristocratic participants themselves had of course been rather different. It involved, in the pursuit of *noblesse oblige*, a number of technical preoccupations recorded by Channon as long before the event as the previous November – 'conversation has taken on a Gilbert and Sullivan quality. Coaches and robes, tiaras and decorations. Winnie Portarlington announced at luncheon that she has harness but no coach; Circe Londonderry has a coach but no horses; Mollie Buccleuch has no postillions but five tiaras. People are obsessed by their Coronation prerogatives. There is something unreal about it.' Unreal or not, they could be relied on to do their stuff when the day came, with a certain inborn confidence which might not have been matched by Mr Shinwell's eminent scientists or salty railwaymen. And as usual, all went well. The night before, 30,000 citizens bedded down twelve deep in the Mall. It was a wet, bitterly cold English June night. And the rain continued to fall relentlessly. Across the front pages of the sopping newspapers the following morning could be discerned the news of the conquest of Everest. There was much talk that day and for some weeks afterwards of a new Elizabethan age. 'What a day for England, and the traditional forces of the world!' sighed Chips Channon. 'Shall we ever see the like again?' A few days later, the Archbishop of Canterbury felt impelled to observe that 'the country and Commonwealth last Tuesday were not far from the Kingdom of Heaven.' Certainly the little children, who we are told form the basis of that kingdom, had enjoyed the proceedings.

If the BBC's figures were correct, nearly half the population saw the Coronation on 2,700,000 television sets, their own or other people's. As an indication of the speed with which the television habit was conquering the nation one has only to compare the fact that when the service was temporarily suspended in the icy winter of 1947 there were only twenty thousand licences. Even by 1949 two-thirds of the population had never even seen a television set. By 1953 sound-only licence holders outnumbered viewers by five to one; in 1954, the year in which *The Archers* reached its thousandth performance, by three to one; and in 1955 by two to one. Although the outside broadcast of the Boat Race in 1952 broke down embarassingly, schools programmes, an important new development, got under way in that year. It was an innovation which aroused a good deal of anxiety and disapproval. The High Master of Manchester Grammar School, Eric James, made a public avowal that a set would only enter his house over his dead body, and on 20 December 1950 *The Times* published the following letter:

Sir,

In your issue of 17 December you announce that the BBC proposes to spend over £4 million during the next three years on the development of television. I have just returned from a visit to the United States, where television (though not, I believe, more highly developed technically) has become an habitual form of entertainment in many more households than here. Among persons of my own acquaintance I found only anxiety and apprehension about the social effects of this pastime and especially about its effect (mentally, morally and physically) upon small children.

Before we endeavour to popularize it still further in this country, might it not be as well if we investigated its consequences for American society and took counsel with informed American opinion about possible safeguards and limitations? The fears expressed by my American friends were not such as could be allayed by the provision of only superior and harmless programmes; they were concerned with the television habit whatever the programme might be.

Your obedient servant,

T. S. Eliot

What was seized on by many as a bulwark against the barbarizing effects of the new medium was yet another Beveridge Report, published a month after T. S. Eliot's letter, which recommended that television should be the exclusive monopoly of the BBC, an organization which could be expected not to countenance mindless frivolity in its programmes. There was one dissenting voice on the committee, that of the relatively unknown Conservative member for the Wirral, Selwyn Lloyd, whom nobody expected would be Foreign Secretary within five years. While Labour was in power, nothing was done to implement the report, but some action was required of the incoming Conservatives as the BBC's charter came up for renewal at the end of 1951. At this point the battle for commercial television began.

Churchill was not especially interested in the matter, though mildly hostile to the BBC, which had kept him off the air for many years before the war. There were, however, some big guns in the cabinet, including Eden, Butler and Macmillan who were opposed to breaking the BBC monopoly. Churchill, by appointing one of their number, Lord Salisbury, to chair the appropriate committee, seemed to be playing into their hands. Salisbury, however, cried off and was replaced by Woolton, who was Lord President of the Council and still party chairman. Woolton, unlike some of his colleagues, genuinely believed in the desirability of eliminating monopolies and responded readily to mounting backbench pressure. By the summer of 1952 a White Paper was drafted, which included the decisive phrase: 'The present Government has come to the conclusion that in the expanding field of television provision should be made to permit some element of competition.'

A glance at the existing television programmes of the BBC suggests that it was in no way unreasonable for the nation to contemplate at least some breath of competition. A characteristic programme for a whole day, as late as October 1953, comprised the following:

3.15 Football: England v. The Rest of the World

4.10 Watch with Mother: The Flowerpot Men

5–5.40 Children's Television

7.20–7.45 A Welsh programme entitled PWY YW PWY

8.00 News Reel

8.15 Inventors' Club

8.45 Music for You: Music, Ballet and Song

9.45 Joan Gilbert's Diary

10.05 Football: England v. The Rest of the World

The outcry by the greater part of the clergy was sustained and predictable, *The Times* giving a lead by explaining that to hand television over to sponsorship would be as unthinkable 'as it would be to give advertisers a decisive say in school curricula'. The Archbishops were against commercial television much as they were against sin, and a great role in the campaign was played by Lady Violet Bonham Carter, whose concern that cultural standards should not be debased by commercial exploitation was echoed less eloquently by Herbert Morrison, who announced that the whole thing was a Tory plot on behalf of big business against the little man. Some backbench Tories were strongly of the opinion that a state monopoly of broadcasting constituted a potential political threat to freedom of expression, and it was backbench pressure which eventually prevailed. Although a Gallup poll showed the nation to be equally divided on the issue, the Act setting up the Independent Television Authority, with provisions aimed at guaranteeing the standard of programmes and advertising, finally received the Royal Assent in July 1954, the first chairman of the Authority being Kenneth Clark. The public had to wait a year before commercial television started on 22 September 1955. The initial programme featured Sir John Barbirolli and the Hallé Orchestra and the first 'commercial' extolled the merits of a brand of tooth paste. Before long the subliminal sensitivities of millions would be battered into acquiescence by advertisements of which the following example earned an understandable notoriety, even in black and white:

> 'Omo improves on perfect whiteness.'
> 'Even on *perfect* whiteness?'
> 'Even on *perfect* whiteness.'

But the public soon learnt to take advertising in its stride. By the end of its first year ITV had captured seven viewing hours to every four of the BBC and between 1954 and 1959 over eight hundred cinemas closed. The pub, the dartboard, and the greyhound track lost ground to the new cultural phenomenon of family viewing, which was even held to account in part for a falling off in the divorce rate, which had quadrupled between 1940 and 1950.

Both the monarchy and television were factors making in their different ways for a certain unity in the life of the nation. The mounting scale of immigration in the Fifties was, on the other hand, beginning to be a divisive factor. Nobody – or at any rate nobody articulate – would as yet have described the British Nationality Act of 1948 in words used by Enoch Powell, as entailing 'upon the home country the calamity of mass African and Asian immigration'. However, a *Sunday Times* leader of November 1953 proclaimed that 'we are threatened with the possibility of a serious colour problem here through the persistent immigration of people from the West Indies.' In December 1954 Henry Hopkinson, a career diplomat turned politician, who was Minister of State at the Colonial Office, answered criticism in the House. He announced that in the first nine months of the year 8000 West Indians had arrived, as compared with 3000 a year in the two previous years. He went on to say that it was most undesirable that the mother country should break with its tradition of freedom of entry for colonial peoples. The situation was being watched.

Neither Hopkinson nor anybody else foresaw that, by the time of Butler's Commonwealth Immigration Act of 1962, coloured immigration would be running at a figure of 136,000 a year. As yet, there seemed little cause for anxiety. In 1953 London, Birmingham, Manchester and Nottingham were the only towns with more than 1500 Commonwealth immigrants, and they were predominantly West Indians with relatively fewer linguistic and cultural difficulties impeding assimilation. There was no large influx of Pakistanis at Bradford, for instance, until 1958. Nor was there any undue pressure exerted by the newcomers on the labour market, since by 1955 there were still more unfilled jobs than persons looking for employment. It was, however, true that the demand for unskilled labour was beginning to drop off, while that for skilled labour was rising, a state of affairs which could lead to difficulties in areas where this trend was most evident.

In the urban areas most affected, tensions were also beginning to develop in the field of rented accommodation. It was curious how frequently landladies declared themselves to be totally devoid of racial prejudice, while at the same time pointing out that the need to have a proper regard for the attitude of the neighbours precluded them from letting the back room to a coloured lodger. Differences of habit and temperament led to misunderstanding. British reserve, a prominent feature of West Midlands culture, could all too easily be interpreted as downright hostility to strangers. In the sunny atmosphere of the Caribbean islands doors were seldom locked and to walk uninvited into one's neighbour's house was the most natural thing in the world. Resentment could easily build up against those Indians and Pakistanis who seemed determined to maintain their cultural identity in the land of their adoption. To many of the new arrivals Britain seemed a land of singularly relaxed moral and religious principles. Whether too solemn or too noisy and ebullient, the immigrants became obvious targets for the not uncommon type of individual who cannot manage life without a hate object. The majority of the population, like Mr Hopkinson, continued to watch the situation but not particularly closely.

Inner city problems, whether of deprivation or racial disharmony were not, however, the focus of popular attention in 1955, as compared with the mounting evidence of consumer prosperity. After ten years of privation, the law-abiding British, as well as the spivs, decided to enjoy themselves in the Fifties. Whereas there was one motor-car for every seven families in 1950, there was one for every three and a half by the end of the decade. Austins, Hillmans, Vauxhalls and Wolseleys, no longer earmarked for export, pursued each other along inadequate roads operating on plentiful imported petrol. The quantity, if not the quality, of beer was back to pre-war standards and Saturday night at the local was followed by ritual car-washing on Sunday to the detriment of the vicar's congregation at Matins. Galvanized iron buckets gave way to plastic ones and the detergents, alluringly advertised on the television in a crescendo of competitive mendacity by 1955, greatly mitigated the domestic servitude of washday. As John Betjeman noted, all was now hygiene and hilarity:

> Our air-conditioned bars are lined
> With washable material,

The stools are steel, the taste refined
Hygienic and ethereal.
Hurrah, hurrah, for hearts of oak!
Away with inhibitions!
For here's a place to sit and soak
In sanitary conditions.

There were new drinks too of a more or less exotic derivation
– lager, Babycham and much more wine – though you could still
see in the darker recesses of the saloon bar the odd superannuated
granny sipping her port and lemon and reminiscing about the
blitz. There was much jingling of coins and endless talk of the
pools which netted £74 million in 1955. It was a bad time for
the once ubiquitous pawnbrokers, whose shops closed down
over a wide area, but still a good one for the street bookmaker.
From 1950 the sums spent on advertising increased by 10 per
cent a year, with great emphasis on the new gadgets which shone
out brightly from the gleaming windows of the radio and electrical shops which had sprung up in every High Street. Every
item proclaimed itself as being easily available by way of hire
purchase. Half the television sets and probably a third of the
vacuum cleaners acquired in the early Fifties were on hire
purchase. Much ingenious advertising was slanted at the
juvenile end of the market, where wages were now 50 per cent
above what they had been before the war. The LP disc arrived
in 1950 with its revolutionary cultural and commercial potential.
The radio blared on incessantly, most of it only half listened to,
though an increasing amount of attention was being paid to the
goings-on in a fictional village called Ambridge, to which listeners
were introduced in 1951.

Many more households than ever before included more than
one earner. In 1954 nearly four million had two breadwinners
and nearly two million had three or more. Consequently, the
paid fortnight's holiday, now nearly universal, increasingly involved something of a splash in more senses than one. Butlin's
holiday camps, which had started in a small way in 1937, did a
roaring trade, catering most successfully to the curious desire
of the otherwise staid British for the greatest possible amount of
noise to be provided for them when on holiday. But the more
enterprising now began to take their holidays abroad in ever
increasing numbers, with the first cheap air-tickets becoming

available in 1952. Bemused Europeans, who had long learnt to identify John Bull as a rather stand-offish gentleman wearing a discreet alpaca jacket and a panama, accompanied by his spouse in a diaphanous frock generally unsuitable for her age, were now confronted with something very different. However, since there was nothing they didn't know about tourism, they sensibly came to terms (usually rather advantageous ones) with their new visitors, whose holiday ethos derived from Bridlington rather than Harrogate. None of this was to have the slightest effect on the settled British determination never to acquire a foreign language. Apart from the usual holiday mishaps, lovingly described with photographic illustration during the ensuing winter months, it was all great fun. It is to be doubted whether a great deal of the mind-broadening traditionally associated with travel occurred. The one exception was the creation in the Fifties of a new British attitude to food.

The need to make the rations more or less palatable had marginally improved British cooking during and after the war. It had at least induced domestic cooks (who now included virtually all middle-class housewives) and restaurateurs to think what they were doing in the effort to make a little go a long way. Now there was comparative abundance and the man matched the hour in 1951 in the person of Raymond Postgate. Postgate combined stern left-wing politics (he was married to George Lansbury's daughter) with much conviviality at the Savile Club with among others Gerald Barry, Gilbert Harding and Stephen Potter, the former English don, who enlivened the dark post-war years by developing the concept and practice of Gamesmanship (1947). Postgate's enduring monument to British happiness was *The Good Food Guide*, the first edition of which containing more than five hundred entries appeared in 1951 and thereafter annually. Christopher Driver in *The British At Table* links Postgate with two other powerful influences – Mrs Elizabeth David, the daughter of a Conservative MP, who produced four of her trend-setting cookery books between 1950 and 1955, beginning with *A Book of Mediterranean Food*; and George Perry-Smith, the proprietor and chef of the Bath restaurant called the Hole in the Wall. Few middle-class housewives with pretensions to entertaining could afford to dispense with Elizabeth David's elegantly produced volumes, though the vastly more voluminous Mrs Beeton (1861) still had her clandestine adherents. Perry-Smith in his delectable small restaurant never strayed beyond the confines of the Elizabeth David recipes. Driver quotes one of his many pupils – 'up here in North-East England, restaurant customers are easily impressed by vulgar display and pretentious menus. We are looking for what we learnt about in Bath; real cooking in a white-washed room.' And with the good cooking, increasingly widespread, went a new appreciation of the wine which was its natural accompaniment. Nor was it necessary to dip extensively into capital gains to enjoy the new sophistication and abundance. A veteran *bon viveur* in the person of Evelyn Waugh entertained Ian Fleming's wife at the Ritz in November 1955. Between them they consumed caviare, *crème Germiny*, *tournedos Rossini* and pears, washed down with white and red burgundy (followed in his case by 'some spurious Chartreuse'). The total bill was £10.

For the generality, however, the end of rationing meant for the moment the return of substantial British meals to British tables. A survey, quoted by Driver, claims that six out of every ten men were eating their midday dinners at home with substantial quantities of potatoes, washed down with tea. The evening meal could be a superb 'high tea' in country districts, or something a good deal less inspiring, with much addition of HP sauce, in the suburbs. Chicken, a middle-class preserve before the war, became cheaper and more accessible but constituted no threat to the primacy of roast beef or roast lamb on Sundays. The adjective 'good', as in 'good, plain English cooking', continued to be applied to the milk pudding and anything which was not a milk pudding was felt to require a liberal admixture of custard. The word 'starter' was not yet in use but for the younger and more adventurous the prawn cocktail acquired popularity. There were still few Oriental restaurants, but the Italians were beginning to make a considerable impact with the Espresso bar. Indeed by the mid-Fifties the biggest single difference in British eating and drinking habits since the war was the emergence of the coffee-break for the white collar worker to match in popularity, if not in frequency, the manual worker's tea-break. Nescafé and its sedulously advertised rivals like Maxwell House not only broke the monopoly of the tea habit but were precursors of the 'instant' food revolution which was

228

about to break out. In 1954 there were only 100,000 packets of frozen fruit and vegetables on sale as compared with 360 million in 1960.

Writing in 1951 Seebohm Rowntree and Lavers were of the opinion that 'at this point in our national development the educated and thoughtful sections of the community are still not only a minority, but even a small minority of the whole.' Such an unpalatable truth, to say nothing of the tone in which it was delivered, would not have been pronounceable by a sociologist after Richard Hoggart's *The Uses of Literacy* came out in 1957. But in the early Fifties the word 'educated' carried with it straightforward and commonly held notions of literacy and articulacy, and working-class culture was usually seen as something to be transcended rather than venerated. The grammar school was still widely regarded as the best available instrument open to working- and lower-middle-class boys and girls with intellectual ambitions. At the Labour party conference at Margate in 1953 Crossman noted that the Trade Union delegates vigorously heckled Jennie Lee, Aneurin Bevan's wife, for attacking grammar schools. By the end of the Fifties, by and large, the general public was less interested in the organization of the school system than in whether their own child had access to a good or a bad school of whatever type. The politicians, for their part, had not yet accepted the provision of education as something to which a substantial proportion of the national income need be allocated. John Vaizey, a young economist, was busy demonstrating that, whereas in 1938 2·7 per cent of the national income was devoted to education, in 1955 this had only increased to about 3·4 per cent, most of the increase being attributable to school meals and the provision of free milk. In 1948, not long before his death, George Orwell agonized about the education of his son in a letter to Julian Symons: 'I would like him to start off at an elementary school. If one could find a good one. It's a difficult question. Obviously it is democratic for everyone to go to the same schools, or at least start off there, but when you see what the elementary schools are like, and the results, you feel that any child that has the chance should be rescued from them.' Hugh Gaitskell in 1956 was similarly equivocal on this particular issue in a broadcast discussion – 'unless you happen to have a very good state school fairly near it is difficult' – and sent his daughters to a Direct Grant school.

Other middle-class parents continued to patronize the public boarding schools. These had changed very little in ethos despite or perhaps because of the war, which had given a new lease of teaching life to elderly veterans of the 1914 conflict who were now being replaced by ex-service men of that of 1939. National Service in many cases gave a great spur to the inculcation of the martial virtues. By dint of underpaying their staff, even the most celebrated schools had kept their fees within reach of middle-class incomes, augmented by not infrequent capital gains – Eton cost £360 a year, Winchester £354, Harrow £345, Wycombe Abbey £300. They combined much excellent teaching with vestigial barbarity.

As yet two provisions of the 1944 Education Act had remained unfulfilled. The school leaving age still stood at fifteen and the County Colleges designed to provide compulsory part-time education for the fifteen–eighteen age group had not come into existence. Some 400,000 fifteen-year-olds annually entered employment with average earnings which seemed startlingly higher than comparable earnings before the war but which in all probability merely reflected the effects of inflation. It could fairly be assumed that a high proportion of these would belong to the majority categorized by Rowntree and Lavers as not belonging to the educated and thoughtful sections of the community, and might indeed engender families with similar limitations. It was now learnt with dismay that one girl in fifty might expect to give birth to a child before she was seventeen. R. Morley, a Labour MP, evidently felt that the way to increase the nation's stock of educated and thoughtful persons was to spend more money when he declared in the House in April 1951 that he did not 'accept the Honourable Gentleman's hypothesis that there is only a limited amount available for education'. But the author of the 1944 Act was now Chancellor of the Exchequer, a shift in responsibility which led him in a broadcast in January 1952 to state that 'to say there is no room for economics in education is wrong'. It would be some years before that part of the national purse-strings would be significantly loosened.

There were mounting anxieties too about the efficacy of new teaching methods in the schools, typified by the schoolmaster with five years' service in two secondary modern schools who wrote to *The Times* in 1953 that 75 per cent of their output was at best semi-literate. 'Formal instruction in spelling and grammar has been abandoned in favour of "free" drama, "discussion", quiz games and many an "activity" that involves no penwork, in the belief that our children will pick up a command of their mother tongue without conscious effort.' At a higher level, C. S. Lewis pointed out that we had lived to see the second death of ancient learning. Influential voices at Oxford and Cambridge continued to complain of undue noise and bustle, the former now admitting 7000 undergraduates a year and the latter 8000. Four per cent of the appropriate age group were receiving university education. Those fortunate enough to be among the select few continued to conduct themselves with impressive decorum, rarely receiving any publicity except periodically in Scotland, where they had a habit of electing persons deemed to lack academic gravity to positions of high dignity.

By the Fifties the newspapers were beginning to be once more recognizable in size and scope after the long years of restricted newsprint when the tabloids were reduced to twelve small pages. Of the mass circulation dailies, the *Daily Mirror* and the *Daily Express* sold more than twice as many copies as did their nearest rivals, the *Daily Herald*, the official organ of the Labour party (with 49 per cent of its shares owned by the TUC) and the right-wing and old-fashioned *Daily Mail*. On Sundays nearly eight million regular purchasers settled themselves down to the sensations and salacities of the *News of the World*. There were still three London evening papers from which to choose. The left wing *Star* commanded a wider readership than Beaverbrook's *Evening Standard*, though the *Evening News*, from the Harmsworth stable like the *Daily Mail*, was the most popular of the three. *The Times*, the *Daily Telegraph* and the *Manchester Guardian* – the quality press – commanded between them some two million daily readers. Rowntree and Lavers, sharing its liberal philosophy, considered David Astor's *Observer* (a very different organ from what it had been under the ultra-conservative J. L. Garvin) as a 'paper of which any nation might well be proud'; whereas they dismissed the *Sunday Times* as 'a frankly right-wing paper'. But neither the finer shades of political opinion, as expressed in Laurence Cadbury's *News Chronicle*, nor the unrelieved militancy of the Communist *Daily Worker*, had much to do with the secret of mass-readership. Whereas the

Daily Worker was read by one per cent of the adult readership, the *News of the World* was probably read by every second adult. The *Daily Mirror* was beginning to set a trend in popular political journalism. Its headlines after the 1955 election read as follows:

> because its leaders are TOO OLD, TOO TIRED, TOO WEAK
> because the Labour movement has been BAFFLED, BEWILDERED and BETRAYED by INTERNAL FEUDS
> because its organization is RUSTY, INEFFICIENT, pathetically INFERIOR to the slick Tory machine.'

'Labour lost –

The Fifties witnessed the decline of the post-war literary orthodoxy, which had derived from a marriage of minds between pre-war Bloomsbury and the heirs of what can conveniently be termed the Auden generation, although the exiled Auden, who had long since relinquished Marx and Freud in favour of Niebuhr and Kierkegaard, was something of a lost leader. The tone was urbane, politely radical, belle-lettrist, Voltairean but without Voltaire's passion; the *illuminati* included Desmond McCarthy, Cyril Connolly, Harold Nicolson, Vita and Edward Sackville-West, John Lehmann, Raymond Mortimer, G. W. Stonier, Edward Shanks, George Rylands, T. C. Worsley and Philip Toynbee. Many, though not quite all, of them had out-lived the radical attitudes which had earned them their fame in the Thirties when there had been much baiting of what D. H. Lawrence had called the beastly bourgeois. Literary comment and reviewing in the late Forties was bland, 'civilized' and genteel.

A change was perceptible around 1951. Book-reviewing in particular took on a new and waspish tone, often from the pens of younger writers. There was a sudden urge once again to upset the proprieties. A best seller of that year, *The Cruel Sea*, was 'explicit' in a manner hitherto largely confined to the paperback Tauchnitz editions spirited through the Customs. By 1955 the publication of Nabokov's *Lolita* presaged the early demise of anything resembling the existing code of censorship. The popular poet of the day was no longer the elegant ex-Communist Cecil Day-Lewis but the comparatively ragamuffin Dylan Thomas, whose collected poems were published in 1952. The posthumous *Under Milk Wood* in 1954 was an instantaneous and uproarious success. A sculptor with the proletarian name of Reg Butler produced a prize-winning work incomprehensibly entitled 'The Unknown Political Prisoner', which the Institute of Contemporary Arts thought a masterpiece. It prompted Evelyn Waugh to write to Randolph Churchill to enquire 'what relation "Reg" Butler, the notorious sculptor is to the politician' of the same name. The hero of a prize-winning work entitled *Casino Royale* seemed to enthusiasts for that sort of literature to be a rather more interesting cad than the pre-war Bulldog Drummond. In 1954 C. P. Snow, who had already made his reputation with *The Master* in 1950, published *The New Men*, which seemed an appropriate title in a year which also saw the appearance of both *Lucky Jim* and *Lord of the Flies*. The clash of old and new aesthetic attitudes was highlighted the next year by the controversy surrounding Annigoni's portrait of the Queen and the popular acclaim accorded to John Bratby's *Still Life with Chip Fryer*. Just two years after Terence Rattigan had demonstrated the relationship of his middlebrow Aunt Edna to the world of the box office, Peter Hall produced in 1955 *Waiting for Godot*, described by Rupert Hart-Davis as 'the ugliest, dullest, most meaningless twaddle' he had ever endured. The New Men thought differently. The star of Christopher Fry finally set with the production of his *The Dark is Light Enough*, which despite a star part for the greatest actress of the day, Edith Evans, seemed to many to be just as opaque as *Waiting for Godot* without benefit of tramps. Already the iconoclastic young critic Kenneth Tynan had characteristically announced that Christopher Fry bore the same relationship to a first-class playwright as the man who carves the Lord's Prayer on pin-heads does to a sculptor.

However Rattigan's Aunt Edna still had her moments. She would have been intrigued by an ingenious thriller called *The Mousetrap*, which was playing to full houses in 1952, and there were still well-constructed plays of the type she appreciated – N. C. Hunter's *A Day by the Sea* in 1953 or Enid Bagnold's *The Chalk Garden* in 1954. But above all, there were *The Boy Friend* and *Salad Days* in 1954, which tunefully and unexactingly evoked a long lost mood of pre-Freudian romance. There was nothing, however, at all innocent about Max Ophuls's *La Ronde*

(1951), which pursued its elaborately amorous course across the screen of the Curzon Cinema for well over a year. As books and plays and films (though not the BBC) became more 'daring', it seemed to Seebohm Rowntree and Lavers, as well as many others, that the nation was living on what might be called 'the moral capital of the past'.

Pessimistic Catholics like Evelyn Waugh and Graham Greene were much in vogue. However, it was still possible to escape from the prevalent preoccupation with the *noirceur* of the human predicament with C. S. Forester and especially the immensely popular Nevil Shute, who had left his native England in 1945 because of what his obituarist described as 'high taxation and what he felt to be the decadence of Britain, with the spirit of personal independence and freedom dying'.

Although the general public still did not buy books extensively – a poll in 1950 showed a figure of less than £1 a head per annum – the Fifties saw a huge increase in borrowing from public libraries and the paperback revolution was by now well under way. A particular vogue was for wartime escape stories, of which the prototype was the phenomenally successful *The Wooden Horse* by Eric Williams. Women's magazines flooded on to the market, it being calculated that by 1955 12 million women were reading two women's magazines a week from an available field of fifty*.

The world of the early Fifties was, then as ever, sufficiently full of the unexpected to throw up a succession of short-lived wonders. There was much tap-room conversation about the many sightings of flying saucers, and at a more down-to-earth level the whole countryside in 1953 was littered with the gruesome carcasses of dead rabbits smitten with myxomatosis. Every winter in London the noxious fumes labelled 'smog' carried off scores of victims. No fewer than 1,300,000 people attended in 1954 one of the meetings organized at Harringay stadium for the square-jawed, clean-cut American evangelist Dr Billy Graham. Few people seemed as a result to be much 'changed', but the phenomenon indicated that religion could be effectively marketed like soap-powder. Those of a more sceptical disposition had had their consolation the year before when it was discovered that the Piltdown Man had been after all a hoax.

* Harry Hopkins, *The New Look*, Secker, 1963, p. 328.

234

Crime and particularly crimes of violence, aroused much public attention and newspaper comment. There were a good many of them – 7083 in 1953 as compared with 4743 in 1945, although cases of larceny and breaking and entering had slightly diminished during the same period; it was noted with alarm, however, that half the convictions for breaking and entering related to juvenile delinquents. One school of thought put the blame for this 'fairly and squarely' on bad discipline in family and school, while others thought it attributable to social deprivation. The question of youthful crime came into lurid prominence with the Craig-Bentley case in the winter of 1952. The sixteen-year-old Craig, incited by his nineteen-year-old mentally defective accomplice, had shot a policeman between the eyes. But it was Bentley who was hanged, although recommended to mercy by the jury, and not Craig who was under age. Bevan led a deputation of two hundred MPs to appeal against the sentence, in vain.

The Labour government had allowed a free vote on a motion to suspend capital punishment for five years. Although Gallup poll evidence showed that hanging enjoyed great popular support, the politicians were much divided. On the free vote the Commons favoured abolition by a small majority; the Lords voted for retention. By 1955 the execution of Ruth Ellis and the discovery of new evidence at Rillington Place in the Christie–Evans case, together with the report of the Royal Commission set up by Labour, ensured that the controversy would move swiftly to a climax. An influential Pelican paperback called *Sex and Society* by Kenneth Walker was also published in 1955. It argued that the imprisonment of consenting adult homosexual males was barbaric and that the law should be changed.

EPILOGUE

'It is a folly to expect men to do all that they may reasonably
be expected to do.' ARCHBISHOP WHATELEY

IT HAD BEEN a strange and momentous decade, by the end of
which it was possible to look back on some impressive national
achievements. While the dismantling of the war economy had
been too slow a process in the eyes of many, it was undeniable
that the demobilization and resettlement of many millions from
the armed forces and munition industries had been carried
through with exemplary fairness and efficiency. The withdrawal
from Burma and India, though too precipitate for some, had
been achieved with reasonable dignity, and since the Commonwealth had not yet been put to any sort of test it was possible, if
not necessarily desirable, to entertain modest hopes for its
future. If optimism about the United Nations scarcely survived
that organization's birthpangs, a strikingly bi-partisan British
foreign policy had had its successes and the United States had
not reverted to isolationism. It was widely believed that the
problems of unemployment, acute poverty and uncared-for
sickness had been finally solved, and after sustaining much
misery and privation the populace was at last beginning to feel
well fed and well housed. Something too of a bloodless social
revolution had been consolidated after the war. If Jack and Jill
were not yet altogether as good as their masters, they were no
longer to be found in the servants' hall. If Ernie Bevin could
make a success of the Foreign Office and Herbert Morrison
could dominate the business of the House of Commons, then
the career open to the talents – or at any rate male talents – had

become a reality in British public life as never before. At the same time the excitements of the Coronation and the popularity of the young Queen seemed to reflect an underlying cohesion in the social fabric. Traditional British institutions and habits had unobtrusively resumed their sway. Justices of the Peace continued to be Justices of the Peace as they had since the fourteenth century; the policeman on the beat was still affectionately known as a bobby; there were 400,000 members of the Women's Institute and 115,000 of the Townswomen's Guild; and *God Save the Queen* was still played at the end of the performance in provincial cinemas. The spring of 1955 was the zenith of Britain's post-war boom and it seemed legitimate, after all that had gone before, for the average Englishman to feel entitled to relax and anticipate the fulfilment of Butler's prophecy of a dramatic and imminent rise in the standard of living.

Any such mood of complacency was to be rapidly dissipated during 1956, one of the most momentous years in post-war history and one which sharply and uncomfortably upset many of the attitudes and assumptions established in the ten years we have been examining. Before its close Nasser had seized the Suez Canal, just over a month after the last British troops had left, and Anthony Eden, broken, humiliated and morally discredited, had limped off the political stage. The implacable Soviet grip on Central Europe had been grimly re-emphasized in Hungary and the special relationship, for so long the keystone of Churchill's policy, seemed to be in tatters. The year began with the bank rate rising to its highest level since 1932 and ended with the reimposition of petrol rationing. In August the first Aldermaston march took place, precursor of so many duffel-coated crocodiles footslogging through Berkshire villages behind the Co-op van. The comfortable consensus which had only recently cocooned the post-war cultural scene was rudely shattered by Osborne's *Look Back in Anger* and Colin Wilson's *The Outsider*, closely followed by Richard Hoggart's *The Uses of Literacy*. Rock and roll had arrived with a vengeance and the young were abandoning docility for rebellion.

What had gone wrong and what was the way forward? For their part, the Socialists were much concerned to discover how the momentum of their cause, which seemed to have run into the sands in 1950, could be revived. There seemed to be so much

237

unfinished business. A group of their young intellectuals started a searching re-appraisal, which was published in 1958 as *Conviction**. A common theme was the extent to which nationalization seemed to have fallen short of the high hopes entertained for it. For Peter Shore, already author of *The Real Nature of Conservatism*, 'the peaceful revolution of post-war Britain turns out to be no more than a managerial semirevolution;' for the *New Statesman*'s Norman Mackenzie the country seemed to have entered a phase of 'social-bureaucratic State capitalism'. The sociologist Peter Townsend recalled the mood of 1945, when he was seventeen, as one of 'a pervasive faith in human nature' and 'a prevailing mood of self-denial'. Five years later 'the momentum following the war was spent and the Labour party's victory at the polls was a hollow one, the succeeding year before the defeat of 1951 being one of the most painful and degrading in recent political history'. It was particularly disturbing that, as Brian Abel-Smith put it, 'the major beneficiaries of the post-war changes in the social services have been the middle classes.' There seemed, furthermore, little of what came to be called worker participation. 'I do not want a society,' proclaimed Peter Shore, 'in which an élite, viewing the world through board-room windows, makes the big decisions, collects the big rewards, while the mass of men deprived of power and responsibility dig their gardens or watch the telly.' Unfortunately neither then, nor since, did the mass of men show any inclination to desert their gardens and their tellies in order to make big decisions. They preferred to leave that sort of thing to the trade union leaders whom they could hardly be bothered to elect.

Above all, what had happened to equality, the moral essence of socialism as defined by Professor Arthur Lewis of Manchester University with his dictum 'Socialism is about equality'? Did this mean more and better nationalization and the overthrow by peaceful means of the capitalist order, as the Left and the

* This left-wing symposium interestingly contained essays from Hugh Thomas and Paul Johnson, then prominent among the *nouvelle vague* of Socialist intellectuals. Paul Johnson's contribution advocated the abolition of the monarchy and the House of Lords and the expropriation of the public schools and the Oxford and Cambridge colleges; Hugh Thomas pleaded for a radical overhaul of foreign policy.

fundamentalists continued to assert? Crossman in a 1955 Fabian lecture seemed to think not: 'Labour's real dynamic has always been a moral protest against social injustice, not an intellectual demonstration that capitalism is bound to collapse.' More importantly, Hugh Gaitskell had become convinced that the moral aims of socialism were much more likely to be achieved under a mixed economy, lubricated by the appropriate application of Keynesian demand management, than by further irrelevant nationalization.

The formulation in print of Gaitskell's ideas was left to Anthony Crosland, whose *The Future of Socialism* (1956) set out to chart the future in the light of the experiences undergone in the post-war decade. Crosland was full of ideas for diminishing inequality, inspired by a genuine idealism and a desire to jerk socialism out of its ideological rut and project it in the direction of an almost Comtian fervour for positive action – what came to be called social engineering. He fully accepted the new formulation of socialism, which on the right of the party was rapidly consigning Clause IV of Labour's constitution to the dustbin of history. 'Is it not then clear that the ownership of the means of production has ceased to be the key factor which imparts to a society its essential character? Either collectivism or private ownership is consistent with widely varying degrees of liberty, democracy, equality, exploitation, class-feeling, planning, workers' control and economic prosperity.' These were brave words but, unfortunately, he seriously misread the signs of the times by proclaiming that 'we stand in Britain on the threshold of mass abundance.' Given that presupposition, all that was required would be a redistributive programme based on taxation and the elimination of privilege. Orwell, in his perspicacious way, had, however, put his finger on the underlying fallacy in discussing the world, East and West, as a whole in a 1949 article on Wilde's *The Soul of Man under Socialism*. There he wrote: 'Actually the problem for the world as a whole is not how to distribute such wealth as exists but how to increase production, without which economic equality merely means common misery.' What had been left out of account was the awkward fact that if, in a competitive world, the leaders of a country, dependent on exports for survival, tacitly agree to condone restrictive practices and massive overmanning and decide to ignore the necessity for capital re-equipment, then the wealth to be redistributed will never be generated. To quote Orwell again: 'Even if we squeeze the rich out of existence, the mass of the people must either consume less or produce more.' If, *pace* Anthony Crosland, Britain was not standing on the threshold of mass abundance, then it might begin to seem as if socialism had little to offer except comprehensive schools and internecine arguments about unilateral nuclear disarmament.

The trade union leaders in the early post-war period, despite being mocked and vilified by the Labour left, were much more realistic than their detractors. Deakin, in particular, was fully aware – as Attlee was – that all that had been gained could be put at risk by inflation, and Lincoln Evans knew that quasi-theological disputes about who should own the steel industry were unimportant compared with the efficient production of steel. This was a far cry from Morgan Phillips, secretary of the Labour party, who had written at the time of the steel debates, 'The battle for steel is the supreme test of political democracy: a test which the whole world will be watching.' The trade union leaders – and Attlee and Morrison with them – also knew all about the enemy within and were prepared to speak out loud and clear about the power of the Reds in the movement. They were the heirs of Ernest Bevin, who had set his stamp on and directed the nation's labour force during the war as he did on foreign policy and much else after it. But for the twenty years from 1954 to 1974 the trade unions under very different leadership would succeed in exercising unfettered industrial power to the extent of unbalancing the constitution.

It was confidently charged against the Conservatives in opposition in the Forties that they would be incapable of getting on with the trade unions. In the event they got on with them rather well, much as King Ethelred got on with the Danes. Psychologically, this was more or less inevitable. A confrontation between two forces, one of which is consumed by guilt, as were the post-war Conservatives, while the other is devoid of any such emotion, is likely to be very one-sided. It was not only in their dealings with the trade unions that the Conservatives turned a blind eye to disagreeable reality, but it was a particular failure in a Conservative government to pretend not to be aware of the vital connection between a commitment to full employment and the disruptive potential of union monopolies. They compounded their guilt further by euphorically stoking up excessive expectations in circumstances in which there was already an imminent danger of leap-frogging wage claims. Samuel Smiles, with his emphasis on thrift, inventiveness and hard work, had somehow dropped out of the Tories' Saints' Calendar. Instead it was to be a free for all – and as Frank Cousins grimly observed, 'if it is to be a free for all, we are part of the all.' It would take twenty years and a Chicago economist, together with the party's most improbable political leader since Disraeli, to re-establish the truth that there is nothing free in the world of goods and services.

As we now see, the course laid out by both political parties could only have led to social and economic ruin, but for the uncovenanted mercy of North Sea oil. However, it did not feel like that at the time. Nor did the British nation as a whole reflect the view of Michael Foot, in the aftermath of Labour's third successive defeat in 1959, when he described British society as 'evil, disgraceful and rotten*'. No doubt there was, as usual, less concern than there should have been about the more unfortunate members of society, but the inner cities of the Fifties, still scarred with weed-infested bomb sites, presented fewer social problems than they do today. Smaller schools, smaller shops and much less high-rise living made for more social cohesion. In an inarticulate way, the British working-class family believed that the war had been fought to preserve essential freedoms and that, give or take a bit, such freedoms continued to exist – the rule of law, a free press, freedom to grumble about 'them'. Just as decent medical care was fully available, so the Labour government's introduction of Legal Aid had widened the bounds of justice. People took for granted that, however many jokes circulated about the civil service, it was both industrious and uncorrupt. If its higher echelons were inclined to overvalue the Commonwealth and regarded the 'defence' of sterling as Moses regarded the tablets of Sinai, these were arcane matters, not much contemplated by the average working man. He, like Michael Foot, enjoyed walking his dog on the heath. By American or European standards he was a late riser

* *The Age of Affluence*, 1952–64, V. Bogdanov and R. Skidelsky, Macmillan, 1970, p. 95.

and a lazy worker. There were better things in life for him than the competitive struggle. With imported petrol now in full flood, he either owned, or planned to own, a motor-car or took the coach or even 'cadged a lift'. Britain is a small island and a trip to the seaside or the dales or the lochs made an easy expedition. Whatever his choice, it involved the ritual picnic with a cheerful scattering of litter over the chosen beauty spot. For the enterprising holiday-maker, and there were more and more of them, there was the day trip to Boulogne or ten days on the Costa Brava. The nation was mad about sport. Commercialization and media adulation had not yet turned its heroes into the sulky and petulant prima donnas who often replaced them in the Sixties and Seventies. Some of the most illustrious sporting stars had been favourites before the war, such as Stanley Matthews, Len Hutton and Gordon Richards (knighted in Coronation year, in which he won the Derby on Pinza with the Queen's horse Aureole second). Although Britain as host nation had cut a lame figure in the 1948 Olympics, by 1954 there was the phenomenon of the young medical student Roger Bannister running the mile in under four minutes. In British sporting parlance there was always a hope of 'a turn up for the book'. In more and more walks of life women were consolidating and expanding the gains they had made during the war. Although much remained to be achieved, especially in education, the diminution of household drudgeries was an unmixed blessing and released much creative energy. Those with longer memories continually remarked on how much better dressed the children were than before the war. If the nuclear family and even the stability of marriage were clearly under threat, there was a greater ease and informality between the sexes, as there was between the age groups and indeed between the different strata of society. There was much of the spirit of live and let live – for one, the top-hatted enclosure at Ascot, for another a day's fishing on the canal. Rancours and animosities existed as always in society at large, as in the family, but they rarely surfaced, as they did in the Sixties.

There was, as always in human affairs, much to worry about in the Britain of the mid-Fifties. But the prevailing wisdom held that, just as we had muddled through the war, so we would muddle through the peace. As, on the whole, we have.

BIBLIOGRAPHY

General studies covering this period include notably *Post-War Britain* (A. Sked and C. Cook); *British Society since 1945* (Arthur Marwick); and *A History of Post-War Britain 1945–74* (C. J. Bartlett).

I have listed below a number of books which I have found in varying degrees helpful and stimulating. Among works of reference I have had much recourse to *The Dictionary of National Biography* and to Butler and Freeman's invaluable *British Political Facts 1900–1960*. *The Times* obituaries were often helpful, as was the *Annual Register*. Among a wide range of periodicals *The Listener*, *The New Statesman*, *The Spectator*, *The Economist*, *Tribune* and of course *Picture Post* provided considerable grist for my mill. I more than once reflected that the shortage of newsprint which characterized much of the period had the useful effect of averting the minds of editors from the wholly ephemeral.

AUTOBIOGRAPHY, MEMOIRS, DIARIES

Butler, R. A., *The Art of the Possible* (Hamish Hamilton, 1971)
Channon, H., *Chips, The Diaries of Sir Henry Channon*, R. R. James, ed. (Weidenfeld and Nicolson, 1967)
Coote, C., *Editorial* (Eyre and Spottiswoode, 1965)
Crossman, R. H. S., *Backbench Diaries*, Janet Morgan, ed. (Hamish Hamilton and Jonathan Cape, 1981)
Dalton, H., *High Tide and After, Memoirs 1945–60* (Frederick Muller, 1962)
Einzig, P., *In the Centre of Things* (Hutchinson, 1960)
Harris, R., *Politics Without Prejudice* (Staples Press, 1956)
Hillary, R., *The Last Enemy* (Macmillan, 1961)
Hodson, J. L., *The Way Things Are* (Gollancz, 1947)

Hodson, J. L., *Thunder in the Heavens* (Wingate, 1950)
Hopkinson, T., *Of This Our Time* (Hutchinson, 1982)
Lees-Milne, J., *Caves of Ice* (Chatto and Windus, 1983)
Lee, J., *My Life with Nye* (Jonathan Cape, 1980)
Lyttelton, O. (Lord Chandos), *The Memoirs of Lord Chandos* (Bodley Head, 1962)
Mayhew, C. P., *Party Games* (Hutchinson, 1969)
Muggeridge, M., *Like it Was* (Collins, 1981)
Nicolson, H., *Diaries and Letters 1945–62* (Collins, 1968)
Pliatzky, L., *Getting and Spending* (Blackwell, 1982)
Sitwell, O., *Laughter in the Next Room* (Macmillan, 1949)
Thompson, A., *The Day Before Yesterday* (Sidgwick and Jackson, 1971)
Waugh, E., *Diaries* (Weidenfeld and Nicolson, 1976)

BIOGRAPHY

Birkenhead, Earl of, *Walter Monckton* (Weidenfeld and Nicolson, 1969)
Blackburn, F., *George Tomlinson* (Heinemann, 1954)
Boyle, A., *Poor Dear Brendan* (Hutchinson, 1974)
Bullock, A., *Ernest Bevin, Foreign Secretary* (Heinemann, 1983)
Carlton, D., *Anthony Eden* (Allen Lane, 1981)
Donoghue, B., and Jones, G. W., *Herbert Morrison, Portrait of a Politician* (Weidenfeld and Nicolson, 1973)
Foot, M., *Aneurin Bevan* Vol. II (Davis-Poynter, 1973)
Harris, K., *Attlee* (Weidenfeld and Nicolson, 1982)
Hoggart, S. and Leigh, D., *Michael Foot, A Portrait* (Hodder and Stoughton, 1981)
Martin, K., *Harold Laski* (Gollancz, 1953)
Rolph, C. H., *Kingsley, The Life, Letters and Diaries of Kingsley Martin* (Gollancz, 1973)
Thomas, H., *John Strachey* (Eyre, Methuen, 1973)
Toole, M., *Mrs Bessie Braddock M.P.* (Robert Hale, 1951)
Vernon, B., *Ellen Wilkinson* (Croom Helm, 1982)
Wheeler-Bennett, J. W., *King George VI* (Macmillan, 1958)
Williams, P. M., *Hugh Gaitskell* (Jonathan Cape, 1979)

GENERAL

Addison, P., *The Road to 1945* (Quartet Books, 1977)
Allen, V. L., *Trade Union Leadership* (Longmans Green, 1957)
Atkinson, A. B., *Unequal Shares: Wealth in Britain* (Allen Lane, 1972)
Barnes, E. W., *The Rise of Christianity* (Longmans Green, 1948)
Beer, S., *Modern British Politics* (Faber and Faber, 1965)
Beveridge, W., *Full Employment in a Free Society* (Allen and Unwin, 1944)

Blake, R., *The Conservative Party from Peel to Churchill* (Eyre and
    Spottiswoode, 1970)
Boardman, H., *The Glory of Parliament* (Allen and Unwin, 1960)
Bogdanov, V. and Skidelsky, R., *The Age of Affluence* (Macmillan,
    1970)
Brogan, C., *Our New Masters* (Hollis and Carter, 1947)
Brogan, D. W., *The English People* (Hamish Hamilton, 1943)
Butler, D. E., *The British General Election of 1951* (Macmillan, 1952)
Butler, D. E., *The British General Election of 1955* (Macmillan, 1955)
Calder, A., *The People's War* (Jonathan Cape, 1969)
Calvocoressi, P., *The British Experience 1945–75* (Pantheon, 1978)
Carmichael, J. D. and Goodwin, H. S., *William Temple's Political
    Legacy* (A. R. Mowbray, 1963)
Chamber, P. and Landreth, D., *Called Up* (Allan Wingate, 1955)
Childs, D., *Britain since 1945* (Ernest Bevin, 1979)
Cole, G. D. H., *The Intelligent Man's Guide to the Post-War World*
    (Gollancz, 1947)
Cowles, V., *No Cause for Alarm* (Hamish Hamilton, 1949)
Cox, C. B. and Dyson, A. E., *The Twentieth Century Mind.*
    Vol. III (O.U.P., 1972)
Crosland, C. A. R., *The Future of Socialism* (Jonathan Cape, 1964)
Crossman, R. H. S., ed., *New Fabian Essays* (Turnstile Press, 1952)
Crossman, R. H. S., *Planning for Freedom* (Hamish Hamilton, 1965)
Cudlipp, H., *Walking on the Water* (Bodley Head, 1976)
Currie, R., *Industrial Politics* (O.U.P., 1979)
Davidson, C., *A Woman's Work is Never Done* (Chatto and
    Windus, 1982)
Deane, P. and Cole, W. A., *British Economic Growth 1688–1959*
    (C.U.P., 1962)
Driver, C., *The British at Table* (Chatto and Windus, 1983)
Duff, P., *Left, Left, Left* (Allison and Busby, 1971)
Eatwell, R., *The 1945–51 Labour Governments* (Batsford Academic,
    1979)
Eldon Barry, E., *Nationalisation in British Politics* (Jonathan Cape,
    1965)
Eliot, T. S., *Notes Towards the Definition of Culture* (Faber and
    Faber, 1948)
Emmett Tyrrell, ed., *The Future that Doesn't Work* (Doubleday,
    New York, 1977)
Glass, R., *The Social Background of a Plan: A Study of
    Middlesbrough* (Routledge and Kegan Paul, 1948)
Gorer, G., *Exploring the English Character* (Cresset, 1955)
Grafton, P., *You, and You and You* (Pluto Press, 1981)
India – The Transfer of Power Vol. XI (HMSO, 1982)
Hancock, W. K. and Gowing, M. M., *British War Economy*
    (HMSO, 1949)
Harrington, W. and Young, P., *The 1945 Revolution* (Davis-
    Poynter, 1948)

Hartley, A., *A State of England* (Hutchinson, 1963)
Hemming, J. and Balls, J., *The Child is Right* (Longmans Green, 1947)
Hennessy, P. and Arends, A., *Mr Attlee's Engine Room* (Dept. of Politics, University of Strathclyde)
Hewison, R., *In Anger. Culture in the Cold War 1945–60* (Weidenfeld and Nicolson, 1983)
Higginson, N. & J., *Great Adventure* (University of London Press, 1945)
Hoffman, J. D., *The Conservative Party in Opposition, 1945–51* (MacGibbon and Kee, 1964)
Hollis, C., *The Rise and Fall of the Ex-Socialist Government* (Hollis and Carter, 1947)
Hopkins, H., *The New Look* (Secker and Warburg, 1963)
Hopkinson, T., *Picture Post 1938–50* (Harmondsworth: Penguin, 1970)
Hunter, L., *The Road to Brighton Pier* (Barker, 1959)
Jay, D. P. T., *The Socialist Case* (Faber and Faber, 1937)
Jewkes, J., *Ordeal by Planning* (Macmillan, 1948)
Kelf-Cohen, R., *Nationalisation in Britain 1945–73* (Macmillan, 1958)
Koestler, A., ed., *Suicide of a Nation?* (Hutchinson, 1963)
Law, R., *Return from Utopia* (Faber and Faber, 1950)
Levy, H., *The Shops of Britain* (Kegan Paul, Trench, Trubner, 1947)
Lewis, R. and Maude, A., *The English Middle Classes* (Phoenix, 1949)
Lewis, R. and Maude, A., *Professional People* (Phoenix, 1952)
Longmate, N., *How We Lived Then* (Arrow Books, 1973)
Lyttelton, G. and Hart-Davis, R., *Letters*, Vol. I (John Murray, 1978)
McCallum, R. B. and Readman, A., *The British General Election of 1945* (O.U.P., 1947)
Mackenzie, N., ed., *Conviction* (MacGibbon and Kee, 1958)
Marchant, J., ed., *Post-War Britain* (Eyre and Spottiswoode, 1945)
Marsh, D. C., *The Changing Social Structure of England and Wales* (Routledge and Kegan Paul, 1958)
Marwick, W. H., *Scotland in Modern Times* (Frank Cass, 1964)
Mass Observation, *Peace and the Public* (Longmans Green, 1947)
Mass Observation, *Report on Juvenile Delinquency* (Falcon Press, 1949)
Middleton, D., *The British* (Secker and Warburg, 1957)
Moore, R. W., ed., *Education – Today and Tomorrow* (Michael Joseph, 1945)
Morgan, K. O., *Rebirth of a Nation, Wales 1880–1980* (Clarendon Press/University of Wales Press, 1981)
Morgan, K. O., *Labour in Power – 1945–51* (Clarendon Press, 1984)
Newby, H., *Green and Pleasant Land* (Penguin, 1980)

Nicholas, H. G., *The British General Election of 1950* (Frank Cass, 1956)

Orwell, G., *Collected Essays, Journalism and Letters*, Vol. IV (Secker and Warburg, 1968)

Pelling, H., *A History of British Trade Unionism* (Macmillan, 1976)

Perrott, R., *The Aristocrats* (Weidenfeld and Nicolson, 1968)

Powell, J. E., *Freedom and Reality* (Batsford, 1969)

Priestley, J. B., *Postscripts* (Heinemann, 1940)

Priestley, J. B., *Letter to a Returning Serviceman* (Home and Van Thal, 1945)

Pryke, R., *Public Enterprise in Practice* (Martin Robertson, 1981)

Richmond, A. H., *Colour Prejudice in Britain* (Routledge and Kegan Paul, 1954)

Rogow, A. A., *The Labour Government and British Industry* (Blackwell, 1959)

Schwarz, G. L., *Bread and Circuses* (Sunday Times, London, 1959)

Scott, J. D., *Life in Britain* (Eyre and Spottiswoode, 1956)

Seebohm Rowntree, B. and Lavers, G. R., *English Life and Leisure* (Longman, 1951)

Seldon, A., *Churchill's Indian Summer* (Hodder and Stoughton, 1981)

Sissons, M. and French, P., ed., *The Age of Austerity 1945–51* (Hodder and Stoughton, 1963)

Temple, W., *Christianity and the Social Order* (Penguin Special, 1942)

Thirkell, A., *Peace Breaks out* (Hamish Hamilton, 1946)

——, *Love Among the Ruins* (Hamish Hamilton, 1948)

——, *County Chronicle* (Hamish Hamilton, 1950)

——, *The Duke's Daughter* (Hamish Hamilton, 1951)

——, *Private Enterprise* (Hamish Hamilton, 1947)

Thomas, I., *The Socialist Tragedy* (Latimer House, 1949)

Titmuss, R. M., *Problems of Social Policy* (Longman, 1950)

Turner, G., *Business in Britain* (Eyre and Spottiswoode, 1969)

Vaizey, J., *The Squandered Peace* (Hodder and Stoughton, 1983)

Vaizey, J., *In Breach of Promise* (Weidenfeld and Nicolson, 1983)

Wakeford, G., *The Great Labour Mirage* (Robert Hale, 1969)

Watt, D. C., Spencer, F. and Brown, N., *A History of the World in the Twentieth Century* (Hodder and Stoughton, 1967)

Wickenden, J., *Colour in Britain* (O.U.P., 1958)

Wiener, M. J., *English Culture and the Decline of the Industrial Spirit 1850–1980* (C.U.P., 1981)

Ziegler, P., *Crown and People* (Collins, 1978)

Zweig, F., *Labour, Life and Poverty* (Gollancz, 1948)

Zweig, F., *Women's Life and Labour* (Gollancz, 1952)

INDEX

256